Real

A Mom's Journey from Expectation to Reality

Charlotte Gatlin

WESTBOW
PRESS®
A DIVISION OF THOMAS NELSON
& ZONDERVAN

This book is a work of non-fiction. Unless otherwise noted, the author and the publisher make no explicit guarantees as to the accuracy of the information contained in this book and in some cases, names of people and places have been altered to protect their privacy.

Scripture quotations marked (NCV) taken from the New Century Version®. Copyright © 2005 by Thomas Nelson. Used by permission. All rights reserved.

Scripture quotations marked (NIV) are taken from the Holy Bible, New International Version®, NIV®. Copyright © 1973, 1978, 1984, 2011 by Biblica, Inc.™ Used by permission of Zondervan. All rights reserved worldwide. www.zondervan.com The "NIV" and "New International Version" are trademarks registered in the United States Patent and Trademark Office by Biblica, Inc.™

WestBow Press books may be ordered through booksellers or by contacting:

WestBow Press
A Division of Thomas Nelson & Zondervan
1663 Liberty Drive
Bloomington, IN 47403
www.westbowpress.com
1 (866) 928-1240

Because of the dynamic nature of the Internet, any web addresses or links contained in this book may have changed since publication and may no longer be valid. The views expressed in this work are solely those of the author and do not necessarily reflect the views of the publisher, and the publisher hereby disclaims any responsibility for them.

Any people depicted in stock imagery provided by Getty Images are models, and such images are being used for illustrative purposes only. Certain stock imagery © Getty Images.

ISBN: 978-1-9736-6549-6 (sc)
ISBN: 978-1-9736-6550-2 (hc)
ISBN: 978-1-9736-6548-9 (e)

Library of Congress Control Number: 2019907538

Print information available on the last page.

WestBow Press rev. date: 06/25/2019

Acknowledgments

This book is dedicated to all of the Charlotte, DK, Peter and Anna's of this world.

Writing this has been a dream of mine for eighteen years. The process has brought me healing, purpose, and joy. My hope is to encourage others in similar situations. While I feel extremely vulnerable putting my truth out there, I am also excited to share it. I pray I can be used for His Purpose.

I would like to thank my beautiful colleague and editor, SK. Your time and effort is a gift. And for all of those who have encouraged me in this process, I am grateful.

I'm working on loving this person staring back at me in the mirror.

This is about my journey and how I got here.

I'm kind of a hot mess these days. I'm trying to figure out how to wait patiently for the things I want in life, but I can't make these things happen just because I want them to. I need to wait; wait on the Lord to see what He has planned for me. I've never seen it more clearly than I do now. It has taken everything in my forty-one years on this earth to get here.

Do I wish some of the hardships had never happened? That I could have skipped the hurtful, gut-wrenching parts? Absolutely. However, without all of it, I wouldn't be here now with so much clarity that it hurts.

Now that I've been inspired, and felt prodded by the Lord to share, here it is... me being real, raw, and honest... through the good and bad.

Preface

I have been given so much in my life. My years have been full and happy... well, for the most part. I've wrestled with self-worth and confidence in myself for as long as I can remember, but I know that it is not worth the air I breathe to think negatively about myself. I am happy in my own skin now; it's taken me a long time to be able to say that.

The things I've wanted to change, or pleaded with the Lord to change, have all become part of my story, my journey. As I sit here, curly hair frizzing in my face, pale skin, and a few pounds heavier than I'd like, I'm ready to tell my story. Not as a way to hurt anyone else who has crossed my path, but for myself. This process has been cathartic for my healing, my growth. This is proof that the Lord hears our prayers and is ever present in the joys and the heartache of life.

Chapter 1

I got my first job right when I turned sixteen. It was at a convenience store where I met my future husband, Danny. We didn't run in the same circles or even attend the same high school. But as the Lord would have it, after a six-year time span of dating, breaking up, having other boyfriends, and experiencing character-building moments, we were married. The weather on our wedding day was less than ideal - as was being walked down the aisle by my dad, who was facing his second battle with adenocarcinoma (lung cancer). Although he was losing his hair and felt puny, I was honored to be walked down the aisle by him. On that rainy, emotional day, I became a missus.

We experienced the usual bumps along the way as newlyweds, including some disagreements over money and when to have babies, but we had a great beginning. There was lots of love, house projects, camping, laughter, and hope for our future. We bought our first house after being married for just three months and soon got a puppy I named Dutch. He was hysterical, naughty, and taught us a lot about what having patience means.

After a few years of both of us working full time, (me) longing for a positive pregnancy test, and living life, we moved into an old farmhouse close to my parents. We knew it was an emotional buy but that big green-and-white farmhouse had something we both loved. We knew we would make it a home.

In 2002, I finally got the positive pregnancy test I had been longing for and was able to fulfill my lifelong dream of becoming a mom. I quit my full-time job one week before Daniel King (nicknamed DK) arrived at a whopping nine pounds and three ounces. I was instantly in love and excited to stay home to raise our little family.

Except our little family of three grew faster than anticipated. DK was just five months old when I found out I was pregnant again! As I cleaned the house and got prepared for DK's first birthday party, I anticipated baby 2 popping out at any time. Thankfully, he hung in there, making it twelve months and ten days between their two birthdays. In the summer of 2004, we were blessed with Peter Willis. He was an even bigger boy at nine pounds and six ounces. While DK came out with his eyes wide open and head bobbing to check out the world around, Pete just kept his eyeballs shut for two days and chilled out.

It was just after Pete was born that emotions were at an all-time high. I was sore, tired, and unsure about how to balance a one-year-old and a newborn. I didn't know which end was up. Tears were streaming down my face, and I just needed a moment to vent. I didn't expect Dan's reaction at all. I knew he was struggling with the stress of it all, too, but from my point of view, I was the one doing the work. He took my emotions and quadrupled them in that moment. He began yelling at me and I was struggling to make sense of it all.

"This is why we aren't having any more children!" he screamed.

I felt small and insignificant, but at the time, I also believed maybe he was right. I wasn't handling it very well. Maybe I was being irrational. How I was feeling made sense to me, and his reaction did not. I resolved at that moment to keep my thoughts quiet and just buck up. Being so overwhelmed, I always felt the need for help, but I never knew the right ways to ask for it.

All the sleepless nights, bottles, diaper blowouts - I handled them. My husband had a job and I didn't (as was told to me), so he needed his sleep. And to be honest, the years of having two boys that close in age were fast and were one of my favorite times in my life. We spent countless hours playing with Little People and cars from the movie *Cars*; we went to play groups and spent time at parks with picnics. We also spent all kinds of time with my folks, who lived about thirteen miles away on the lake. And we spent time with Danny's parents, who eventually moved closer to be near their grandkids.

As the kids grew, so did my understanding that I needed to be very careful of what I expected, or thought should be normal, based on what families around us had. I was living my dream of being a mom. Why wouldn't I do it all on my own? My husband had a good job and a lot of responsibility at work, so I could make sure home ran smoothly. Over time, though, I felt I wasn't meeting the expectations of a stay-at-home mom. I began making sure the house clutter was picked up and the floor was vacuumed nearly every day by the time he got home from work. I started fearing I would upset him if it wasn't.

In late 2006, I found out we were expecting baby number three. I was really excited, but Danny struggled with the news. I would sit in the gliding rocking chair, in the prepped violet-and-white gingham nursery, while clinging to my oversized belly and sobbing. I'd look out of the side yard window and cry to the Lord for help in what was to come. He had given us this child, and He would provide. I went to all but one of my prenatal appointments by myself. Danny came to see if it was a boy or girl. As he saw it, I did this on purpose. So, I resolved I would just have to raise this little girl on my own.

As time clicked on by, Danny would spend more time away from home, either hunting for a week or weekend here and there or going to the bar with his buddies. It got to a point where having him gone actually made it easier. We could do our daily routine of lunches, naps, playtime, dinner, and bedtime. At the local gym, we started trying new things like soccer and tumbling classes to keep busy. It was easier to do it on my own, and when Dan would show up, it was a bonus. I was asked where he was the times he didn't show up. I'm thankful that over time, people just stopped asking.

When Anna came along, I struggled with some postpartum depression (and acne - yuck!) after she was born but tried to soldier on so that I wouldn't hear about it from Dan. One real positive to having Anna Rose was that she corrected my vision, both literally and figuratively! After giving birth to her, I no longer needed to wear my contacts or glasses. I could now see how she completed our family.

During those years, we fixed up and tried selling our prized farmhouse so that we could get into something that didn't require as much work. Mom and Dad chipped in a lot to help with the kids, even giving me a day off during the week to run errands, take a nap, paint a room, or have lunch with a friend. Having that time really helped me recharge my battery.

As the days turned to weeks, weeks to months, and months to years, soon it was 2010. Looking back, I do believe that was the most difficult year of my life. I kept a journal close to the bed to keep track of my thoughts and hopes and to cry out to the Lord in prayer, for help, for guidance, and for provision.

Chapter 2

January 8, 2010

We had a house showing today. I'm remaining hopeful that we'll get to move into the new house we put money down on. A whopping $7,000; that's a lot for us. Having the previous "buyers" back out just before closing really hit us hard. But we'll keep trying.

Both boys had a good day at school today and stayed on green, which is the stoplight system they use for good behavior. Dad always teases them about getting on red. I think that has only happened once this year for DK in kindergarten. With Petey-Wheat being so squirrely, I'm surprised he doesn't get on yellow more in young fives.

Anna is so precious with her talking and the things she says. She learned today that my name is Charlotte. I'd ask her, and she'd say, "You Mom, Momma, Charonine," in her little two-year-old voice. I need to record it more. It seems the video camera got a lot more use on the first two!

January 10, 2010

I truly enjoyed playing games with the kids tonight. We had a sock ball fight, built a fort, tickled, and tackled. They are so fun. Now they are in bed and conked. Anna keeps saying she's going on Mama's potty as she climbs on the toilet. She's so cute.

DK impressed me so much today. He's so smart; he picks up on things so quickly. Pete is tenderhearted and wanted me to carry him up to bed tonight. Dutch is lying next to me on Danny's side of the bed because he's still not home yet. I'm not sure where he is, but the quiet house is just fine by me.

January 11, 2010

Most people have cushy lap dogs who love to go on car rides. Perhaps they like to nuzzle their noses out the half-opened window and feel the cool breeze on their furry faces. Or perhaps they like to look out the window longingly at the world of unknowns, wondering what smells are out there, and what other dogs they might meet. This is *not* ours.

I drove around for two hours with Dutch, only to find out the people were a no-show to our house showing. They were running late and didn't make it. If they only knew what work went into it! I drove anywhere I thought possible to occupy Dutch's mind. He kept hopping onto our groceries in the back. Three times he jumped on the loaves of bread and squashed anything in his path. He was nervous, whining, and hopping from back to front, front to back. He even tried to roll down the window with his paw. I have learned to lock the windows because he has nearly decapitated himself by rolling the window up on his own head. The dog knows how to work power windows.

Here he is, hopping from DK's seat to Anna's to whine and to stick his nose out the window. And to find out the folks never showed up! This is the not-so-fun part of trying to sell a house.

January 25, 2010

I feel like I am acting discontent. I'm trying so hard for it not to show, but it's really difficult. Dan has been struggling quite a bit, and I don't know what to do. I'm not supposed to talk about it with anyone; he told me I can't. Instead, here I sit, writing in my journal by the light of my cell phone because he's in bed, and I'm not allowed to turn a light on. I'm not sure where to turn or what to do.

Lord, please help me know when to intervene. I know he is struggling with his own feelings and thoughts. I haven't quite figured out how to help him when he's like this. It seems easier when he's not home, though. I feel awful admitting that. When he is home he seems more and more disconnected from me and the kids. *Oh, Lord, please guide me!*

January 26, 2010

Tonight I had this overwhelming feeling of guilt for getting after the kids today. I got after Pete to *think* because he gets so wrapped up in his own la-la land sometimes. And DK kept asking, "is this the right decision?" when coming up with ways to spend his allowance. I ended up getting Anna back out of bed after bedtime so I could sit with her on my lap. She sat with me to watch *American Idol* and kept turning to smile at me, looking me dead center in the eye. My eyes filled up with tears. I treasure that genuine love she shows me in her sweet, two-year-old face.

Another night of doing it all solo. Sometimes I get nervous not knowing what to expect when he's out so late like this. This is becoming the pattern; it's every other night he is away from home. I'm not sure where he is or who he is with. As difficult as this is, when he is home there is still this feeling that it's just me and the kids. He sits with his laptop on his lap, earbuds in his ears - watching something different than us. He is becoming so disconnected. It seems like he is a million miles away from me, from these precious humans who bring so much joy. I'm not sure how to fix this, how to change it.

January 31, 2010

I really want to sell this house! I am trying my best to keep it clean all of the time in case we get a showing, but between the kids and Dutch, that is a challenge. The fun part is looking for a new house. Something bigger and in a neighborhood would be great. With the kids this young, we don't need to worry so much about what elementary school they end up at. I just want it to be the right house where we can have memories and grow.

I hope, after Danny and I's lengthy discussion yesterday, that he can meet some of his personal goals. He said he wants to quit drinking so much beer. I want that, too. I've never had a drink before in my life, so the idea of having alcohol out of the house is just fine by me. Tomorrow is a new day, a new month.

Chapter 3

February 1, 2010

The song "Seek Ye First" is in my head right now. *Thank you, Lord, for another day of healthy kids, for Dan's and my relationship, and how You continue to bless us. It feels great to see You are working in our lives, oh Lord. We are wanting to grow and learn. Please show us how to pray together as a family and how to seek You in these hard times.*

I am grateful, Lord, for the genuine smiles on our children's faces. For how excited Anna gets when she sees me. She loves her mama.

February 2, 2010

Anna is putting on any hat, gloves, and mismatched shoes she can find. She thinks she's going outside to play with the boys.

"Where my oder one gwub, Mom?" (where is her other glove)

The other two are outside, burning off some energy. We've had a typical sort of day. Pete, Anna, and I slept in until 8 am, which is some kind of miracle. DK was up before that but stayed nice and quiet. He's a really considerate kid.

DK wanted to go to Target to spend some money from his piggy bank. On these days during the week, when the boys don't have school, it's a challenge to keep busy. There we were, walking up and down every aisle at Target, both boys having an impossible time deciding what they want to spend their fortunes on. Anna kept saying she had to pee, so we ended up in the restroom several times, which I'm guessing haven't been cleaned in a week. DK finally decided on a Lightsaber, and Pete: A Nerf gun.

Once we were home and the kids were playing with their new found items, fighting ensued along with crying and *accidentally* hitting each other in the face. Let's just say my irritation level went up about three notches and the yelling began. I always regret yelling after the fact, but in the moment, I'm not sure what else to do! Needless to say, we got creative, and they went outside.

February 5, 2010

Last night, around 12:36 am, (roughly - Dad and I joke because we pay attention to the exact time), Anna started crying.

I hopped out of bed to check on her, and she had barfed. She was standing in her crib telling me, "Mommy, akkies on it, dare puke on my pillow. Dare puke on my bwankie, dare puke on my arm."

I picked her up out of bed, cleaned her up with new jammies, and replaced her sheets. By this point, she was shaking from being cold in *yucky* jammies. So I wrapped her up in blankets as I sat on the floor and rocked her back and forth. Then we started talking.

"Where da moon go, Momma?" I told her it was hiding.

She wondered, "The dun-dine hide-een too, Momma?"

"Yep, the sunshine is hiding, too, Anna." Then we talked about how Jesus is up in the sky, too.

She looks out her window and says, "I can't see De-dus Mom?"

We talked a few minutes about where He is and how He's in our hearts. She finally stopped quivering, and I put her back in bed. Being as particular as she is, she had to have all new blankets. I got her all set, gave her a kiss and said, "Ni-nights." She pulled her little hand out from under her covers and curled her precious fingers into a wave with a big smile.

"Ni-nights moon and dun-dine too... Ni-nights De-dus."

February 8, 2010

I lost count of how many times I was up last night lending a hand to any one of the kids or helping Danny out of his bad dream. Pete had to cough and kept trying to swallow to make it go away. Yet, he just *had* to report to me every five minutes that it was "still in his throat!" Anna woke up a few times needing Kleenex and DK woke me up simply to see if I had checked on him yet.

That, and each time I got up, Sunny got all excited and started slapping his tail against the dresser. We like dog-sitting for Sunny; he's so sweet, and it gives Dutch a buddy. Dutch also kept whining when I got up. So in addition to the humans' needs, I had to cater to Dutch with getting him a drink in the bathtub. He will literally pull back the shower curtain, hop in the tub, and wait until I turn the faucet on. He's a *freshwater snob*. If I don't know that he's in there waiting for me, he will get out of the tub and nudge the closed toilet seat until I respond.

February 9, 2010

I feel like Danny is very sensitive tonight. The kids are so precious, and I wish they didn't have to be picking up on mood swings. Yet they do, and they handle it. It's something I'm proud of, and, at the same time, it makes me sad. He has been struggling this week, and it's getting harder to come out of it. We got a chance to talk this morning, and I told him how I am at a loss for words when his mind is in that dark place.

I don't blame him - I just really don't like where it leads. And it seems when things start going downhill, they can spiral. When things change back to normal, there is a sense of peace. Like I can breathe; we've made it. But I'm not there right now.

Dear Lord, please help Dan every moment and our incredible kids as they grow. Thank you for the gift each individual one is to us. They are so amazing; they are so special.

February 16, 2010
Yesterday on our car ride home, Pete said, "Mom, I never want your face to change." He's so cute. We got into a conversation about someday, when he is a professional singer, he will get me tickets to sit "in the very front and after he sings a song he will come give me a hug right away."

DK fell asleep in our bed again tonight. When he gets scared, it's where he feels safe. I say, "Ok, I suppose," but it always makes me smile.

I have been wondering how I can help my husband. I feel like he doesn't really want to talk about what's on his mind. It's hard and doesn't make sense to me, but I'm trying to be supportive. It really scared me tonight when he threw his cell phone up against the garage in a rage-filled moment. It shattered into all sorts of pieces, and he thought it was funny. I stood there with a blank look on my face. *What about this scenario is funny?*

I've been feeling like I'm in the way, so going to bed earlier on these nights is my best option. I am leery of the conflict or anger I may otherwise face. Perhaps it is not the best thing to avoid it, but I can't find the strength to handle it some days.

February 17, 2010
I'm a tad irritated.
I'm irritated that I've put on a few pounds.
I'm irritated that I can't ever have all of the clothes in the house clean and put away at once.
I'm irritated that no room stays picked up for more than four minutes.
I'm irritated that every single time Anna sneezes, I have to run for a Kleenex.
I'm irritated that we haven't had showings on our house.
I'm irritated that I have to vacuum again.
I guess I'm a little more than a tad irritated...

February 18, 2010

I had the opportunity to help in Pete's class at school and it was wonderful! What a fun bunch of five-year-olds. All different, yet the same. I got to sit in the library with them, and one of the little girls in Pete's class asked to sit on my lap. I loved it.

Afterwards, I headed for Mom and Dad's house to pick up Anna. Mom asked if I would stop at the pharmacy to get Dad's new prescriptions. She finally convinced Dad to see the doctor this morning and, sure enough, he has pneumonia. Since his two bouts of cancer, his immune system isn't what it used to be.

When I got to their house, Anna was up from her nap, and Mom was visiting with her friend, Rosemary. I noticed on one of Dad's medications that he should probably start on it right away, so I headed to find him downstairs sleeping. He was lying there in my old bedroom, shirt all undone, covers tossed to the side, with his eyes closed, and he was moaning.

I said, "Dad?" and that startled him awake.

I don't usually call him *Dad*. We have never called each other *Charlotte* or *Dad*. If he calls me by name, I know it's something serious. It's typically a name out of love, something silly and light-hearted. But this occasion called for *Dad*. We visited for a minute, in between him trying not to cough and trying to get his bearings. I felt awful seeing him like that. I didn't stay too long because I didn't want to wear him out, and I had to get home in time for the school bus.

In a quick decision, I thought, I'll go the back way home, it will be quicker. Little did I know, taking that way home would prove quite the entertainment. Anna and I ended up in a ditch, met a tow truck driver who gave us a free tow and free show - his pants fell down to his knees while hooking us up to his truck! Fortunately, I was able to get ahold of Mom, who drove to meet the bus in the knick of time.

While Nan and the boys were waiting for us to get there, Dutch and Sunny managed to destroy the dining room blinds again. They were so excited to see humans and wanted to come out to play, but Mom didn't have a house key. So that was neat.

I'm happy to report that Dad seems to be feeling stronger. I pray he'll feel back to normal soon. And as for Mom, she's having a biopsy tomorrow.

February 20, 2010
We went to see Mom and Dad today and had a very nice visit. Glad to see Dad up and around! Mom looked sore from her biopsy, but they are both on the mend. The kids were thrilled to see them both and did a nice job going easy on Papa. They usually tackle him and *pretend* punch him in the gut. But they didn't today.

I also learned a new fact - Peter doesn't like to be kissed on the lips anymore. He says it's too wet, so when we kiss him we do as they do in England, or wherever they go *moo-wah* on each cheek. The kid is so rare.

February 23, 2010
I was downstairs watching TV when I heard a horrific, loud *boom* come from upstairs. I went running and found Danny weeping, laying half of his body over DK while he slept. DK was sound asleep until the weight on top of him woke him up. Puzzled, he looked at me and then dozed back to sleep. I sat down next to Dan and kept whispering, "what happened?"

He couldn't even lift his head, he just laid there. When he eventually got up, he walked into our bedroom and fell to his knees. I asked him how many beers he had, but he wouldn't answer. He just wept, and I didn't know what to do.

He finally gathered his wits and told me his doctor diagnosed him with Bipolar Disorder. So many thoughts came racing through my mind. I felt a sense of clarity, *of course that's what it is.* The mood swings, anger, impulsivity, and aggression. I guess I wasn't surprised. My heart went out to him, seeing how hard it hit him. Having a title makes it hard to swallow, I understand that. I don't want him to get caught up in the title, though. As much as it made sense to me, I'm at a loss for words. He won't let me in. What can I do? How can I help him move forward from this spot?

Lord God, please show me how I can be used in this, how I can be helpful to him during these upcoming days. I know he is struggling to find peace, and I want to help him. Show me, Oh Lord. Please give me wisdom and patience.

February 24, 2010

Dutch, being more calm in the car this time, made for a pleasant surprise and gave us more time to enjoy ourselves. We needed to be out of the house for an hour for the showing. Unfortunately, the showing time was also bedtime. So this called for a lot of drive-bys to see if there were any cars in our driveway. Dan drove around in his car, while I did the same with the kids, and we kept trying to find each other around town. The kids liked making it a game and it helped make the time go by faster.

February 25, 2010

Seems it's been a crazy week! I pulled a neck muscle while trying to shave my legs. Apparently I need to do that more often, to stay limber, because now I can't look to the right without turning my whole body. It didn't help having to unclog the upstairs toilet with everyone claiming they have no idea how it happened.

Now the dog is outside barking at his own shadow, and the boys are supposed to be doing quiet time (QT) while Anna naps. But she saw me in the bathroom upstairs and started talking. I just went about my plunging business and came back downstairs thinking that the house will give me some peace, but then comes Peter to tell me Anna wants a drink of water. Oh, and she has to go potty. How do kids learn how to *stall* at this age already? I asked Pete to get her up and help her go potty. He did, and they were just a bowl full of giggles until I went up and broke up the fun. I think they now realize I mean *quiet* with QT. Here's to hoping my sanity will return this afternoon. And maybe, just maybe, our next house will have more than one working bathroom...

Mom and Dad headed to Arizona today. Honestly, I always struggle it when they leave. Before they left, I went over to send a few things with them in the car – diapers and such – so I wouldn't have to fly with that extra baggage. I told them about Dan's diagnosis, and Dad didn't even blink. He wasn't the slightest bit shocked, and it took me back a little. So much of what we have been dealing with at home, I've kept secret and felt ashamed. I've been convinced it was something I did.

Chapter 4

March 6, 2010

The kids and I are flying to Arizona tomorrow and Danny will come join us in about a week. I worry about him and pray he'll take things one day at a time. If he needs anything, he can reach out to friends or neighbors. Since his diagnosis, he has been all over the map. I'm trying to be sensitive to his needs right now, and I want him to know I'm here, but then he shuts me out. I'm working on my patience and need to allow him space to process it all. We can talk it through when he's ready, and hopefully, I can figure out what his needs are.

I'm nervous to fly with all three kids tomorrow. At six, five, and two years old? *Oye*. Praying I will have patience. There is a version of myself that comes out at the airport, lovingly named "Airport Charly." What can I say, I get crazy stressed, time crunched, and feel the need to be at the gate six hours beforehand! Not really, but that's how I feel. This time with me plus three kids under six years old? Somehow, I've got to keep my cool.

I pray for more patience in all of this, not just the flying. I pray I can take a step back and feel lighter than I have been. I feel a weight on my shoulders that's been mounting. I'm struggling to keep my smile these days, I want to feel *joy* again, just simple ease and joy instead of up, down, and all over. How do I maintain being the mom I want to be and take on the super supportive wife roll? I struggle to know where I fit. How can I get the support I need?

Lord Jesus, I need You. I am having a difficult time stringing words to prayers together, Lord. You know my heart. I know you hear me. Lord, You know my heart. I know You hear me, I just need to whisper Your Name.

March 18, 2010

Now that we're home, here comes the mess, laundry, dishes, and smooshed snacks on the floor. It sure is good to be home though, especially for Dutch. We missed him and he goes on a serious hunger strike when we're gone. He refuses to eat his stockpiled dog bones he has hidden for later. That first few minutes we walk in the door, he is gobbling up those bones and emptying his food bowl. He is so funny.

We had a little airplane incident yesterday...

We're in the air and the "fasten seatbelt" light is off. I look over to Anna who has *the look* on her face. She proudly announces, "I fart-een!" but I can tell by the look that there is more going on. Sure, she's somewhat potty trained – but not fully by any means. Changing dirty pants in a pull-up has become my nemesis.

I tell the boys to stay put and ask the person across the aisle, whom I've already struck up some conversation with, to keep an eye on them for me. Anna and I head to the back of the plane - which seems to be a narrow three-mile walk. We bumped some people along the way, who apparently have never experienced a two-year-old on an airplane by the look on their faces, but alas, we made it. I get her in the tiny, square bathroom, and what do you know...she hasn't pooped in her pull-up yet! After throwing her a little "yippee" party, I get her situated in the three inches of space we have, and she poops on the potty. Wonderful! Happy dance again. Except for when she stands up and smears it on the side of the toilet. Then it becomes dry-toilet-paper-doesn't-get-poop-off and someone-opens-the-door-on-us situation. I'm trying to remain calm while we hit turbulence, and poop gets on my fingers.

Fortunately, I had brought the wet wipes with me (along with a new pull-up, of course) and I'm trying to wipe the remainder from her rear-end. After all was said and done (and we about went through the entire package of wet wipes), I thought I had poop on my jeans. So I try to look at the area behind my right knee in the two inches of space we have, and, fortunately, didn't see anything. We get back to our assigned seat, and I notice a lingering smell. I check all around me and Anna. Finally, I notice it. I have poop under my fingernails.

March 19, 2010

Arizona this year wasn't a complete bust, but it sure wasn't what it has been in the past. I feel like Danny is having a hard time living with what he sees as a *title*. I'm trying to help him understand that it doesn't define *who* he is. There was an incident while we were there that threw me for a loop...

Danny took the boys on a golf cart ride while Mom, Dad, Anna and I stayed back at the condo. After awhile, they came back, and Pete walked right past us and into the bedroom. This was totally out of character for him.

Dad put in the movie *Lion King,* and the kids were enjoying it, except Pete. He was hiding. When he finally came out from under the bed, he threw up. His face was pale, and he looked different. At first, he wouldn't say, but then admitted; he had fallen off of the golf cart when they turned a corner and hit his head on the curb. Dad and I were puzzled and upset that we didn't know sooner. We packed up the kids and headed to the nearest Emergency Room.

I just, I don't have words. I wish we would have been told what happened. *Why didn't Dan come tell me*? I'm still so confused on that piece. But after a CAT scan and some tests, thankfully, Pete didn't have a concussion (but we had to watch him closely). He was thrilled by the flow of grape popsicles that nurses kept handing him, in between Dad and I working to keep him occupied. We sat with him at the ER while Danny thought he needed some time alone; he decided to go golfing. *What the...what?*

The feeling of desperately wanting a normal family vacation was fleeting. Time in the community pool or hot tub was mostly just me with Mom and Dad. I loved the time we got to spend with them as always. They focus so much on the kids, and that brings me peace (and time to pee alone!).

I know the kids had fun, and that is always at the top of the priority list. I just felt like Danny wanted more and more time away from us, be it golfing or going to coffee shops for some alone time. I'm thankful to have had some time in the warm, dry heat, though. Even with the sunburned shoulders and all...

Fast forward to today – I finally had the nerve to sit down with Danny and talk out all of my own feelings. He said he had felt my anger towards him. So, I was honest and expressed my feelings. I felt he heard me and agreed with what I was saying. I'm so glad. It was a relief to be able to open up and be honest.

He didn't have the best time in Arizona, he admitted. I told him how I felt stuck between "where he was at" and a protective and loving dad who would do anything to make things right. Dad was all about the kids while we were there, and that truly helped me out, but Dan said at times it made him feel like he wasn't enough. It feels so good to have talked tonight, to have an open dialogue. Now, I don't feel quite as stuck. When we can talk hard times out like that, I feel so relieved.

"Trust in the Lord with all your heart, and don't depend on your own understanding. Remember the Lord in all you do, and He will give you success" Proverbs 3:5-6 (NCV Mom's Bible, God's Wisdom for Mothers).

March 24, 2010
It's been another one of those days. Today it was harder to control the patience factor, as it seemed to jump out the window early on. I woke up in a good mood. The boys got on the bus, and I waved them off to another day of school.

Then things went downhill when little incidents kept happening. We needed to get out of the house. My day went a little something like this:

1. I've been watching the neighbor baby every so often and didn't realize, when we went to get into the truck, that I hadn't installed his carseat yet. That's a two handed job, and I only had one

available. I managed to lose some skin off my knuckles but got it in there.

2. Anna took my keys from my purse and threw them into the backseat - took me twenty-five minutes to figure that out.
3. A sippy cup dumped all over the backseat. It wouldn't have been so bad if it wasn't cottage cheese-milk from last week.
4. I risked my life trying to obtain a potential mold sample from the ceiling of our root cellar.
5. Mold was confirmed but can be treated for the potential home buyers. Fabulous.
6. Wearing my stylin' cowboy belt wasn't the best idea when it came time to take Anna and the baby into a dirty public restroom.
7. I took the little ones to a restaurant for lunch where we could sit down and have someone else bring the food. All went well until Anna dropped her apple juice and punctured a hole in the side of her Styrofoam cup and juice came guzzling out.
8. Other than living a full week in one day, it's been super relaxing.

April 3, 2010
This morning I didn't feel like getting out of bed. I am feeling so tired lately. Danny wasn't awake, so I got up like normal to tend to the troops. I took the kids to open gym and then to Grace and Joe's house for pizza later on. Danny didn't join us because he didn't feel like being social. It felt good to talk to Grace. I haven't had a chance to share with her in a while. I feel like I can spill all of my feelings to her. From the days of sharing a bedroom growing up until now, she's always been a good listener. Even though we view some things differently, she really has compassion and understanding.

April 7, 2010
I had to get out when Danny got home from work this evening. I needed to go someplace where no one needed me. Everyone was finding fault in everything I did *all* day long. And when Dan got home, dinner wasn't good enough or done on time. Anna was literally pulling at my pant leg. I just needed to leave before I lost it. I told him I needed some time alone, went out to the car, and left. I just drove around town for a while and ended up

in an empty parking lot. I wanted peace; I didn't want anyone to see me cry. I sat there sobbing and crying out to the Lord.

What do I do, Lord? No one wants me, they just need me. How can I keep at this when I feel so worn and underappreciated.

Once I collected myself, I sat up straighter in my seat, took a few deep breaths, and headed home. I pulled in to see the boys' faces smeared on their bedroom window, just waiting for me to pull in. Pete's shirt was totally visible and appropriate, "Trouble finds me even in camouflage." When their little boy eyes' met mine, I knew I could do it. *I can make it through this day.*

April 20, 2010

"Mom, the upstairs toilet is clogged! Oh, and I dropped my applesauce on the floor and now it's all sticky, so I covered it with a towel!"

When I asked DK to clean it up, he said, "I don't want to get started on a huge project right now."

April 22, 2010

The funniest thing happened last week during a house showing. Danny's folks were kind enough to let Dutch come over to their house for a bit during the day so that I could run errands in peace. Great, that's a win-win. Sunny is there, Dutch and Sunny get along great, and they will keep each other company.

Long story short, they broke free from the confines of the screened in porch and had a *Ferris Bueller* experience. We heard from neighbors, and the mailman, that they were spotted taking a dip in the river, walking about Main Street like two old men, wagging tails as they strolled along. We would have had no idea if it weren't for the tear in the screen and people sharing the story around town! They came home, went back into the porch, and waited for Danny's arrival as if they wore a watch. Either way, hearing the story piece by piece? Legendary.

April 28, 2010

I feel like everyone needs something from me when all I want is peace and quiet. I went upstairs to steal a few moments to myself and found our bed covered in Anna's dolls. All of those eyes staring at me. I wanted to hide to process my feelings. I can't always pretend I'm one-hundred percent. But the slightest change in my mood can set Dan off. Especially when it comes to the patience needed for the kids. If he thinks I'm stressed about a little thing, he'll come at it with a sledge hammer. And we can't have that. I just need to steal a few moments of peace when I can to breathe and regroup.

I just heard the coolest song and downloaded on my iPod, *God's Will* by Martina McBride:

"I've been searchin', wonderin', thinkin'
Lost and lookin' all my life.
I've been wounded, jaded, loved, and hated
I've wrestled wrong and right"

I love the story this song tells. I think that's why I like country music so much, nothing like a good story.

April 30, 2010

Our house still isn't sold and I'm OK with it. All of the work for showings that are no-shows, keeping the house clean and smelling like fresh baked cookies is exhausting. Dutch is at peak anxiety on car rides, and I find I'm literally tackling him, Sumo style, to get him to relax. Also the laundry, clean or dirty, doesn't matter, it gets loaded up, and out we go. All of it is getting old.

I've had about every emotion this week. Between learning that Dad now has prostate cancer, and trying to be patient with all that is going on at home, I'm *drained* emotionally and physically. Dad has decided not to monkey with treatment for the prostate cancer. He is stubborn, but also quick to say, it won't "take me out." It's slow growing and common. Danny has been sleeping a lot. I know I need to have patience, but it's so difficult when all the time, that *is* what I'm doing, *being patient*. Can anyone have patience for me when I feel overwhelmed or my feelings neglected?

Chapter 5

May 6, 2010

Danny just doesn't care right now. He was doing so well for weeks but then something yesterday made him upset, and the words that he spoke to me were *beyond* comprehension; they cut me so deep. I hoped we could reconnect and talk about it. I had dinner going in the crockpot all day, and it smelled amazing. When he got home, he refused to eat with us. He left to go get himself some Burger King right at bedtime.

I did bedtime all by myself... *again*. He has been committed to a diet and eating healthier, so I'm trying to follow that with meals for all of us. I feel defeated, like the air has been let out of my balloon. When he gets so frustrated like this it honestly scares me. I'm really trying my best to do what's needed for everyone, and it still falls short.

I've had a headache most of the afternoon and I know stress doesn't help. I've been tracking food and dairy items to see if there is any connection with those things. I do think stress is my biggest kicker, though. I've been texting with Grace, and she is very understanding and told me I can lean on her. Sometimes now, I feel so forlorn. Dan said he cried his eyes into his pillow last night after falling asleep fully clothed, in case Anna coughed in the night. Sometimes he doesn't make sense, and as much as I try to be patient, he gets angry with me if I don't see it from his point of view. I'm trying hard to understand and to have compassion. But the truth is, I don't understand him when his thoughts are all over the map. This is so hard.

When things are good, they are good. But when they are bad? It's really, *really* hard.

I don't know what tomorrow is going to be like. I need to try to rest and get some sleep. I just can't keep up with this pace. *Help me Oh Lord, fill us with hope (like I feel on good days).*

May 10, 2010
Defeat has been creeping up on me again. I love to blog and tell stories. It's a great creative outlet for me, but I'm finding I need to keep some pieces of my story hidden. I wish I could tell it all and express how I *really* feel, deep down inside. But if I told all of the good, along with the bad, people would know the truth about Danny. It's easier to tell the fun, light-hearted stuff. I live in this shame, like I need to hide it away. It's a dark and lonely place to be.

As much as I try to keep a smile and remain positive, sometimes it's forced. Not all of the time, though. I know the true joy down deep that can't be snuffed comes from the Lord. That deep down hurt has me wondering how I can change this situation. I try to be upbeat but then get impatient and angry. And that's not who I am. I waver and try to muster through all of these layers.

Lord, please give me the courage to handle these times as I should. To follow You and Your ways, not my own. I know You will provide me with the tools I need to manage all of this. Sometimes I just don't know what way to turn. I need to turn this over to You.

May 15, 2010
DK lost his first tooth today while eating a Taco Bell taco. He ended up swallowing it, but the Tooth Fairy still needs to come. Hopefully the tooth doesn't need to be present for the Tooth Fairy! Another fun roll I get to take on. I'd better be sneaky, though; he's a suspicious kid!

May 21, 2010
Danny is gone for the weekend golfing with some buddies. I pray he is safe and that he will keep with what we talked about before he left. He said

he is going to cut back on his beer consumption. I reached out this week to ask some questions to better understand Bipolar Disorder. Uncle Nate was very gracious in his response, and I know he will keep it between us. I want to learn how I can help my husband cope and manage.

DK has a stomach bug and threw up all over the family room. Anna has Croup. Every few hours we are sitting on the closed toilet lid, bathroom door closed with the shower kicking out full steam to help Anna breathe. I sure hope we can all get some sleep tonight.

There is *hope*, and I know it. Hope for our marriage and for our children. *Please forgive me, Oh Lord, for the ways I am selfish. I love you, Lord, and thank You for our family. I pray I can continue to cling to this hope and know it only comes from You. Truly, from You.*

May 23, 2010
I'm just reading in my devotions about asking *Why? Why did this happen?* There is so much more hurt in this world, awful pain and suffering. I have found myself asking *why* when it comes to mental illness. Sometimes I wonder if I made the wrong decisions. I feel terrible to even think that.

Tonight's devotion titled, "But Why, Why, Why?" was great insight. The prayer at the end really spoke to my heart:

"Sometimes I get discouraged over such things. Help me to reach out toward Your ever-loving arms that want to enfold me and give me comfort in the midst of my pain." (Daily Devotions inspired by 90 Minutes in Heaven, Don Piper and Cecil Murphey). Encouraging words.

Dan and I had some good conversation about friendships, who he perceives as good and who not the best influences. These conversations get really hard to work through, so I'm glad we did. He is willing to put distance between himself and those who don't help steer him on a good path. I'm not sure how or when he'll start, I just want to support however I can.

May 28, 2010

We've made a final decision to pull the house off the market. So many ups and downs with trying to sell this old, colonial farmhouse, but we have decided to stay. The truth remains: this place needs help. Right now it seems more than we can possibly grasp. But it's doable. We can continue to make this dream a reality. We already had blueprints drawn for an addition five years ago.

So we are back to dreaming, pondering, and wanting to be here. This one-hundred-year-old house has a solid structure and provides for modest living. Nothing fancy, but hey, look at us; we aren't all that fancy ourselves. Shoot, DK had dried ketchup, black marker, and a crusty booger on his face when we went into the hardware store today. I did the ol' lick my thumb trick to try to help him out, but my hand was pushed aside.

June 6, 2010

What a week last week was. I shed so many tears and felt hopeless. I felt betrayed and even got thinking more along the lines of *what if. What if I left.*

Danny was very angry with me last week. He was late getting home one night, and I accused him of hiding his beer because I found it in the laundry. How else would it have gotten there? He got so mad at me and started yelling awful, hurtful things. Then he yanked off his cross necklace and threw it out the upstairs window. That was hurtful on so many levels. I had gotten him that cross with our names engraved on the back so he'd always know he had the Lord and his family here for him.

I became genuinely afraid. I started crying and stood there feeling all of my emotions, raw and exposed. My vulnerability and sadness didn't even matter to him. Soon I heard the lawnmower and realized he was mowing over where the cross necklace landed in the grass. Dan came back inside and punched the dining room wall. He hit it so hard it dented the plaster. He stormed over towards me and began telling me I had to punch him. He even grabbed my hand, made it into a fist, and used it to hit himself in the chest.

I just stood there in shock. He finally started to come down a bit and admitted he was upset that I called his counselor. How could I do that to him? I did it because I've been fearful and kept at arm's length, I needed to know what I was missing and how I could help. Instead, I got this rage turned on me and was told I had no business contacting her, that I had overstepped.

I thought he was coming down off of the manic episode when he headed back outside. I found myself standing in the bathroom staring myself down in the mirror. "Ok Char, it's ok, just breathe, you're trying to help, breathe." I collected myself.

I then calmly opened the back door and called his name. He didn't answer. I kept calling to him with no response.

When I finally found him out back, my eyes locked on the rope hanging securely to a tall tree. He stood there, next to it, acting surprised that I found him. I reached him just in time. *How do I make sense of this?* All of this because I was trying to contact his counselor as a means to help him. A part of my heart broke in that moment, and it isn't ever coming back.

These are hard times, but God is good. I'm remaining thankful, even in the ugliest of moments. The Lord continues to provide for and protect us. When Danny is in this state of mind, it's not him. It's so hard to put into words, but it's like an out of body experience. I pray he will come out of this place and return to us.

June 8, 2010

Today was a wonderful day. I felt like I gave my best to all three kids and managed to keep my patience. We made pancakes for breakfast, and I even let them all help. We got some chores done around home and then went out to spend some of my birthday money. I patched and primed the walls in the dining room so they are ready to be painted. We ordered some pizza, watched COPS, and before we knew it, it was bedtime.

It's kind of sad to me that a wonderful day doesn't include Danny anymore. He has been going about his business, staying out all hours with friends at the bar. I wouldn't ever *want* to live like that, yet it does make me mad that he shows no sense of obligation to his family. These kids are growing up fast, and he's missing it. When he gets home late at night, he tries to get intimate with me. I'm not interested in having him kiss me with his cigarette/beer mouth, yet I don't want to set him off. It's so hard to be in this spot. I'm fearful of a repeat of last week. I feel trapped in my own home.

Thank you, Lord, for keeping us safe today. For simply keeping us safe.

June 12, 2010
I made the decision, after thinking about it for a while, to move our master bedroom downstairs into what was our family room. I know if I just keep waiting for help, it won't happen. Part of the beauty of a farmhouse, with these big open rooms, is they don't have to be just one thing. I love that. I gave the room a fresh coat of green paint, took our furniture apart, and moved it all down the stairs myself. Now each kiddo has their own room upstairs. Mission accomplished!

I downloaded a song today called *You Lost Me* by Christina Aguilera. It's like the lyrics speak to me. I've listened to it over and over:

"And we had magic, and this is tragic.
You couldn't keep your hands to yourself.
I feel like our world's been infected, and somehow you left me neglected.
We've found our life's been changed. Babe, you lost me"

June 22, 2010
I'm glad he's home safe, I'm always glad for that. But I literally got sick when he walked in the door. He had to get a ride home from a co-worker because he was too drunk to drive. Our car is parked somewhere downtown, forty-five minutes from home. He even admitted he drank more knowing he could probably get a ride home with Steve. I'm embarrassed and fuming. Yes, it was the right call to get a ride with someone because there is no way he could have even driven a mile. Where and when is *he* held accountable for his actions? What if he gets a DUI or worse, causes an accident and hurts someone else? I bet he doesn't even think of any of those

consequences. I know a lot of the time he chooses to drive home, even if blackout drunk. I'm just sick over this.

I never thought this would be me, doing life alone. Yet, here I sit dealing with all of this heaviness. I need to choose my words very carefully and protect myself. I'm so grateful that none of this comes out on the kids, but I know they feel it. Our marriage is less of a partnership and more of me parenting him. My heart and head hurt so bad. *Do we even matter to him?* We had a family gathering tonight that I took the kids to. Just me plus three, like everyone expects. They've stopped asking where Danny is.

Here come the tears. Will this ever change, and will he commit to help? How do I keep on this cycle, this roller coaster that has become life?

Lord, please give me strength and rest. I need you, Lord God. Heal our hearts, heal our minds. Show me how to keep at this. How to be a supportive wife and good mom. Give me clarity each day anew. Please, Oh Lord, I need You. I am desperate to find how I can keep at this.

June 25, 2010

After planning this trip for months, it's here-our girls weekend away! Nothing but shopping, eating out, and good company. Leading up to this, I've had so much more patience at home knowing I had a break coming. Danny was supportive of me doing this up until two days ago when something changed. He belittled me and told me I was awfully selfish for leaving him with the kids, and I'd better think through what this said about me. He also set the stage that I'm not to speak of what has been going on at home.

Just as we got onto the expressway, I received a text from Danny that simply said, "GOODBYE." My heart jumped into my throat and I started to quietly panic. In my head, horrible thoughts and images were circling. Do I ask Alison to turn around or call 9-1-1? *I don't know what to do.* I took a few deep breaths, as quiet as possible, so as to not interrupt the fun conversation going on in the car. The only things that should be on my mind in this moment are which curtains to buy and who's going to pass the peanut M&M's.

With one deep breath, I calmly text back, "Are you ok?"

No response. Meanwhile, my heart is *pounding* so loud it can be heard beating outside of my body.

I turned toward the window to dial his cell number, unassumingly, and he answers. I ask if he's ok and he claims to have no idea what I'm talking about. Arguing at that point would only draw attention to it. I am relieved that he didn't hurt himself, yes. But *why* did he do that only to mess with me and bring me worry? I'm not going to buy it or play his game. I quickly texted Dad to make sure all was well and he told me not to worry; he'd make sure of it.

Lord, clear this mind, let it be filled with simple things. Let me laugh and be in the moment here with these beautiful, God-fearing friends of mine. I'm so thankful for them in my life.

Chapter 6

July 12, 2010

We had a pretty decent week camping with friends. These are the memories I want for our kids, and I love that we have the trailer. Bunk beds in the back, and there's plenty of room inside for rainy days and playing games. I loved camping as a kid, and we did it the old fashioned way, in a tent. I don't think I ever truly appreciated the amount of work that goes into it! I love how simple it is, being outside, dirty bare feet, good food, laughter, and campfires. I love simple. I like to think I'm a simple person. Dad and I have had this conversation a lot. He and I see ourselves as a Chevy, not a Cadillac. Give me a pair of rain boots, a comfy sweatshirt, and my hair in pigtails. That is all I need to be in my happy place.

I think that's part of why I struggle in the difficult moments with Danny. Is it something I said or did to make it so hard? I am all about talking through conflict and learning how to take criticism better. I've always been called sensitive, but I feel like I'm tough.

Now that we're back home, I can feel and sense in the air, a change coming. As much as I've tried to deny it in the past or stay positive, with this, comes survival mode. I can see in his eyes that he's not himself. His pupils get large, and it's a fight or flight response. I swear in these moments; I see Satan in his eyes.

For who knows how long, it's not like I can say, "Just wait twenty-four hours or a week, and we'll be all good." I just want to speak my heart, but

I need to wait. I want to share my feelings but have to wait until the time is right.

Gracious God, I feel incredibly broken during these times. Place on my heart, Lord. What do I do? Please make my heart whole again; able to fill back up and feel like myself. I feel so honestly lost right now. "I love you, Lord, and I lift my voice. To worship You, Oh, my soul."

July 14, 2010

Danny threw my prized front porch chairs into the woods behind the barn tonight. I spent a lot of time refinishing these chairs that an old friend gave us by repainting them yellow, my favorite color. They match the cute rug I found at a garage sale. He just picked each one up in a fit of rage and threw them as far as he could. Then said awful, hateful things to me as I stood there in utter shock. *What on earth did I do to be treated this way?* That's what I keep asking myself. I know he isn't in his right mind, but thinking that doesn't fix this damage he's doing to my heart. It's so pointed at me, so intentional.

As he started to calm down, he admitted to not being truthful about who he's been hanging out with. He wouldn't say who he's been with, just that he wasn't being honest with me. I stood there shaking like a leaf not knowing what was coming next. I pray he will come back down to earth and be himself again. This weekend is important to me. My sister Grace is getting married.

I want him to try his best to be a part of this. If for nothing else, for me. I need to pray for healing in my heart after hearing awful things about myself; about my body, how disgusting he finds me, and how much my hips have grown. I've birthed three children! I know this, but it hurts. From the man I married, and who is supposed to hold me up and support, he makes me feel so small. He doesn't apologize or regret saying these things. Yet I'm supposed to be more understanding of him. I feel so embarrassed and hurt.

July 17, 2010
We headed for Frankfort yesterday, and Anna hasn't been sleeping well. She has been running a fever and can only say, "My belly hwerts." Poor soul. It seems like every time we head out of town someone ends up sick or injured!

At the rehearsal dinner last night, Anna was vomiting on my lap. I managed to turn her so it went under the table, but there went my cute sandals and new capri pants. Danny wasn't even around; he was sitting up at the bar. The boys were sitting on Papa's lap at another table, so I quietly got up and took her to the bathroom to wash up. I didn't want to draw any attention, this was Grace and Joe's day. I was just so grateful to be a part of it.

Hopeful that Anna will feel better and Dan will see the need to help out with the kids.

July 18, 2010
The weather was amazing, as was Grace and Joe's wedding yesterday. I am so happy for them. Anna hasn't fared so well, her fever won't break, her little cheeks are rosy, and she's exhausted. Today is Pete's birthday, and even though I had thoughts of this trip being *fun,* quality family time, it's not.

Between the wedding and reception, Danny insisted I take him and Anna back to our hotel. He claimed it was so she could rest, but I know he has a few six-packs in our room. What am I to do? I don't want to miss Grace's reception, but I knew Anna wasn't going to make it, so we took the forty-five-mile trek back to our hotel. Not without a speeding ticket, though. I suppose being distracted by Dan's anger, and Anna being so sick, I wasn't paying attention to the road signs.

Oh Lord, give me the strength to balance all of these feelings and emotions. I'm angry, sad, frustrated, but also thankful. Does that even make sense? It does in my head. No matter what, I hope Grace and Joe felt special on their day.

July 24, 2010
Poor Anna, she is asleep now, and it looks like her fever is finally coming down. What a whirlwind this week has been. After days of wondering

why her fever wouldn't break, and calling the doctor's office four times, we landed in the children's hospital. After several tests and an ultrasound, they found her appendix had ruptured! She's only two-years-old. *How is this even possible?*

Since being admitted, she's had a few different drains put in her belly to get the infection out. Watching nurses wheel her down hallways, when I had to stay put in the waiting room, was hard. Mom, Dad and Grace were right there with me, though. Grace drove through the night to be with Anna and me when she heard the news, even though this was her honeymoon week! She's simply amazing.

Both boys were kept occupied today by friends who agreed to keep them for the day. Danny has come up to visit once since we were admitted. I haven't yet showered in peace or eaten an actual meal in days. I'm so overwhelmed by everyone praying for us, bringing cookies, magazines, coloring books, and games. Praising God for bringing her through this!

July 25, 2010
Anna had a tough night last night. I don't feel like she's quite out of the woods yet. The fact that the infection was able to leak from her appendix into her little body, is scary. The longest nap she's gotten was two hours today. Pastor D. came up to pray and visit with us, along with several others throughout the day. No Danny today, but we're managing like usual. Both boys have been occupied by Nan and Papa or at friends' houses, and for that, I'm grateful. People like to help. I need to be better about asking for it.

July 27, 2010
Tonight Anna was treated by the therapy dogs stopping by her room. She got her fingernails painted; she's a new woman! It's been a constant flow of white coats in and out. They had to flush her drain again, and she cried her eyes out. I wish they could just poke and prod me instead. There's nothing worse than seeing your kids in pain and not being able to fix it.

July 28, 2010
I thought we were going to become crispy critters after the fire alarm situation in the middle of the night! I was woken up to the annoying alarm

going off in our hospital room and fluorescent lights flashing across the courtyard. At first I thought it was a drill, but when the fire trucks pulled up; it was no joke.

I was told by the floor nurse when I poked my head out in the hallway that they'd let me know if we had to evacuate. *Seriously?* So I did what any other woman would do at that time of night/morning. I put my bra and a sweatshirt on and sat in the dark, waiting. Thoughts of unplugging Anna and wrapping her in a blanket, making a run for it down the seven levels of stairs, filled my head. I probably sat there in ready position for over an hour. But we never got even a knock on the door, and despite all the commotion, Anna never woke up.

July 29, 2010

I'm beyond exhausted right now from the hospital and all of the emotions that came from our stay. Anna did amazingly well. In six weeks they will remove her deflated appendix after she's had some time to heal. Reflecting on all of it, I'm so thankful Anna did so well, that it wasn't a worst-case scenario. Grace being there with us, Mom and Dad being there and helping with both boys, was a blessing. We made it. Now I feel like there isn't enough caffeine to keep this mama awake any longer. I need a seventy-two-hour nap.

Please call on me, Jesus, because I need to hear from You… please give me peace that passes all understanding.

Chapter 7

August 2, 2010

While DK was dinking around in the lake in front of Mom and Dad's this morning, he stepped on something sharp and called out to me. I went running to find a big ol' hole in the bottom of his foot! We threw a Ziploc bag over it and headed to the medical center.

Five stitches later, it looks like football will be on the back burner for now. I told him when I got my first stitches while carving a pumpkin, how Papa took me for a new toy afterwards because I was so brave. Naturally, I did the same with DK. He never even cried. I'm so proud of this kid.

August 11, 2010

I have never been so afraid *in all of my life*. I thought for sure he was going to kill me last night.

We have been camping with friends and their kids all week. This is our third campground in five days, and we've had a lot of fun, that is, up until yesterday morning when Danny locked us out of the trailer. Fortunately, I had all of the beach gear out and ready so we didn't need to get back in. I was trying to keep my composure while packing up and walking to the beach, but Ashlee knows me so well. She knew I was struggling. Her and her husband, Chris, chipped right in and helped make the day a good one, despite what I was feeling underneath.

After spending the day at the beach, we were all whipped. I knew there was a lot of alcohol in the trailer, so I was dreading what I might to walk into. He finally opened the door after knocking four or five times. I managed to put the kids to bed and started for the front of the trailer. I saw Danny laying in bed and decided I would sleep on the sofa instead. As I was laying down, I felt my arm being yanked as I was lifted up off the couch by hand. "You are sleeping with me. You're my wife, you will sleep in this bed."

He stood over me while scolding me about how useless I am. I was so terrified, but got into the bed with him anyway. He was listening to satanic sounding music raging on his earphones. It was so loud; it was as if he was the only one listening to it.

I laid there wondering who to call, who would rescue us. He needed professional help, but who could get there fast enough? I could call Uncle Nate. He knows the situation, but it'd take too long for him to get here. I don't know where the nearest hospital is or if I would even have a phone signal to call 9-1-1. What would he do if I tried to get back out of bed? I was paralyzed with fear and waited for his breathing pattern to change so I knew he was asleep. I stared at the ceiling all night long. Every sound or movement made me hold my breath. I started calling out to the Lord *Please keep us safe, please Lord, please.* I didn't sleep a wink.

The next morning was Chris' birthday and they were making a big breakfast to celebrate. I got up early so I could tell them we wouldn't be joining them, since I wasn't sure what Danny would do. Before I had the chance, Dan got up as if the night before never happened. He was super joyful and went about eating eggs and pancakes while thanking them for breakfast.

WHAT. JUST. HAPPENED.

August 19, 2010
"...so your Joy is independent of circumstances. This is how you trust Me in the moments of your life" (Jesus Calling: Enjoying Peace in His Presence by Sarah Young).

I love that. I want to *trust* even in these hard times, in moments of fear, unknowns, and complicated situations. *I trust you, Lord. I do. Please continue to keep us safe.*

August 23, 2010

I painted all three kids' bedrooms in two days, and I love how they turned out. Mom and Dad helped a ton by taking the kids during the day. Then, in the evenings, we went out on their boat with snacks and small cans of Sunkist. The weather has been amazing, and it's so relaxing to just sit and chat. I love the feeling of the wind blowing through my hair. It's a great way to clear my mind. This ability to spend time with the kids and my folks is priceless. I'm thankful for being able to stay home and be *Mom*. I know these days of the kids being young are fleeting and I want to enjoy it all. Doing house projects makes me feel good, too. It makes me feel like I serve a purpose.

August 24, 2010

It's been an up-down-all-around week. Danny has been really happy, giddy actually, but he is starting to level out. Yesterday I wasn't sure which way things would go, but we're getting there. I'm thankful we are moving towards being on the same page. I have been enjoying this version of him; he is motivated and attentive to me. I'll take it because it's not often that he makes eyes at me or even says thank you.

Last night felt a lot different, though. I had a flat tire while I was out running errands, and Danny told me to find someone else to help. There I was, with only a few other cars in the parking lot, left to figure it out. By God's grace a young man and his dad saw my predicament and offered to help. The young man drove to his house to get some tools and came back to change my tire for me. I was so overwhelmed by his kindness! There are still good people in this world.

August 26, 2010

Things have been going so well that I'm hit with this fear that it will all go downhill soon. Danny continues to be present and aware. He even did the dishes tonight. He hasn't done housework in months. He is like a new man, the man I married. If only this could last longer than a few days at a time.

We heard from the insurance company that we would have to put up a fight to get continued counseling treatment. There are only a certain number of visits covered each year under Danny's insurance, and he doesn't want to feel forced to disclose his mental health diagnosis to his employer. What a frustrating process. Since that news, he's been struggling. He asked that I keep the kids out and busy for a while so he could have some quiet. I understand needing alone time. I'm just hopeful it doesn't turn into anger.

"I go to bed and sleep in peace, because, Lord, only you keep me safe" Psalm 4:8 (NCV Mom's Bible, God's Wisdom for Mothers).

August 29, 2010
I'm afraid he's slipping tonight. He's distant and keeps saying, "C'mon, just play along you know this, c'mon," while I'm trying to make a grocery list for school lunches. I'm sitting here writing as my husband is slipping away. He's making no sense and trying to coax me into an argument. There went his mood. There went the good. Time to prepare for what tomorrow may look like...

August 30, 2010
Pete and I had a date last night, just the two of us. It was wonderful, and he had me laughing the whole time. He chose to have dinner at a steak restaurant where we shared a salad. He wouldn't venture to my side of the plate with his fork because he doesn't like sharing germs. He's hilarious. Afterwards, we walked around town, got a hot fudge sundae, and played at the park. He kept thinking of things to do to make the night last longer. It was priceless. He's such a special boy - I enjoyed doing this with DK a few weeks ago, too. I love that they'll still hold my hand in public, and we talk about anything and everything. If only these days would last.

August 31, 2010
Why can't the good stay? Why can't my husband be the same as he was two short days ago? I knew it and felt it underneath, the need for some "quiet time." I was hopeful it was only quiet he needed, but it's more than that.

Why? There's that question again. *Why?* At this rate, I don't know how we will make it until February when counseling starts back up. Now he's saying he thinks he can wean off his medications and get back to normal. That's a terrifying thought.

Earlier today, cousin Sylvie made me cry. She stopped along the side of the road and picked me wild flowers. They are sitting in a vase on my nightstand. Such a simple gesture that meant the world.

Lord God, have mercy on us. Show Danny he needs some help in whatever form he is willing to receive. Why can't the good just stay, Oh Lord, why? And Lord, thank you for these glimmers of good in the world through your servants like sweet, sincere Sylvie.

September 4, 2010

Dan told me this morning he is needing more time to himself, so he packed up and headed east. What about my time and my feelings? I continue to hold down our family alone while he figures himself out. I can't help but feel he's selfish with his time. He won't let me in, and yet, I feel like a prisoner. I do whatever I can to keep the kids busy and so that they don't notice, but I'm sure they do. I wish Danny would think of *us*, but he doesn't. *Lord please give me what I need to make it through this day. Just today, be gracious to us. Please.*

September 8, 2010

Anna has her appendix out tomorrow morning. *Oh Lord, please keep her little body safe and strong. For healing her little body. I praise You oh Lord.*

Danny has been on and off crabby again. Well, angrier I would say. I'm wondering if I enable him too much. I've been doing some serious thinking about starting to take instead of give. It's against my nature, but I think I need to start standing up for myself more. I always fear the consequences. That doesn't make me wrong, though.

Last night he was so mean to me, mad over nothing, so I questioned his alcohol consumption. He denied it and told me I was a lazy wife who just lives off of his paycheck while I sit at home doing nothing. This morning he admitted he had been drinking last night. So he can admit it but not apologize for lying and humiliating me?

It was really neat that a mysterious person got poop all over the bathroom upstairs, and now I get to clean it up. Not that I can't handle poop, it's just that I'm emotionally and physically spent. I've been working so hard to get the house ready for a women's retreat I'm hosting, and it's wearing me out. I'm stressed over the details. *Lord, please meet me here, in the details.*

September 10, 2010
Yesterday morning was an early one. I set my phone alarm to go off at 4:30 am. I woke up a few times in the night, like usual when I know I have an early morning coming, but managed to get enough sleep. I grabbed a bowl of Anna's favorite cereal, Alphabets, and then went out to start the truck. Once everything was set, I went up and scooped Anna out of bed, and we headed for the hospital. Hard to believe it's been six weeks already since her appendix ruptured. Today is the day that deflated balloon comes out, or as Anna says, "go to the hospickle to get da ackies outta my bwelly."

After giving her medication to make her loopy, off she went for surgery. She insisted on wearing her pink cowgirl boots. The doctor and nurses got quite the kick out of her. Mom and Dad came to sit with me in the waiting room and all went well. I still can't believe it's an outpatient procedure. We left the hospital after a few hours with a polaroid of her appendix and a lot of gas pains from anesthesia.

September 13, 2010
I just put Anna in her bed for a nap and Petey-wheat is in his room for some QT. I'm not sure either will stay where they are, but we'll see. I'm finding my patience is worn thin again today after the constant "Mom? Mom? Why? Mama? Mom?"

Pete told me today that his eyes *are* bigger than his belly button. He doesn't quite get why we keep telling him his eyes are bigger than his stomach. This kid!

September 16, 2010

Everything's coming together so nicely for the retreat. I'm having a blast setting up, the neighbors offered their driveway for more parking, and I got Dutch anxiety pills. I got the ingredients for all of the meals and some fresh flowers to put out. I love fresh flowers; they add so much to a room. The little touches are coming together, and I'm excited.

The boys are at school, and Anna just went with Nan. Mom and Dad stopped by with the tables and chairs for me to use, and now I need to do some more cleaning. Before he left, Dad said, "I like this house. You want to know why? Because it feels like a home." It really does.

(*Later that same day*) I feel lonely and lost tonight. I've repainted the family room, moved our bedroom downstairs, and rearranged our house for this retreat. I've painted bedrooms, touched up trim work, and done laundry until my arms fell off. So much work, so much pride. The kids are situated at my folks so the house could stay clean, and I finished setting up.

Dan pulled in from work, and I immediately knew something was amiss. This was a different episode than I've seen. He was really excitable and quite angry at the same time. Out of nowhere, he stripped down to his underwear and went outside, shaking his head and cussing me out. He began moving our trash barrels and recycling containers around in the driveway while sputtering hateful words. Cars were constantly driving by with heads turn in our direction. When he came back inside, he sat down at one of the tables I had set up and started lecturing me about how this is *his* house, and I have no right to have people come over.

I wish my husband encouraged me, but instead, is cunning and malicious in his words and actions. He made me feel worthless and humiliated. He told me it looks *sloppy*. In these times I'm not sure where to turn. I tried my best to de-escalate him. Nothing was working. In the end, I'm left feeling devastated yet again.

September 17, 2010

I called and made myself an appointment for counseling today. I think it's time. I have never been before but am hopeful having someone to hear my side helps. I am getting discouraged by having to hide my feelings all of the time. I'm packing them down deep so I can maintain the patience and smile I want to have. Although, sometimes the smallest things become mountains, and I start yelling. I know what's at the root each time. It's not fair of me to lose my patience on the kids when they aren't the true cause.

Chapter 8

September 22, 2010

I've weighed my options in my mind, and I'm thinking about leaving. *Would that make me a failure?* Where is my happiness though? My joy, my ability to hold my head high? That is the constant battle in my head.

Oh Lord God, I come before You with my heart open. Pouring it out to You. Help me have discernment. Clarity. Contentment. Peace in my heart. Please move my feet one in front of the other. Hear me as I drop to my knees with palms lifted to You, heal my heart, show me how, Lord.

September 23, 2010

It's been another crazy day with packing lunches, showers, getting everyone up and out by 8 am. Anna had her follow up with the surgeon and all is well. Praise the Lord!

Afterwards, we headed to the grocery store when she informed me from her car seat that she just peed her pants. *Great.* After I got her cleaned up and in a new pair, we went to school to pop in and surprise the boys with McDonald's lunch. Even though DK was the one who begged me to come, when he saw us, his face didn't hide his embarrassment. Oh, and I backed into our cow bell with the truck. Now it's loose.

On a day like this, I tend to look back and laugh. Life is too short not to laugh through the day-to-day happenings. I think that's why when Danny is looking to hurt me with his words, calling me lazy and useless, it cuts deep. The fact that I don't have a job outside of the home does not make me lazy. I've never been needed more than at home with these three humans. This has always been my dream job, to be at home with my babies. It's what my mom did, and I've always admired her for it. No job could pay me nearly what this one does.

September 25, 2010

Things have been different. Last week I was at a complete loss of how or where to turn. My feelings, that have bottling up for *seemingly* ever, came out. I told Danny I'm thinking of "separating things" and taking the kids somewhere. I told him I worry about how his moods are affecting the kids, especially DK. He said he always feels the mood shift. It was powerful; I felt like he listened. I said what I've been needing to say and how we can't move forward like this. He said he agrees and understands.

Lord, I need patience and guidance that only You can provide. Please point me in the ways in which I should go. Every moment, guide me in how to calmly react and speak my mind.

I am starting to see my counseling appointments as a blessing rather than with resentment. I usually just sit and cry the whole time, but now I'm starting to open up.

September 26, 2010

Pete lost his second tooth today, or should I say, allowed Papa to pull it out. Papa is the only one Pete will let anywhere near his mouth! When we went to pack up from nephew Matt's lacrosse game, I realized I left the headlights on again! We left the truck there and went to grab some dinner with Nan and Papa. When we got back, the engine started right up! The kids joked that Papa jumped it, and they all started to jump. So cute.

September 29, 2010

Danny just left home to head east, pulling the trailer. He usually leaves it parked at a friend's place until spring. I understand why he brought it there, but it just gives him more freedom to leave and have his own place. He's becoming more and more removed, not just from us, but friends, too. I want to support his health and wellness but also need something from him. I can't be the one who holds everything together all of the time. Does that make me selfish or lacking compassion? I don't think so. If he would just work together with me, I want to help him get the right balance of medication and treatment. But as I've learned, I'm not to touch either topic.

September 30, 2010

I drove Dan's car this morning to an appointment, and it is filthy. I got a few miles from home when the car started beeping and flashing the *check engine* light, relentlessly. I pulled over and called Danny with no answer. Three calls and repeated texts later, still no response. There I sat waiting, getting more upset over the fact that I'll be late for my appointment. After several more calls, he finally answered and downplayed the whole thing, saying there is nothing wrong with the car, to keep going. If he had told me this happens to his car on occasion, I wouldn't be running ten minutes late and in such a foul mood.

October 6, 2010

I've been thinking about how thankful I am for Dad. He is serving these kids as if he were their father. As much as I wrestle with them feeling fatherless, I know they have Dad. My dad is their father here on earth. He's gone on their field trips, taken care of them while sick, tucked them in during naptime, made them meals, and reads and shares what the Bible says to them. If they are naughty or out of line, he gently pulls them aside and talks them through. And for this, I am grateful.

"He is always ready to offer assistance; all you need to do is ask. When the path before you looks easy and straightforward, you may be tempted to go it alone instead of relying on Me. This is when you are in the greatest danger of stumbling" (Jesus Calling: Enjoying Peace in His Presence by Sarah Young).

So powerful, oh Lord, please carry us right now. For not knowing what lies ahead is hard, but my trust is in You!

October 14, 2010

Danny opted to head out east again. Not that we have a lot going on at home, but it makes me feel like I'm a single mom *again*. Why we can't we just take a weekend to relax as a family of five? Looks like we'll spend some time at the lake helping Dad take the boat dock out. I recall the first year helping Dad do it. It was mid-October, the water was freezing cold, and we didn't have waders. We went waist high in jeans. Good times.

October 24, 2010

I am enjoying my time with my counselor more than ever. I'm digging deeper with her and being totally honest. To have an objective point of view helps, and so does knowing she isn't judging me. Danny and I have talked again recently about separating for a while. He finds ways to talk me out of it by being understanding, and I want to believe what he's saying is true. But there's always that doubt. Oh well. Tomorrow starts a fresh week. We can do this.

Lord, please watch over us, lead us, protect us, please be here with us, Oh Lord God. Lead us not into temptation, but deliver us from evil. Danny has had a good day today, and I'll take it.

October 26, 2010

I just went up to check the kids. Tears filled my eyes as I watched each of them sleep. I dropped to my knees and cried out. *Please protect these pure and innocent minds from harm and danger, Lord Jesus. They are so beautiful.*

Anna has been wanting me to hold her all the time, sit on my lap, and be right by me. I know this time will pass and she won't want to anymore, but sometimes I am consumed with doing other things and don't have the patience I should.

DK said to me tonight before bed, "You are the second most beautiful thing in the whole world." I asked him what was the first and he said, "God." So precious. As he's getting older, he doesn't say things like that just to say them. That made it even more heartfelt.

Danny struggled with a lot of anxiety last week leading up to taking the boys to the OSU football game. He had been promising to take them for weeks. The night before, he bailed and said I had to take them and "they will have more fun with you." Around and around we went. He was really angry with me. It turns out the root of his anxiety was that I mentioned to Mom that he was going to give sobriety a try. While I meant him no disrespect, his reaction was quite harsh. This expectation that I am to keep my mouth shut, about even this, is unreasonable. I have internalized so much. I'm not even allowed to tell people I'm in counseling.

"So don't worry, because I am with you. Don't be afraid, because I am your God. I will make you strong and will help you; I will support you with My right hand that saves you" Isaiah 41:10 (NCV Mom's Bible, God's Wisdom for Mothers).

Chapter 9

November 2, 2010

I've been awake since Anna came downstairs crying at 3:30 am. I scooped her up and put her in bed next to me, only to find she was soaked in pee. We quickly went up to her room, got her changed, and tucked back in bed. By then, I was wide awake, so I started pondering life.

I thought about dates Dan and I went out on when we were teenagers, our early married days, jobs I've had, and finally started to doze off. No sooner was Pete standing next to me saying something about glow sticks and "I didn't mean to." As a mom, that's never something you like to hear. I head on up to Pete's room to find his quilt glowing along with the other four blankets, sheets, and sixteen stuffed animals on his bed.

Later on, DK informed me that I'm not allowed to be outside to watch him and Peter get on the bus in my bathrobe. He has a reputation to protect. I must watch and wave from inside from now on. *Noted.*

November 4, 2010

My headaches are coming around so often; it seems I have more time with them than without. I'm trying to function like normal because, well, I *have* to. All three kids have been sick the past few days, too, so I'm exhausted. Mom and Dad to the rescue. They are picking the boys up from school and grabbing Anna from me, so I can have a breather.

The kids love it when Papa picks them up at school. They anxiously await to see his grey pickup truck in the parent pick-up line. He's a celebrity.

November 12, 2010
Getting the kids to bed was no joke last night. It was quite the process because Pete wanted to sleep in Anna's room. DK tried but couldn't because she talks too much. Once everyone was settled, I sat down to catch up on emails and surf the web. Even though my head started telling me it was time for bed, I was bent on enjoying the rare, quiet house. My headache kept gaining steam, and before I knew it, I couldn't even read the clock. I tried taking some sleep medication, but the headache only grew. Fearing vomit and my head popping off my neck, I got up to take two heavy-hitter migraine pills. I could hardly walk or shut my eyes because they wouldn't stop moving back and forth, causing me to reach for the puke bucket. I just lay there in the pitch dark with my eyes open, staring at the ceiling while rocking myself like a baby.

Next thing I knew, Anna was in my face telling me she needed a hug, followed by Pete in my face saying, "It's 7:01 Mom, *when* are you gonna get up?" Although the headache was gone, my skull hurt so bad it was like someone took a baseball bat to it. *Where is Danny?* He decided he needed a break, so he went to a friend's cabin.

In this season of pain, Oh Lord, I pray for quiet, for healing, for the ability to manage what's needed of me while trying to listen more closely to my body. I pray for patience with the kids as I do this on my own. Help me Lord, reach my heart and heal it, please.

Chapter 10

November 15, 2010

Yesterday I yelled repeatedly for peace and quiet and tried having Anna lay down with me. Instead, I ended up giving a ten-minute lecture on what the word *quiet* means. Seeing as how well they are doing today, I would say that talk was effective.

This song has been playing on the radio lately and it catches me every time, *You're Gonna Miss This* by Trace Adkins.

"You're gonna miss this, you're gonna want this back.
You're gonna wish these days hadn't gone by so fast.
These are some good times, so take a good look around,
You may not know it now, but you're gonna miss this."

I will surely miss these days of mass chaos. I know I will.

November 17, 2010

I'm feeling blah right now, that's the best way to describe it. I have a headache and needed to be honest with Danny about what I've been feeling about our relationship. He has been so distracted, and I finally had the courage to talk to him about wanting him to be present when he's home. He thought I was being too harsh and didn't like what I had to say. What about when I need a minute? *I am raising these kids alone.* I want him to be here, mentally and emotionally, to be a dad.

November 18, 2010

I have been overwhelmed with God's presence and peace. What talking to Him more and being more prayerful has done! Things are day-to-day and sometimes minute-to-minute with Danny. I have been praying for a miracle that only God's hand can provide with Danny's anxiety, anger, and mood. Today I have felt peace amidst the pain.

Jesus Calling today read, "You already know the ultimate destination of your journey; your entrance into heaven. So keep your focus on the path just before you, leaving outcomes up to Me" (Jesus Calling: Devotional Journal by Sarah Young).

November 21, 2010

Bedtime was fun tonight. I smiled as I sang the A-B-C's with Anna. Her little 3-year-old voice ringing out, not pronouncing her X's right, is so stinking cute. *Thank you Lord for each of these three humans; they are so precious.*

This morning I woke up feeling like I needed some time to myself, just peace in the valley, time to regroup. We went to church and out to lunch with Nan and Papa before heading home. Dan isn't feeling good, so he took a nap and the kids all had quiet time. Bingo, I got the Charly time I needed. I sat and wrote in my journal and read devotions. When everyone got back up and around, I was ready for it. We ended up watching *The Incredibles* together as a family.

I'm sitting here thankful for today, for this evening, and for our family. Praise God for the gifts He gives. Like we heard at church this morning, we will "thank Him now."

November 22, 2010

I know my tears won't make my kids younger again, but when Danny talked to me tonight about how big DK is and how he can't really fit on our laps anymore, I got choked up. They are growing so fast. They are their own people. I pray they keep their innocence, for their future, their decisions, their wives and husband someday. I pray they will each outlive me by a hundred years. I miss them already while they are still here.

November 24, 2010

Why in the world do I keep getting calls from 1(234)5? That's how it shows up on my phone, but no one is on the other end. "That's amazing, I've got the same combination on my luggage." (classic line from the movie *Spaceballs*).

I went to the doctor a few days ago for my headaches. I'm glad I went. Without a doubt, the worst part was stepping on that scale. Weight scales at doctor's offices are liars. I felt like the doctor heard me and answered my questions. He ordered an MRI and is going to double check that the titanium piece from ear surgery won't be an issue. I'm hopeful they confirm that I have a brain and can help get to the cause of these awful headaches.

Overall it's been a good few days, but things are gradually going downhill. I can feel a difference in a half hour time. He's different, I can feel it; I see it. I am sick because of it.

November 27, 2010

"I sure do like those Christmas cookies, sugar. I sure do like those Christmas cookies, babe..." One of my favorites by George Strait. I'm loving the Christmas music on. Who am I kidding, I love everything Christmas. It doesn't bother me one bit that things seem to get an earlier start every year.

The kids and I went bowling this afternoon. My patience was already fleeting, so when Pete chucked the ball so hard it went two lanes over, and Anna needed to go to the bathroom every third frame, I nearly lost it. Danny not joining us really hurt DK's feelings. I had to try to explain to him that when Dan is having a hard day, he just needs some time to himself. It's nearly impossible to explain and not show my own sadness over the whole thing.

November 30, 2010

And so it begins. He is angry tonight after getting home from a night out with his buddy. He's had too much to drink and anxiety has been here since last Friday. He's trying to curb it, but I can feel it, and I know the kids can, too. They have had to see and accept their dad is having a hard time and it's left them disappointed. I have such a hard time explaining that when their dad is not doing well, it's best that we just keep away and give him time. I'm not even sure that's true.

To me, this feels like he gets to make decisions for all of us, on his terms, no one else's. *Oh Lord, Oh Lord, Oh Lord, I am speaking your name, please come and rescue him before he gets so far away.* Why is he so angry? I feel it's because of me, even though I have no idea why. DK stayed up extra tonight and said that made his day. He smiled so big. When Danny got home, I sent DK up to bed soon after. Dan flashed an awful look in my direction and scolded me for doing that, sending DK to bed. I just want to cry.

December 3, 2010
"You are a very strong woman." Dad said to me today. "You are a strong, strong woman." I was in tears last night because of all of the inappropriate and irrational things Danny was saying at the dinner table. It scared and angered me. I was left feeling terrified and raw, exposed. I went into the bathroom, shut the door, and stared myself down in the mirror. Once I collected myself, I walked into the family room and told Danny how that made me feel and how his behavior is affecting the kids. I said what I needed to say. I felt stronger and some pride because of it. *Thank you, Lord, for providing an opening for me to speak.*

December 6, 2010
Another headache all day. They seem to be more frequent now. I've wondered if it's a food allergy or has to do with dairy, so I've been cutting things out and charting it. Nothing seems to help except Excedrin and sleep. In a perfect world I could take a nap when a headache came on, but in this world, I'm a mom.

Danny had an unusual episode late last night. The fire alarm kept going off from the smoky oven, and he went crazy with a laundry basket, smashing the ceiling. I had to vacuum up the parts of plaster that fell to the floor. He was filled with rage (his words) and asked me to shoot him in the chest. He told me where the gun was and pointed to where on his chest to pull the trigger. He even got the bullets out. After my initial shock, I convinced him to go to bed and lay down. Then I lay down next to him and wrapped my arms around him to try to calm him. He kept asking why I stay and called himself a monster.

It was hard, but with God's peace and grace I was able to function just fine today. I don't think he's quite back to normal yet. We didn't really talk about it. I have felt like a single parent for so long now, but how else can we function? The kids have needs and wants that are important, too. I wish he would do more with the kids. *This* right here is their childhood. *This* is molding them. I pray for his physical wellness as well as mental. For him to seek the help he needs. For our family, one day at a time.

Grace recently introduced me to Nickel Creek. This song, *Reasons Why,* really hit me with the lyrics:

"I'm holding my heart out but clutching it, oo, feeling this sort of a love that we once knew.
I'm calling this home when it's not even close. Playing a role with nerves left exposed.
And standing on the darkened stage, stumbling through the lines
Others have excuses, but I have my reasons why."

December 11, 2010
Chills literally came over me while reading my devotions tonight. *"Make Me the focal point of your search for security"* (Daily Devotionals from Jesus Calling by Sarah Young).

I want to; I need to. When that feeling comes over me, I want to throw up. Tonight, he was watching a movie on his laptop while the kids and I were sitting in the same room watching TV. He was a million miles away. Truthfully, I don't always want to watch kid shows either, but it's not about me; It's about this family.

Soon enough we headed upstairs where I put the kids to bed, like always. DK got up from bed to go to the bathroom and tripped on a Lego. Danny whipped his earbuds out and yelled ragefully up to DK, "What are you doing?!"

I quickly chimed in from the couch that he was picking up a few Legos. Danny turned his head to look straight through me and said, "Do you have something to say to me? Do not undermine me with *my* kids." Fear gripped me as I swallowed back my tongue. He'd been drinking since noon.

I know he has a mood disorder, extreme moods, but what he says cuts right to the heart. I told him earlier that I'm worried about him. He told me not to scrutinze him and said it was none of my business. This is hard. *So hard Lord, please grant me what I need here, You.*

December 13, 2010
Between me and Dutch, we have enough hair falling out to make a series of puppets. Good thing the Lord knows how many hairs are on my head!

It's a snow day, which DK wasn't exactly thrilled about. He knew if the weather was bad enough for a snow day, then he probably wouldn't get to do his one-on-one time today. All three kids have been working towards a different personal goal. They get to do special one-on-one time with someone of their choice when they meet it.

DK chose to do his time with Papa. And with that, there was no way a snow day would keep it from happening. Papa will pick him up around 3:15 pm for a movie and dinner. DK and Papa's relationship is special. Pete also met his goal and chose to spend his time with me. He wants to go to dinner and get dessert - he's mentioned it sixteen times. I pray Anna is safe with Danny tonight and they enjoy spending a bit of time together, just the two of them.

Chapter 11

December 15, 2010

Yeah, I've got some things I should probably do today, but right now, I'm enjoying sitting here at home, just me and Dutch, with my winter coat still on, cross-legged with my journal on my lap. I had the pleasure of helping in DK's class this morning at school. I am getting to know the kids more, and they are so cute. There is a little, plain jane girl, who always amuses me with the dramatic way she reads books. DK has come so far this year in his reading, I'm so proud of him. He is growing up so quickly.

I have been wanting to talk to Danny, even made a list of things to say. So last night I told him some of my feeling. I held back some not knowing what I would get in return. He continues to pull away and isolate himself. He sat there, listened, and said he would try to be more aware. I pray he will actually think on it, even just a little bit.

"I pray that the God who gives hope will fill you with much joy and peace while you trust in Him" (Romans 15:13). *Please Gracious Lord, fill this place with joy and peace.*

December 17, 2010

Last night, I left with the kids. We packed up as fast as we could and fled to Mom and Dad's. Danny was out of his mind.

I had rearranged a coffee date with my friends three times due to Danny's behavior. Tonight, I was going. I even talked it all through with Grace and she confirmed, "You need this. You can go."

I made dinner, the table was set, so when Danny got home from work, he simply had to eat and hang out with the kids. I could tell he was in a mood but also knew he only took it out on me, not the kids. I went into the bathroom, stared myself down in the mirror and repeated, "You're fine, you can do this, you can go, it's ok." I said my goodbyes and headed out the door. I wasn't even five miles from home when I got the call. It was Danny. He said, "You'd better come home, the kids are afraid of me." Click.

I was hysterical. I have never pulled a faster U-turn in my life, and the drive home was a tearfilled blur. I got inside to hear Dan belittling me, telling me how useless I am and noticed the dinner I had prepared was on the kitchen floor being eaten by Dutch. Dan was cocky and condescending. He said feeding the dog dinner was his representation of how I made him feel. While the tirade continued I resolved we had to go, right then. I took the kids up the steep staircase, threw a few essentials into a pillow case, and left. It wasn't until I bolted out of our driveway that I called Dad.

The only words I could speak were, "Dad, we're on our way."

No questions asked, he said, "We're here."

Dad took over with the kids, found a silly cartoon they enjoy called *Arnie the Donut*. All three kids assumed their positions on Papa's lap while Nan got some snacks and I hid in their bedroom. I was rocking, sobbing, and crying out to the Lord in the pitch dark, *"Please Lord, please, don't let him kill himself."*

The whole thing was like an out of body experience. I couldn't believe it. We came back home this morning. Mostly because I hated leaving Dutch there. He feels it all, too. I am thankful that Danny and Dutch were both ok when we got back.

December 18, 2010

After all that has happened in the past few days, Danny wanted so badly to make it up to us. He truly was sincere with his apology and wanting to spend time as a family. I was very raw and honest about needing him to realize his alcohol problem. He suggested we find a hotel somewhere close by with a pool so we could spend quality family time. It sounded like just what we needed, to reconnect.

We packed up a bag and headed to a hotel about an hour from home. It had a water slide, a nice pool, and hot tub. Danny wouldn't get in the water with the kids, but he did come down to watch us swim. I say watch, although more like spend the entire time on his cell phone. At least he was there. We got cleaned up and headed next door for dinner. That's where everything changed. Danny quickly ordered the beer sampler and drank them so quickly that I didn't even have a chance to control the look that surely came across my face. We *just* talked about this. This was contributing to *why* I left with the kids. I just told him this earlier today. There I sat, feeling worthless, so I shifted my focus onto the kids. I couldn't eat a bite of food.

Fortunately, the kids were exhausted from swimming so putting them to bed was easy. Once they were tucked in and asleep, I locked myself in the bathroom. I texted Grace, asking her what should I do. I was trapped. I don't think I've ever felt so alone. Grace helped calm me, offered to call the police. But I knew that wouldn't solve the problem. I stood there, staring myself down in the mirror. Tears falling like rain. "I just need to make it to tomorrow. It's going to be ok. *Lord, please keep the kids safe. Please intervene here, I am at a complete loss.*

I was locked in the bathroom for about an hour before I collected myself and went to check on the kids in the adjoining room. Dan hadn't even noticed I was gone, so I quietly slid into bed with my back to him. By now, he was full on drunk watching TV. I pretended to fall asleep as tears dripped over my nose and onto the pillow.

December 21, 2010

"Live by faith, not by sight" 2 Corinthians 5:7 (NIV84). That was in my devotions tonight. I witnessed a true miracle tonight. While we ate supper together, there was chatter and conversation all the way around. I happily said I would do the dishes so Dan could play some game on the Xbox with the boys. From the kitchen, I could hear laughter and healthy competition. It was the best sound I've heard all week. I closed my eyes as my hands soaked in the sink and just said, "Thank You Jesus."

This was a miraculous sight considering what we've been through in the last week. Danny has been researching Bipolar Disorder and alcohol abuse. Tonight he was saying he needed the help to quit, that he needs the tools because he can't do it on his own. This is music to my ears. I pray he stays on this course and knows what all is at stake. We love him and want to help. He's realizing that. I pray for the days, weeks, and months that lie ahead, for what we face in social situations and friendships, for strength to say *no*, for my follow through and follow up to help keep him on track. I'm tired and ready for rest. I'm grateful for *hope*.

December 23, 2010

Tonight I asked the kids a series of questions… As always, their answers were precious and unique to each of their little outlooks on life. DK had more one word answers, Pete drew out with comical facial expressions, and Anna just kept talking in her precious little voice.

How do you feel about the back scratcher?
DK: "It's silly."
Pete: Smiled and gave a thumbs up.
Anna: "How do I feel about the back scratcher? I watch Oswald and Olivia."

What is your biggest issue?
DK: "Somersaults."
Pete: "Umm, about somebody that I know… Anna."
Anna (squinting): "Going to Bella's house."

Who is your best friend?
DK: "Pete."
Pete: "DK"
Anna: "Bella and Gran and Gramps and Nan and Uppa and Gramma T."

What is your favorite color?
DK: "Green."
Pete: "Can I write two? Red and white. They are Ohio State colors."
Anna: "Pink and purple."

What are you most afraid of?
DK: "Nothing. I'd say nothing."
Pete: "I'm not afraid of anything."
Anna: "Deer, uhh bears."

How do you feel about euthanasia?
DK: "What's euthanasia? I don't know what that is."
Pete: "What is that? Is that the country Asia?",
Anna: "Oh I want you to come with me!"

How many stuffed animals do you have?
DK (quick to answer): "Ten! Actually eleven."
Pete (thinking, scratching his head, picking his nose…): "Three"
Anna: "1-2-3-4-5-6"

Have you ever heard of a pyramid scheme?
DK (funny face): "No!"
Pete: "No."
Anna: "Yeah and I don't like it."

How many brunettes does it take to change a light bulb?
DK: "I don't know."
Pete: "I know about the light bulb part but not the *barnetts* part!"
Anna: "Uh, that light bulb does not work right there."

Where are kiwis made?
DK: "I don't know."

Pete: "Kiwi? I have no idea where they are made!"
Anna: "I don't like those."

How old do you think Santa is?
DK: "A thousand."
Pete (squinting): "Sixty, sixty-one…"
Anna: "I don't know, ok!"

How old do you need to be to retire?
DK: "Forty-nine"
Pete: "My guess is umm, ah any age."
Anna: "I don't know, maybe I turning six."

What would Jesus do?
DK: "Give us freedom."
Pete: "Put someone onto the Earth."
Anna: "He would… Jesus will take us to heaven."

How many spots are on your shirt?
DK: "Zero!"
Pete (looking at his shirt): "I don't have any spots on this shirt. (lifts his shirt to his bare chest) "Oh you mean this shirt? I'd say two!" (looking at his nipples)
Anna (standing to count and looking down): "1-2-3-4-5-6-7-9."

Is your room currently clean?
DK: "Sometimes"
Pete: "Yeah, I try my best to clean it all the time."
Anna: "Uh no… no."

What will heaven be like?
DK: "Nothing else than on earth."
Pete: "I think it'll be brighter than anything in the world."
Anna: "Dutch dog, Anna, Nan, Cyndi…" (Anna went on to list everyone she knows)

Chapter 12

December 24, 2010

It's Christmas Eve, and here we are. Today is one of those that will be remembered forever. Danny took zero part in today's activities. He didn't come to his parent's house at noon for dinner and gifts, nor the Christmas Eve program Anna and Pete have been practicing and talking about for weeks. He told me he wasn't going to participate because of what I said the other night. If he drinks again, I will leave.

I was at lunch with my friend Jessi yesterday, and she saw the pain written all over my face. I did it; I opened up and told her...all of it. She was so encouraging and told me to pray every single moment. Jessi and her husband came to the Christmas Eve program tonight to show support, and it meant so much. Pete played the part of Joseph, and Anna was an angel. Grace, Joe, Mom, and Dad were there, too. At the end of service, as we sang *Silent Night*, I stood there thinking *this is Christmas? And Danny doesn't want any part of it, and it's my fault.* I kept swallowing back the lump in my throat and shifting my focus to the kids. DK, standing next to me, could read me like a book. He was so tender and brokenhearted, too.

As we cleared out of church, Pastor D. approached me and asked how we were doing. I said, "Pretty good… he's not coming tonight." Pastor pulled me in for a hug and whispered in my ear that he's here for us, and we should get together.

December 26, 2010

What a day! It began super early with three excited kids raring and ready to play with their new Christmas gifts. I got up and sat with them while being bombarded with questions and battery requests. Danny slept in because he was tired. I began getting frustrated but managed to get everyone ready for church. He shocked me by offering to join us for church.

I had no idea what would happen next as we took a seat in that church pew. As the service began, Pastor D. went over some announcements and mentioned the need for "prayer for a family member in our congregation dealing with mental illness." My heart sank in an instant, and I could feel his eyes. I looked down at Danny at the other end, and he was already furiously staring at me. He quickly torked his head and stared intensely at me.

I instantly got up, shuffled in front of the kids and into the bathroom where I got sick. It took a few minutes to clean myself up as I stared myself down in the mirror. Once collected and ready, I headed out the door where Danny was waiting for me with the kids. My confused and fearful face mirrored the kids'. We left mid-service in silence and headed home. The only words he said were, "I can't believe you. I can't believe that you would talk about *me* to Pastor D."

I got the kids out of car seats, and we hurried into the house to make some lunch. Danny pulled me aside and scolded, "Listen. I'm going to either the gym to work out or the bar. If I go to the bar? That's on you. I can't believe you did this to me."

With that, he left in a hurry. I dropped to my knees right there and sobbed, praying *"Oh Lord, please, please make him go to the gym."* The kids and I had a quick grilled cheese and headed upstairs to work on a puzzle DK got for Christmas. When I heard Danny get home I stayed upstairs. Danny eventually called for Pete to come see him and said, "Tell your mom she doesn't need to be afraid of me."

December 29, 2010

If I decided to write a book, would anyone buy it? I am honestly thinking about it. I have this headache again. Thankfully, Danny has been doing well today. He went skiing with some friends and admitted he hasn't done that sober before. He followed that statement up by admitting he hasn't had a sober Christmas since he was sixteen. Every year, since I've known him, he's been intoxicated for the holidays.

I pray I can be wise and know how to respond to this type of information. How can I be supportive while I'm feeling lost in the shuffle? *Oh Lord God, please keep us safe and healthy. I know I keep falling short, Lord. Please meet me in my shortcomings and hold me up so that I can be what You need of me in this time. Oh Lord, I long to be an example, a disciple. Even in these hard times.*

January 1, 2011

It's strange to be writing 2011 already. Danny is bugging me tonight, and I just want him to leave me alone. He slept most of the day and woke up in a good mood; I didn't have that luxury. He thought watching the ball drop was dumb, so the kids and I made up some snacks, played games, and watched it anyway.

We talked about his long term goals, his sobriety, how he's hopeful he won't relapse. He even wants to quit smoking; a habit he's picked in the past year. I thought the conversation was heading in a positive direction until he starting saying he doesn't have Bipolar Disorder. He doesn't have an objective view; he can't see it. I've wondered how much he remembers when he's high and manic or when he's in a really dark place. I think he needs to go to a new therapist, someone who actually deals with this specific disorder. I can't fix it. I've been made to feel so much of it is my fault. I'm also seeing and learning more that it's not. I just need to help him get through and manage him best I can.

Chapter 13

January 3, 2011

Here we are at day fourteen sober. We had a date night to celebrate our anniversary while the kids were with Danny's parents for the evening. I felt like we had a good discussion at dinner where I confessed my loneliness. Just saying the word *lonely* made me feel even more lonely. I don't get any affirmation or physical touch that I long for from my husband; An arm rub, a hand held, hug, a gentle back pat as he walks by. Nothing. I know he's been dealing with all of this, but what gets lost is, *so have I*. His response to me being open was, "I'm one (cuss) up away from where we were a few weeks ago."

January 6, 2011

I called Pastor D. earlier. Come to find out, he wasn't even talking about Danny that Sunday morning. He felt awful for what happened because of it. I also decided to share my story at mom's group today. This is such a huge part of our lives, and Danny has not allowed me to talk about it. He somehow finds out when I do and the consequences for it aren't worth sharing. I hope, and do honestly feel, I can trust these ladies though.

Not that this defines who we are, but it is where we are.

January 7, 2011

We got talking at dinner about Danny's and my past; how we dated back in high school, how he broke up with me a few times because he wasn't ready to have a girlfriend. Danny told the boys that he used to get "homesick for Mommy," and someday the boys will feel that way about a girl.

Danny mentioned that during the college years, "Mom went from a girl to a woman and turned into a hottie." With the dinner clearing and conversation, we didn't notice Pete had left the kitchen. Two seconds later, here he comes with a Barbie doll and asks, "Dad, did Mom look like this?"

January 8, 2011
Well the weather outside isn't frightful, it's pretty. Anna and I just came in from sledding and it won't be long before the boys do, too. Her poor little fingers were getting so cold. I started making hot cocoa when Peter yelled for me to come watch him attempt snowboarding on a $5 plastic sled. He's so funny. He did make it standing up the whole way down the hill. Things changed quickly when DK *accidentally* kicked Pete in the face. Hot cocoa for all!

January 9, 2011
I wish Danny's lips didn't taste like cigarettes when I kiss him goodnight. His mood has been better, but he's slipping. I don't feel like we talk much to each other. The deep, open honesty isn't there; it feels like surface level stuff. I think I'm afraid of what is underneath. I don't want to anger him or change his mood. And that is a tall order. It makes me feel awful that I can't be honest and myself because, well, I'm living in fear.

January 10, 2011
I read in my devotions, *"God intervenes and expresses love in the most unbelievable situations"* Daily Devotions Inspired by 90 Minutes in Heaven by Don Piper and Cecil Murphey).

I've always tried to look at life long-term, but once Danny's mental illness crept in, life became day-to-day survival. In these past few, stress-filled, agonizing months it went from hour-to-hour, to moment-to-moment. What a mighty God we serve that He is with each of us, always. Even in these seemingly desperate, unbelievable times. We are safe, healthy, and I am grateful.

I have a favorite song I used to listen to it all of DK's pregnancy and this song would calm him as a baby every single time he'd cry. It was the coolest thing. *Redeemer* by Nicole C. Mullen:

"I know my Redeemer lives, the very same God that spins things into orbit, He runs to the weary, the worn and the weak.
And the same gentle hands that hold me when I'm broken.
They conquered death to bring me victory. Now I know my Redeemer lives."

January 11, 2011
Today is a fun date to write, 1-11-11. I have someone I can talk to, someone who gets it, who is familiar and dealing with the same family dynamic! Can I share this with Danny? That I've made contact with another woman married to a man with Bipolar Disorder? I'm afraid he will be angry with me. I'm wondering if I can meet with her and not tell him, but I'm not a secrets kind of gal.

I saw a photo on Facebook of a friends' new baby and I couldn't stop thinking about her. All morning, I felt a prod to call her. It was a total God thing. We've lost touch, but after chatting for a bit, she told me about a friend of hers who's husband is struggling with Bipolar Disorder. Seriously! She also called me a superhero. She said I am one because superheroes repeatedly put themselves last and others first. It meant so much coming from her.

January 12, 2011
Things are going well, but it's been a busy few days. I'm noticing that I get wrapped up in cleaning the house and on my laptop, so I'm making a conscious effort to be more present. This morning I played Barbies with Anna and built Legos with Pete. Last night the kids and I played Uno and Mouse Trap. With it, came the best sound, good ol' fashioned belly laughs. Just make the plastic dude from Mouse Trap barf into the bucket that the silver marble is supposed to go into, and it's a guaranteed laugh fest.

Last night I was on my knees beside DK's bed. He was all covered up while laying on his stomach facing me. He said, "Mom, remember when your hair was short like mine?"

I said, "Yep."

He responds, "I like it longer."

I replied with a squint of the eyes and a turn of the head, "Is that your way of telling me you think it looks nice?"

DK said, "That's my way of telling you I love you, and I think you're pretty."

Crocodile tears streamed down my face. This is the stuff; this is worth more than any paycheck.

January 13, 2011
I come to the Lord with a thankful heart, knowing these good days are a gift from Him. I'm allowed to feel joy even in these trying times. I'm *choosing* joy despite knowing his mood will change and things will falter. I have hope, though, and I'm clinging to it. *Some days I don't feel Your presence, Lord, but today I do, and I am thankful.*

I downloaded some hymns on my iPod. When I put it on shuffle and one of those songs comes on, I am on my knees, palms raised in reverence to the Lord.

All My Tears (Be Washed Away) by Selah & Kim Hill.

"When I die, don't cry for me. In my father's arms, I'll be.
The wounds this world left on my soul, will all be healed, and I'll be whole.
Sun and moon will be replaced with the light of Jesus' face.
And I will not be ashamed, for my Savior knows my name."

January 18, 2011
"Rehearsing your troubles results in experiencing them many times, whereas you are meant to go through them only when they actually occur" (Jesus Calling by Sarah Young).

Wow, I am so guilty of doing this, of anticipating! I need to wait on the Lord to carry me through when things actually occur rather than being on the defensive all of the time.

We had an amazing speaker at mom's group today, she's come twice now. Wow, Staci sure tells it like it is. No frills. The first time she spoke to our group we all left with makeup running down our faces and crying. Not in a bad way, but in a way that she touched our hearts and truly wants to teach and help us raise Godly children. It's pretty awesome stuff and quite the responsibility! No tears fell today, but equally good conversation. What a cool lady, she's got her stuff together.

Afterward, Anna and I came home for some "butter and jelly", as she calls it. We chatted for quite some time, colored together, and now she's having quiet time. It felt good to shift my focus on her while we were sitting here, rather than picking up my phone or opening my laptop. It's good to have reminders sometimes that these types of things can wait. There is no reason I need to text back right away. Listening to Anna talk about hot air balloons and asking funny questions like, "where are the naughty deer?", are too priceless to miss.

January 24, 2011
Today marks the anniversary of my cousin Amelia's passing. To think she was only six years old; I can't imagine that as a parent now myself. She and I were thick as thieves. She was stubborn and fought the good fight. It was so hard to see, but I truly think I was shown what compassion and love look like through her example. She loved Jesus so much, even sounded like a preacher. What a gift she was.

Anna is excited to have her first playdate with a little friend over to our house next week. She won't have to worry about legs being torn off Barbie or Barbie stripped naked like when she plays with Pete! Anna told me earlier when Pete was taking the clothes off Barbie, "Pete makes me crabby!"

January 26, 2011
Danny took Dutch out to the field at the end of our road a few days back for a little exercise. They got back sooner than expected. I was folding

clothes when Danny called to me from the porch. When I arrived, blood was everywhere.

Danny said he must have caught his ear on a pricker bush, and even though it looked worse, it was only a small knick. I took Dutch by his collar and led him into the glassed-in shower. Of course I was wearing my favorite jeans, so I quickly took them off before I got blood on them. There I was in the tub with Dutch in my socks, undies, and t-shirt. Peter opened the door to look, and Anna's head popped in, too. They wondered what in the world I was doing to poor Dutch! I had Pete go get some gauze and masking tape. Unfortunately, every time Dutch shook his head the bandage flew off, and it looked like a crime scene. I was so happy to see Jessie when she stopped over to take a look. The bleeding finally quit, crazy animal.

January 27, 2011
I just had the coolest talk with DK.

Tonight we are having manicotti for dinner. Not a favorite of DK's, or Danny's for that matter (but it was something different that Pete and I happen to enjoy). Anna was still not sure. DK got upset and didn't want to eat. He was also upset that his video game got interrupted because he and Peter were bickering, so they had to turn it off. Then he went to his room to find Pete had taken apart his Lego ship to put Legos in the "estimation jar" for school. Three pretty big blows to the little man.

We talked about these things and singled each out as to what was bothering him. I told him I understood, and I do. It's OK to be disappointed or frustrated. Then the cool discussion came about. I told him that life isn't always going to be *chicken strips* (his favorite). Sometimes life throws manicotti at you. Something new, or different, or not what you would want if it was up to you, but if you'll try it, you may like it. I told him about the mom's group at church. At first I went because I felt it was something I should do. I took a bite. Once I took that bite, I realized I kind of liked it. I took a little more, chewed on it more, and realized it's great! I've been so blessed by it. Had I not taken that first bite, I wouldn't feel the encouragement, new friendships, and growth I do today as a result of it.

He looked at me with a big smile. He got it. Now let's see if he'll try the manicotti.

"Dear Lord, thank you for all that you did for us today. Please, oh please help us all to have a good day tomorrow, and please help DK to be on green at school so he can get to 10 days green. And Ummm, Amen." -Pete's bedtime prayer

Chapter 14

January 29, 2011
It wasn't until I walked down to the mailbox looking like this, that I laughed at myself.

The morning was filled with:
- being woken up too early by kids running the halls (ahem, Pete and Anna)
- twice going upstairs to tell Pete and Anna to get *back* in bed
- DK feeling sick - but is he too sick for school, or just wanting to stay home?
- reminding Pete 4 times to get pants on
- giving the boys a ride to school

So, naturally, I didn't take the time to shower. I took them to school in my pajamas and bathrobe. Of course I threw a hat on so I *wouldn't* embarrass them or anything. Apparently, the hat didn't help.

January 30, 2011
As I write this, I am convinced my friend and I are staying at the same exact place where the movie *Psycho* was filmed. We're in the middle of nowhere and I'm just so glad I'm not alone! We are here for a women's retreat. We've been looking forward to this since we signed up last August.

What's not cool is how I feel deep down in my heart. On the drive here, Danny called me and told me I needed to do it: be honest and open with Ashlee and tell her he doesn't care for her. After all these years, and time we've spent as families together, Danny just doesn't care for her and wanted me to tell her such. He kept insisting, and I'm feeling torn. Danny has become irritated and disrespectful when we'd spend time together as couples. For days afterward, he'd "dog" my friend. Ashlee and her husband, Chris, are the *most* gracious people we know.

I hung up the phone with him, and she asked what was wrong. We've been friends for so long that we can easily read each other. She's prayed me through awful times and witnessed so much in my marriage. Feeling I needed to be honest, I made the statement, "Dan thinks we should do things separate from now on."

The moment it left my lips, my heart broke. Instant tears on her part, and I felt like the biggest fool in the whole world. How could I do this? *Why* did I say it? I was struck with instant regret.

Danny then called me back and was acting overly hyper and outlandish. This type of behavior is becoming more of the norm. It's like he enjoys baiting and shaming me. I get so mad that I end up getting reeled in. I asked him what he was up to, and he told me he just went out and bought himself a new laptop. For his use only. The kids and I weren't allowed to touch it because we'd break it. We just went over our budget the day before. Money has been tight as we recover from Christmas so we need to watch every dime. Mainly, he was telling me I needed to stop spending money. This was coming from the guy who drained my 401K from my old job to pay down debt *he* got us into.

This very retreat had been paid for six months ago, with money Ashlee and I had made on our own. Yet he spends $800 on a laptop when, just yesterday, he promised he wouldn't.

At this point, I'm shallow breathing, terrified about how his mania will affect the kids this weekend with my absence. I immediately called Dad, and he reassured me that if he sensed the slightest mood from Danny, he would keep the kids at their house. He told me to try to enjoy myself and that he had it all under control. I found out later Dad asked Danny to bring the kids over for supper, and they went. *Thank You Lord for Dad!*

With all of this stress and heartache, I found myself in my usual place: the restroom. First in a stall, bawling my eyes out, then staring myself down in the mirror and having some reassuring self-talk. It took some time, but I collected myself, wholeheartedly tried to apologize to my dear friend and did my best to lift the time to the Lord. I had to give it over to Him. I had to, and, as always, He provided. The kids had a good weekend and when I got home, Danny had returned to his normal self.

February 2, 2011
It's a struggle. I don't understand what it means to be an addict. I don't know what words to use or how to help. I'm feeling so small. I have been going back and forth with the fellow BP wife, and it has been so good for me. I was in tears reading her story. I'm so grateful and overcome with emotion to have found someone who *gets it.* I was relieved to hear her words. I'm still on the fence about telling Danny. I don't feel like I have to, and that's ok.

February 7, 2011
Danny is seven weeks sober today. That's an amazing thought. I pray he's being truthful and it continues. I am struggling, worrying, and wondering if the downward spiral has begun. He was overreacting to some emails I exchanged with Dad. I didn't see anything out of the norm. He got really mad that I wasn't seeing his side and that always scares me. I had plans with a girl from church and was already late.

I got this huge lump in my throat sitting there at lunch, my mind going to, "what if he drinks because I didn't agree with him? Is he ok?" Then I'd flash back into the conversation and put on my smile. *Just get through the next hour, Lord, get Dan through this next hour.* And we did. *Thank you, Lord.*

Danny told me how amazing the love for our kids is. I was so glad to hear him say that. He has already missed so much. These moments of clarity and being present are a gift.

February 9, 2011

I need to take a shower but can't quite yet. The washing machine is running, so I will wait a bit until we have hot water. On Friday we're getting a new hot water heater. Here's to being able to wash clothes and myself at the same time!

I'm feeling better than yesterday. There is definitely something about the month of February that just bites. It's a "blah" month if you ask me, dirty snow and lost gloves, right in the dead of winter. I realize I can't change it, or take February off the calendar, so I'm cool with it. I know my series of headaches doesn't help my attitude either. I woke up with the same one that put me to bed early last night.

February 12, 2011

The hot water heater installer just left without putting one in. This old farmhouse! Come to find out, our house is not up to code, so before we can get a new water heater, an electrician has to come out. It seems nothing comes easy!

For some reason, I've been feeling very lonely again. I'm not sure if lonely is the right word. I feel like I'm going through the motions and waiting for the next day to come. I don't like the feeling of rushing through life when I know it goes by too fast already. Like hearing the kids voices and being asked to play when I don't really want to, but they won't ask me as they get older, so I do it. Then I feel sad. I could just cry for hours. Although, right now I have no idea what I'd cry about. I pray and yearn to shake this feeling. I feel stuck where I am and know that's not the truth. Danny has been doing well as of late, and I'm glad he's sober. So why am I now having these feelings of irritability, loneliness, and sadness? *Teach me, Oh Lord. Guide me in these low moments. I know You are here in this place, help me shake these feelings.*

February 16, 2011

Dutch is getting old, the crazy "aminal", as Anna would say. He got between Danny and I again because he could feel the tension. I had to diffuse Dan last night, and, since then, Dutch has been on high alert.

He's such a smart dog, protective of his mama. Danny is so frustrated and impatient with the kids, so it makes me feel like I'm living under a microscope. If I'm not patient, he feeds off of me and exaggerates it. Even though I know these swings will come and go, it doesn't make it any easier when you're drowning in the deep end.

I shared with Mom and Dad how I had to diffuse Dan last night. It was super scary, but we made it. Dad has pneumonia, and they are leaving in a few days to head south. I miss them so badly when they go. They are always here for me. Dad and I both get choked up when they leave. He especially doesn't like being away from the kids, and I like to think from me, too. I pray they are safe and we are too, here at home.

February 19, 2011
I had to have a hard talk with a friend today. Things have been bottling up. I feel like Danny has control over so many parts of my life. I wish he didn't make it so hard for me to branch out. This friend told me that she feels I have more courage than she could even begin to have in herself. That was the nicest thing. I cling to words of encouragement these days. Sometimes repeating the good things others say helps me get the awful things out of my mind. Being put down and belittled makes you wonder your worth. Goodness and kindness help me focus on the One who made me. *Thank you, Lord God for encouragement in the form of words. I needed that.*

February 23, 2011
I'm feeling the need for a massage or something. I've never had one, but maybe it would help this weight I'm carrying on my shoulders. I can't seem to shake it. The kids and I are going to visit Grace and Joe in Frankfort tomorrow. I've had many conversations with them about how their recent fighting/nagging/irritating each other game has to stop. I don't mind driving, but I don't love heavy traffic. Good thing we have GPS to help us get there!

I ran Pete to the ENT today. Good thing, because his eardrum ruptured again. It's hard to know how bad it is because he never makes a fuss about it. When my ear *exploded* a few years ago, it was the most excruciating pain

I've ever experienced, right up there with childbirth. As a matter of fact, when mine finally blew a hole and I was bleeding from my ear, I thought maybe *it was a boy* that had just forced his way through my eardrum. All of this to say, I'm a wuss compared to my six-year-old.

So now we are just hanging out, Uncle Joe and the boys are playing LEGO Star Wars, and Anna is shadowing everything Aunt Grace does. Anna-banana loves the kitty, Marvin. It's so nice for me to have a break in the action, to sit back and not have to be the entertainer. Whew. I'm thankful for Grace and Joe...

February 27, 2011
The sound of the kids' laughter in the truck today was like music to my ears. Somewhere along the way, home from Frankfort, Pete called DK a "poop" and Anna said he was a "snot." DK sunk down in his seat, and I happened to turn around to see him looking at me in the corner of his eye. I asked him what was wrong, and he shrugged his shoulders and turned towards the window. I asked again, and he told me what Pete and Anna had said. While looking at his reflection in the rearview mirror, I asked, "Well, is it true DK? Are you *lumpy and brown?* Do you come outta noses all slimy?"

They all burst out laughing. It's one of the greatest sounds in the world. Our time with Grace and Joe was amazing. We hung out, ordered pizza, and watched *Popeye the Sailor Man*. They are so helpful with the kids. Anna was stuck to Auntie Grace's side while the boys enjoyed playing Xbox with Uncle Joe. DK and I had a hard time sleeping with all of the noises of fire trucks and city buses. I guess we don't realize how quiet it is at home!

I worried a lot about Dan while we were gone. He didn't want to come with us, which made DK feel bad. DK was feeling really sad that he hadn't yet gotten Dan a trinket or something while on our trip. I told him that was thoughtful but not necessary. He pulled me aside and said Dan had asked him a few times to get him a surprise. So, as DK saw it, if he didn't, Dan would get angry which would turn into bad things. He *had* to find something. A grown man making his son feel this way, and worry this deeply, is heartbreaking. My eyes filled with tears. DK quickly tried to change the subject, but I knew what was on his heart. My tears represented pride and disappointment at the same time. We ended up getting Dan a candy bar at a truckstop. I wish I could tell him how he made our son feel.

March 11, 2011

It's hard to explain. I have kept a brave face, but I just can't do this anymore. I decided to take the kids and leave again. This time for five days. What I missed the most about home was Dutch. I know that is awful to think, or say out loud, but it's the truth.

As far as Danny goes, I needed him to see it, to *feel* it this time.

Yes, he's been sober, at least he claims to be, but untreated Bipolar Disorder makes for a tumultuous home. This has been mounting for weeks, and I haven't wanted to admit how bad it's been. I've been spending time on my knees in prayer, weeping and begging God to fix it. Danny has been experiencing more *mixed episodes* which I can best describe as being high as a kite and agitated and in absolute despair at the same time. His pupils get large and he looks right through me. He is getting more aggressive, and I'm terrified.

We were at dinner downtown as a family last week and as we left the restaurant, he approached a random man in the lobby. Danny was looking for a fight. He was literally goating the man to say or do something, anything so Danny could throw a punch. I was so embarrassed. I kept trying to get him to come with the kids and I out to the truck, but he wouldn't. The stare he gave me pierced my very soul.

I didn't want to be on the receiving end of his fist, so I lugged all three kids out to the parking lot, buckled them in car seats, and waited. I debated leaving him there several times, but I couldn't. I turned on some music for the kids while I stared straight ahead, looking into the window of the restaurant, watching Danny provoke this man. What do I do? We sat there and waited for forty-five minutes. When he finally came to the truck, he was so fired up. I just drove. The kids were silent in the backseat. You could have cut that tension with a knife, but we didn't want to poke that bear. The drive home was in pure silence. Once home, I put the kids to bed and climbed into bed myself. Whew, we made it. We are home and safe. But with that and more, I just couldn't do it anymore. We had to go.

I quickly packed up a bag during the day. I figured that would give us some time to get settled at Mom and Dad's before he found out. Little did I know, he was already on his way home from work.

I called him on the way to Mom and Dad's as planned, and told him I needed *a break*. As expected, he said he didn't understand and demanded a better explanation. I said what I wanted and hung up. Whew, deep breaths. I pulled into the driveway and lugged the kids inside. Dad immediately took over while I went out to move the truck to the other side of their driveway. Just as I got parked, the passenger door swung open and Danny got in. I still have no idea how he got there so fast or where he even came from. My heart was pounding out of my chest.

"Dad, please look outside, Dad, *please* look out the front door," I was repeating in my mind.

The trouble was, where the truck was now parked, it couldn't be seen from the front window. I was trying to remain calm while my heart was coming out of my throat. I kept swallowing it down, but the thought that he was going to kill me, raced through my head. No one would even know. I'm a dead woman. I let him rant and rave while I stared into his massive pupils. When he finally let me speak, I collected my words and simply said, "I just. I just needed a break."

While watching his reaction, I somehow pulled up the door handle, slid out of the truck, and walked as fast as I could inside. Deep breaths Charly, deep breathes. I did it. I survived.

Chapter 15

March 21, 2011

Today was pretty run of the mill. It was one of those days I will look back on and long for. We didn't leave home. I did a lot of stuff around the house, and lunch was leftover burritos. There was quiet time where Pete and Anna weren't always quiet. They fought, played some, and then we turned music on and danced.

I had to get after Pete a few times because he was being crazy, jumping and running all over. At one point, the three of us were dancing and holding hands in a circle. Then I held Anna and we danced together. She just looked up at me and smiled. Once DK got off the school bus, we visited in the den, had some egg bagel sandwiches for dinner, and watched TV. Danny started going to an outpatient program with a dual purpose: to help manage his Bipolar Disorder and alcoholism. It's four nights a week but, at this point, anything is better than where we have been. I want to help however I can. We need to commit to his wellness, for these three precious kids, for himself, and for me.

I want to give the kids my best and be a good example of kindness and love. *I pray I can be those things, Lord. That the kids will see You, Your Hands at work in all of our lives. In this season of unknowns and hardship, that we will see You and get to know You more.*

March 22, 2011
We had a short series of "funnies" happen today. Anna and I laid down for a nap and wrapped up in a blanket like a burrito. I didn't even know I had fallen asleep until my phone rang. Half dazed, I answered it, and repeated, "Hello?" but no one answered. It took me a moment to realize it wasn't a phone call, but the alarm reminded me that it was time for the boys to get off the bus.

As 3:50 pm approached, I headed outside in my short-sleeved shirt. I saw the bus through the trees, and realized it wasn't slowing down. Sure enough, the bus *blew* by at 60 mph. I waved my cold arms in the wind, but the driver never saw me. Argh.

I looked down and saw Dutch's ball sitting there and kicked it in frustration. It went straight towards the road, and he darted after it. I screamed his name at the top of my lungs to stop. He was just inches from the truck passing by. That was a close call. Eventually the bus turned around and the boys got home.

March 24, 2011
Pete had an ear follow-up appointment this morning, so our routine was a bit off - lost snow pants, one boot here, Anna spilling her bowl of cereal. As we were trying to get out the door, Anna tripped and fell in the doorway as DK sat and looked at her. With the chaos of it all, I started to lose patience and yell. Finally, on our way to school, I collected my thoughts and explained, while looking at their faces in my rearview mirror, "To all three of you, when you see someone who has fallen, help them up. If you saw an old woman lying on the sidewalk because she just slipped on the ice, you wouldn't leave her there because it wasn't your fault. You'd help, right? This is the same case. Be it you shut the door on Anna or not, you help her up. Always. And make this your mission. When you say yes, make sure you know what you're saying it for. Don't just say yes, but when you say it, you *mean* it."

As we made the turn into town, I followed it all up by saying, "Always help the old lady and let your yes mean *yes!*"

I went from looking at Pete in the rearview to DK and saw the slightest smile. They heard me and I didn't even have to yell.

March 25, 2011
Whewee! In a few hours, it will be school carnival time! I'll be one of two ladies running the cakewalk. The kids and I spent some time at school yesterday afternoon helping set up. They had fun running the halls while us moms taped down the cakewalk/pop toss lines and set out prizes. It sure is fun to be a part of the carnival this year behind the scenes.

March 27, 2011
I skipped a few pages while reading a book to Anna tonight. I wonder if she noticed.

I'm not sure what I'm feeling tonight, but definitely off. DK was up in the night throwing up, and, unfortunately, the hall carpet didn't fare to well. I'll need to call the carpet cleaner today. Danny just completed his six-week outpatient program. I'm proud of him. It has been a big commitment for all of us. Slow and steady wins the race...right?

New song! *Strong Enough* by Matthew West

"I know I'm not strong enough to be, everything that I'm supposed to be. I give up, I'm not strong enough. Hands of mercy won't you cover me, Lord right now I'm asking you to be, Strong enough, Strong enough, for the both of us, yeah"

March 31, 2011
Even with waking up ornery today, the Lord provided for me in a big way! The kids were with Nan and Papa, so I got to fly errands solo and have lunch with a sweet friend. After some time wasted, watching soap operas and eating leftovers, I headed to Pete's first t-ball practice. Papa had taken all three kids, so I met them there. Typical Pete, he's hilarious when he plays so animatedly. He always runs off the field to go to the bathroom whenever he feels the urge. Even if he's playing first base, it doesn't matter if he has to pee, off he goes. Where's Pete? Where else but in the porta potty?

He surely showed his compassionate side tonight too by going over to see if he could help another boy who was crying and running to pick up baseballs so the coach wouldn't have to. He's a good boy. I had a riot running around the playground chasing DK, after being asked fourteen times to play tag. He's quick! He certainly has me beat. My moves to slither from getting tagged aren't as sharp as they once were. Dad even got a chuckle from the sidelines at Pete's practice. We both broke into the song by Toby Keith, "I ain't as good as I once was..."

I truly enjoyed DK's belly laughter as I ran after him. Anna-banana had to go potty, and I typically try to avoid porta jons like the plague. We ventured on over only to find the jon was locked. "Oh too bad for you!" I thought in my own mind, laughing at my own joke, until I realized that didn't change the fact that she had to go. I had the brilliant idea to hang on to her while she leaned back in a sitting position. Let's just say it was the sprinkler effect, my Ugg boots and her clothes got soaked. Good thing I had a change of clothes for her in the truck.

April 5, 2011

So we've met a few roadblocks, but we're going to keep digging. For the longest time I've wanted to research our house to find out when it was actually built. We were told 1900, but is that accurate? We have reason to believe otherwise. How many families have lived here? We know an old woman died on our front porch at some point and the milkman found her. Also, what walls were original and what was added later? So much curiosity and with it being spring break, we have some time to research.

We found out, "any house built before 1940 doesn't really have the paperwork to say when it was truly built, so many homes that vintage are a guessed year." Also, because they didn't issue building permits back then, there was no way to keep track. Interesting! We went around town, the library, and even a little museum to find out more but was unsuccessful. This project and research is helping the kids, and I have something positive to focus on. Danny is continuing to struggle quite a bit. He told me some days he just locks his door at work so people don't bug him. I worry what other people are thinking. How do his co-workers feel when he gets upset? Does he act like he does at home while at work? I worry about him so much. I want him to heal and grow. I know this process is long, and I want to help and encourage the best I can. Even despite my best intentions, this is all *so* hard.

Chapter 16

April 10, 2011

Yesterday both boys had t-ball practice, so Danny took DK and I took Pete. We decided to go a little early so we could play catch. Pete grabbed the baseball bat too, so we went into a field nearby for him to hit a few of my pitches. I kept covering my face with my hands, afraid he was going to break my nose. An old school fear of mine...1984, when I got hit in the face with a baseball bat while playing catcher.

After Pete's practice I told him we would get a hot fudge sundae. I called Danny on our way home to see what they were doing and they decided to join us. We all sat on the front porch steps and enjoyed. Of course Dutch had to try to get a few licks in. He then barked his head off at some poor bikers. His bark is sounding slower now, more of a, "I'm trying to scare you but I'm seventy-years-old," sound. He doesn't have that agile, take-off-like-a-bullet sort of run in him anymore. We play catch, and after three tosses, he won't bring the ball back because, truth be told, he doesn't want to chase it again.

April 13, 2011

I had fun in DK's class again this morning reading with the kids. DK always reads with me first. He's so sweet. Speaking of his sweetness, last night Danny picked the kids up from his parents' house and on their way home, Danny said something like, "Isn't that a pretty sunset?" To which DK responded, "Not as pretty as Mom."

Not knowing that, I went out to greet them when they got home, and DK ran up the porch steps and tightly wrapped his arms around my waist. As he hugged me tight, he told me what he had said. *So sweet*; it melted my heart.

While reading with the kids today, one of the teachers approached me and told me my name was being thrown around to join the PTA. I guess three out of the four board members are stepping down. I am flattered, dumbfounded, and tickled at the same time. I'd love to be at school more, especially in that capacity. We'll see.

April 17, 2011

Danny has wanted to go to a Reds' game as a family for a while. Doing something fun like this as a family of five sounded perfect. Except Danny started drinking beers right when we got to the ballpark. I was thinking he'd better slow down and even approached it from an angle trying not to make him mad, asking him to slow down, but no luck. Not only did I not want a drunk husband, but I also didn't want the credit card statement for it. After a bunch of kid potty breaks, peanuts, hotdogs, and sunshine, it was time to head home. As we were walking out of the ballpark, Danny approached a random guy on the sidewalk and started arguing with him. I was thinking, "Oh no, here we go again." I got embarrassed and said, "Let's keep moving, we have to walk quite a way to the car and the kids are tired," but he told me to leave it alone. There I stood with three kids, watching, as my husband was trying to bait some random man into a fist fight.

I tilted my head back and took a deep breath, grabbed the kids hands, and we started with the massive group of spectators towards the parking lot. That is until I realized I didn't have the keys; Danny did. So we stood at a distance and waited it out. I was trying everything to distract the kids, but they could feel the stress. Not only was he intoxicated but also manic. He wanted to fight. Thankfully the other guy walked away but not without things heating up quickly. I managed to ask nicely for the keys so I could drive home. This was not the kind of family time I had hoped for.

April 24, 2011

After asking for years, and trying to convince Danny of the need, he finally did it. He built me a clothesline! Out beside the barn, it was the most perfect and peaceful spot. It's visible from the road, so I can wave at cars passing by, I can take in the scenery, and the kids can play out back. There it is, my little slice of heaven!

May 4, 2011

Today I cleaned out the trailer so we can head camping for Mother's Day. I look forward to this weekend every year. We didn't go camping last year because it was cold, and Danny didn't want to, but that was fine. I'm glad we're getting to going this year.

Part of my cleaning today included a refrigerator full of fish, which wouldn't be so bad except the fridge was accidentally unplugged a few days ago. I can honestly say I have never seen so many black flies in all my life. It was like nothing I have ever experienced - 3,422 flies came out of nowhere, swirled my head and attacked that already dead fish. I screamed my head off and went running like a mad woman! Let's just say, not an ideal way to spend my morning, but I survived.

May 7, 2011

Danny's mood changed yesterday, and he said we are *not* camping this weekend. "It's too much work," he said. At first I was mad, then sad, but decided I am still going to take the kids. We have been excited and anticipating this trip for two weeks. It's Mother's Day and I can do this on my own. Dad came and helped me hook up and followed us to the campground where I backed the thirty-two-foot travel trailer all by myself. Boom. I can do this. We will do it anyway.

Danny can decide if he wants to be part of this family or not. I cannot continue to wait on him. He doesn't want to do much anymore, and I'm starting to realize I can do things on my own. This is a personal victory. Once set up, and the kids were happy riding scooters, I gave myself a literal high-five and went about reading my gardening magazine.

May 13, 2011

I was pushing the kids on the tire swing out back when an older man walked up between the house and barn. At first I wondered if he was lost, but then the coolest thing happened. He shared that his great-grandparents used to live in our house! He asked if he could come in and check it out. He hadn't been in the house since he was a kid. The kids and I excitedly showed him around, apologizing for the mess as we went. He didn't see the mess though, he was so intrigued by every room and told us what each one used to be. There it was, some of that history we'd been longing for!

After he left I thought about how the Lord had provided the answers we couldn't have found anywhere else. What an amazing experience.

May 16, 2011

I'm finding that hanging clothes on the clothesline has become my sanctuary. It's peaceful and so beautiful. I actually can't wait for loads to get done in the washing machine so I can grab my bag of clothespins and take a step back in time; no noise except the traffic passing by, leaves twisting in the wind. I find it's my safe place. From socks to sleeping bags, I hang even at dusk.

I found myself on my knees in the dark tonight. When I went up to check on the kids, I got down on my knees and just wept in DK's bedroom. I prayed they will be safe from harm and danger. I didn't feel like my knees truly showed the vulnerability and desperation, so I laid myself flat on my stomach, face in the carpet with my hands stretched, open-palmed over my head, i n absolute surrender. *Lord Jesus, hear my prayer. Please, I am desperate. Please take this burden, please lift my children up, that they will know You and yearn to seek You more every single day. Please keep us safe in these times, the good and the bad days.*

May 17, 2011

I am the new PTA secretary for my kids' elementary school! I guess my name being the only one on the ballot helped! I love being at school. Danny wonders if I'm over-committing my time, but we only meet once a month. I'm excited to some of my creative skills to make fancy newsletters. They also asked if I'd do the bulletin board decorations, which I happily agreed to. The kids get to see me during the day, too. I love this!

May 21, 2011

Danny is struggling big time and it's been a constant downward slope. This is *so* hard. I tried to talk it over with him. He's trying to see himself more clearly and admitted to some anxiety. When he got home from work, he threw the black "FAMILY" sign at me from across the room. He said, "If this is what a family looks like, that's a joke."

I was absolutely terrified. It didn't hit me in the head as he intended. Fortunately, I ducked in time. Afterwards, I lay there in the dark waiting for him to fall asleep. There was no breaking through his anger. I just needed him to fall asleep and wake up new. But will he wake up new, or will this stay? I need to try to sleep.

I pray he will get control over himself. I pray he ask questions and want to seek help. How can he think any of this is ok? I *know* he's sick, but I feel like this goes beyond all of that. I try to support, to stand firm, and to love. But it's not enough. What about what I need? This is supposed to be a partnership, not just a one-person team. But I can't push, I need to have patience.

May 31, 2011

What a busy yet, mostly, fun-filled weekend. We drove to Indy pulling the trailer and camped at a really nice KOA campground we've never stayed at. It's fancy despite being in the middle of nowhere. We decided to camp rather than stay in a hotel for cousin Aubrey's wedding. Miss Anna-banana got to be a flowergirl who shyly pulled and barely made it down the aisle!

On the day after the wedding, Mom invited extended family to come out for a visit at our trailer. I was ok with it but hadn't checked with Danny first. I started tidying up and getting chairs set up when he went hysterical on me. He started badgering and shaming me. He wasn't going to make food, pay for food, or entertain *anyone*. This was *his* time and place to relax and not what he had planned.

I ended up taking a walk to a little playground in the campground with the kids, far away from where he could hear me, to call Grace. I didn't know what to do. She calmed me down and I then communicated with Mom that it wouldn't be a very long visit. I used the excuse that the kids were tired.

I detest not being honest, but what was I supposed to tell my whole family that mean the world to me? Mom was gracious and grabbed some pizzas so we didn't even have to cook. I felt like I wasn't even worth the dollar in my wallet, but forced a smile. As everyone was gathered around to eat, Danny put me on the spot to pray. He knows it's out of my comfort zone in large groups, but I wasn't going to let him have pleasure in making me squirm. I quickly prayed silently, asking for peace, and then asked everyone to bow and pray. I did it! And it actually had the adverse effect! Now I feel like I want to be the one praying out loud before we eat *every time*. What a cool experience. Thank You, Lord!

June 24, 2011
Today DK was trying to explain to me, "When a girl becomes a lady...."
So naturally, I videotaped it. Here's his explanation:

Me: "Ok DK, you were telling me about people who were nice. You consider someone a nice lady...where is it? What age is it someone is considered a lady?"
DK: "Umm, aren't you going to do girl first?"
Me: "Well, you tell me the timeline. So girl, then…"
(In walks Pete from the kitchen with a cheek full of food, like a squirrel saving it for later)
Pete (blurts): "It's considered...considered a lady, twenty…"
DK: "A lady, then woman."
Me: "And what am I?"
Pete (now jumping on the ottoman): "A woman."
DK: "You're thirty-four?"
Me: "Right."
DK: "Umm, so when you start being a girl is when you are born. Until about the age of eighteen."

(Anna comes clomping in the room now to see what we're talking about).

DK: "When at the age of eighteen, you start being a lady."

Me: "Ok."

DK: "And then at the age of twenty-seven, you get, you...you're a woman."

Me: "Where does twenty-seven come from? Just a number you think fits?"

DK: "Yep."

Me: "Ok, you make a very good point."

Pete (still squirreling the food off to the side of his mouth): "Can I do it?"

Me: Peter? Yeah, what...how do you feel about it?

Pete: "You start as a, ah..."

Me: "An octopus?"

Pete (giggling): "No."

Me: "As, ahh, baby bird?"

Pete: "As a be, be, you start as a bebe."

DK: "Well, Pete..."

Pete: "You start as a baby girl, then you start as a mother, a girl," (DK puts his hand over Pete's mouth and they start talking over each other).

Me: "Ok, one quick question, one quick question. Anna, what are you?"

Anna: Umm. A little boy."

Chapter 17

June 28, 2011

We figured it was time to get the septic tank cleaned out because we haven't since we moved in. I went out to show the guy where our septic tank is and sat on the front porch in case he had any questions. Plus, it was a beautiful day, and I don't really like strange men walking around the house unattended.

He gets things hooked up and moving along, and I'm sitting there on my pretty yellow chair watching cars drive by when, all of a sudden, it starts raining. Wait, what is this mist? I stand up and realize it's coming from the septic truck! Our own waste being sprinkled all over the side of our house... and me. I get up and yell for the guy who's standing there like Uncle Eddie on *National Lampoon's Christmas Vacation*. He comes running up the side yard and yells, "Oh, oops!"

Oops? That's all ya got?!

July 21, 2011

It's been such a busy month, but ahh, I do love July. The weather has been great. We celebrated both boys' birthdays, and spent a lot of time on Nan and Papa's boat. These memories are going to last for a long time - bathing suit sunburn lines and small cans of Sunkist.

July 22, 2011

Tonight when Dan got home from work, he was physically and mentally exhausted. He went right up the stairs and straight to bed. I had dinner set, and Pete had been anticipating one-on-one time with Danny all day. But there it was, the elephant in the room, the obstacle that is Danny's mood. At dinner, my mind was racing. Is it enabling him to say he can skip tonight? Would that actually be doing Pete a favor? But he wasn't angry or out of control, just tired. So I went upstairs and sat on the bed next to Danny.

"Do you mind if I take the kids in our new car to show Nan and Papa and then out for ice cream?"

Danny asked, "Well, what about Pete? Will he be disappointed? If it means the world, I'll still take him to the movie." That was good, he was thinking of Pete. I ended up pulling Pete outside onto the porch to see what he wanted to do. I spelled it all out and asked if he was disappointed. He said no. I told him to be 100% honest, to tell me how he *really* felt.

He finally admitted he was bummed but followed it up quickly with, "If Dad needs to rest, I want him to get some." I told him that was sweet but that he doesn't always have to worry about everyone else. His feelings matter too. He hemmed, thought on it, and chose the car ride and ice cream.

I reminded him that I'll always have his back. I pray he knows that and he heard me. I pray that he clings to the truth that *his* thoughts matter. He is important. No matter what age, he deserves respect too. I pray Danny will see what these kids are willing to do for him. They are so compassionate, and as much as it makes me sad, they have learned this due to our circumstances. I am a very proud mama.

July 27, 2011

I had to write this down because it was a total God thing. Just a few hours ago, I was talking to the kids about how there is no such thing as a coincidence.

Fast forward to when Danny got home from work tonight and joined me sitting on the porch in the rain. He began encouraging me in my friendships and individuality. The more I listened to him, I realized he was saying the complete opposite of what he's said about these things the past two years. Where did this change of heart come from and how long will this version last? As I tried to make sense of it all, I found myself standing and staring into my bedroom mirror. I was asking, doubting, then reassuring myself.

"I am good. I am doing the best I can. I am trying my best. What more can I do but take life moment-to-moment?"

I felt God give me the resolve to stop the negative thoughts I had about myself and decided, "I need to take the high road and move forward with *hope*. Hope for Heaven and all of this stuff can't consume me."

Now at bed, I'm reading, "the glorious view you can see from the high road" (Jesus Calling by Sarah Young).

AMEN. I love how He tied things back full circle. I smiled as I closed my bible.

July 29, 3011
This verse is incredible when I read it tonight in my One Year Bible, I think it's the whole lesson I'm learning…

"Love must be sincere. Hate what is evil; cling to what is good. Be devoted to one another in brotherly love. Honor one another above yourselves. Never be lacking in zeal, but keep your spiritual fervor, serving the Lord. Be joyful in hope, patient in affliction, faithful in prayer. Share with God's people who are in need. Practice hospitality" Romans 12:9-13 (NIV One Year Bible).

July 30, 2011
I want to begin to heal and to trust. My mind feels consumed with seeing everyone else in their "perfect" family with loving and encouraging husbands. Husbands who read devotions with their kids, play catch, put them to bed, and help around the house. I'm not looking for perfection,

I know I'm not, but certain things need to change to help our family. I'm feeling like most days I just go through the motions. I don't feel happy deep down inside. I feel like some of my joy is gone and won't come back. I have major trust issues with my husband.

This came out a few nights ago when he was acting like he was encouraging me. As I expected, tonight he started to ridicule and shame me about the very things he had seemed sincere about. It's like a game. I want to trust him, but when these things happen, and I feel mocked, how am I supposed to come back from that? I can't just snap my fingers and have it there. I'm not even allowed to talk about any of my feelings with anyone. If Danny knew what Dad knows, I'm sure he would hurt me.

I feel so alone in this place. People ask me, "How's Dan doing?" They ask because he doesn't join us anywhere anymore. I feel like it's such a padded question. I don't know, honestly. I can't answer that.

Dear Lord, please fill my mind with good today. With joy and patience to handle right this minute; not to dread or worry about what may come. My fears of being shattered again grow by Danny's later indecision and anger. Please God, fill me back up so I'm not lonely but am filled with the hope that only You can provide.

Mighty to Save by Hillsong Worship reminds me:

"My Savior, He can move the mountains.
My God is Mighty to save; He is Mighty to save.
Forever, Author of salvation, He rose and conquered the grave,
Jesus conquered the grave."

August 1, 2011
I don't want to be in this space anymore, waiting and holding my breath. I want to be carried through the day without worry or hopelessness, wondering when and how it will end. I feel like I'm trying to understand and support what Danny needs, I know he struggles. I understand that, but I feel like it's raining down on me. *Please lift this cloud, oh Lord! I feel like the weight of the 10,000 pounds on my shoulders.*

August 9, 2011

He says he's doing great, but I know he's not. The good thing is, here at home, things are a bit better. I'm trying to coast back into, "easy does it Charly," and to take it as it comes.

I was given advice to "get off the roller coaster." The roller coaster, that is life, living with a husband who's struggling with Bipolar Disorder. Even with the ups and downs of Danny's mood, I need to stay level; right here with this flat horizontal line I'm drawing in my hand. I have to be conscious of not being happy or excited when he's up, nor sad and down when he's depressed. I was born with my heart on my sleeve, so this feels against my very nature. I will dig really deep to do my best. It's one of the hardest things I've ever had to do in my life.

August 10, 2011

I want to encourage our children to be humble, to listen and ask them, "What do you think God is saying to you today?" *Please Lord, help me to be your servant and be filled with hope and peace, no matter what. And to pass these on to DK, Pete, and Anna. The truest of gifts ever given.*

Dad and I got a chance to sit on the boat today, just us. He sees my suffering - I can't hide it from him. Not since I opened up and let him in. Telling Dad everything has taken some weight off. Dad wants what is best for the kids and me. He's protective and wise. He told me today that I need to get out of my marriage. He told me that I need to file for divorce. I understand, I do. This has been a tough road. But I'm not at that place yet. In my gut, I just can't do it. I'm not ready.

August 14, 2011

To think it was about two years ago now that I had to gather the courage to approach Danny about his alcoholism...We were camping and the kids and I were on a long bike. When we got back to the trailer, there were seventeen empty beer bottles on the counter, and it wasn't even 1 pm.

I was so fearful in that moment, vulnerable, and petrified. I didn't know how he would take it. I feared anger or outburst, but he listened. I reluctantly started the conversation telling him I was concerned about how much he'd been drinking, and it went from there. I felt like he listened, and it went a lot better than I had imagined. I was able to be open and honest. I spoke my truth. I thought things would change, that is, until the next day when he was drunk. I was foolish to have felt confident. My words, feelings, and courage were lost in it all.

August 30, 2011

I took a pregnancy test today. I didn't tell Danny because I don't want to get a reaction out of him. I haven't been feeling right but honestly am thankful it was negative. It got me thinking for a few moments about a baby, and as great as a gift as they are, I was not disappointed. I can't imagine what that would do to Danny if I was. It hurt to feel that way about it. That feeling was a reality check.

Chapter 18

September 2, 2011

I found myself incredibly frustrated tonight. Danny came home from work and went straight to bed. I went into our bedroom and asked what the trouble was, and he said he was sad. He was sad because I didn't want to go to a friend's cabin this weekend. Seeing as I do all of the work to coordinate food, clothing, the dog, bedding, meals, etc., a twenty-four-hour trip doesn't feel worth the work.

The buying/carrying/packing of food itself can take twenty-four hours, not to mention he will be in the woods setting up deer blinds the entire time. It hurts that I'm being made to feel bad for something I wish he would think through. He tends to only think of himself. His disappointment over this weekend poured into dinnertime when he force-fed DK his broccoli. DK was literally gagging, and I felt so bad. I just don't know what to do sometimes.

September 7, 2011

I didn't want to take on the day when I woke up this morning. Danny asked me tonight, if I was depressed. I don't think so, but maybe I am. I haven't been sleeping well. My mind just races when I lay down. I am also getting weary from all of my headaches. These are seemingly non-stop headaches that come every day now, usually holding at a dull one to two on the pain scale, or if I'm being honest, three to four.

What to do during the day with Anna while the boys are at school has been weighing on my mind. How will I find balance for it all? How do I keep her entertained while I do housework? She doesn't have anyone to play with. Then I feel somehow guilty, which turns into frustration. Around and around I go. I want to be present for Anna. I want to be a better mom, even when I don't feel like it.

Having our garage being broken into last night hasn't exactly been what I wanted to deal with today. The window was busted out, someone came in and stole tools, money, and tv monitors out of the truck. Knowing someone sat in *my* seat and tore apart our things has me extremely angry. The police came out and took a report. Apparently there have been a lot of break-ins in the area. I feel violated. I want to be the best version of myself, but I'm not that right now. Sometimes life throws all of these punches. Can we ever catch a break?

September 12, 2011

Anna starts preschool today, and my emotions are all over the map. The social and learning parts will be awesome for her. I'm not sure how she'll do being away from me though. She kind of likes her mama. But this will be good...for both of us.

These years I've been able to stay home with the kids has been the greatest gift. They are our *greatest* gift. Each one of them precious, different, and challenging in their own way. I wouldn't change one second of the time I got with them at home. Now that they are all in school full time, maybe it's time I work full time. I don't know how I would balance it all though. *Lord, please help me to feel some peace as I think about this next chapter in life. How I can help the family financially while still being Mom?*

September 22, 2011

Danny and I are not clicking. And tonight we had some time to chill, just us. The kids were with Nan and Papa - Dad has a cold, and I worry about him. I did most of the talking, and it just seemed so surface-level. We have a plumber updating our pipes in the basement, and Danny made a joke to him about me needing "a shot" to calm down because when I tell stories, I am too animated.

That really hurt my feelings. I didn't think that was very nice of him to say to this guy who doesn't even know me. I know of a lot of people who like how animated I am and think I'm funny. It's just me and how I do things. Given all I deal with, I feel like he should be thankful for me, quirks and all. Instead, he makes fun of me. He claims, after the guy left, that he only said those things because he was hungry.

Truth be told, he does get a little crazy when he's hungry, but still...Then he dropped really inappropriate language over ice cream that dripped on his arm, and I asked that he not talk like that. He said, "What's the difference between saying that and how you talk?"

I don't even know how to respond when he's like this. I'm feeling this distance and don't know how to close the gap. He's being accusatory, and I need to stop helping him feed off of me by being defensive.

We heard a song in church recently that brought me to tears called, *Hold Us Together* by Matt Maher

"He's waiting for you, knockin' at your door!
Every moment of truth when your hearts hits the floor.
And when you're on your knees, now see, love will hold us together
Make us a shelter weather the storm and I'll be my brother's keeper,
So the whole world will know that we're not alone."

September 25, 2011
"I will call upon the Lord, who is worthy to be praised..." (Grace and Love by Deborah Reeves).

I know He is with me and my stronghold.

I want to teach our children about Him and not waiver, even though Danny isn't sure where he is with his faith. We had a talk today, and I didn't realize how much it's been weighing me down. I have been taking the kids to youth group at the reformed church, but Danny refuses to help take them or pick them up. They aren't even allowed to sing any of the songs they are learning because Danny says those songs are political. They can't sing, "In the Lord's Army." I don't understand it, but honestly, it makes him furious.

I've been contemplating a new church, but I think that's because he never goes with us and people are starting to notice. How can they not? Although for me, not having him on his phone watching sports or shaking his head in disagreement during sermons, helps. I recently committed to Adult Sunday School and Danny won't meet me at church, so I have to come home and get the kids in-between for church.

I'm going to keep going. I have to. I need to set this example for the kids no matter what. This is crucial and I will do it alone. These kids need Christ and His Kingdom. I will run them to and from our church and youth group until I'm blue in the face because it's *that* important. It has to happen now.

September 28, 2011
What a day, from sunup to sundown. I've cried, laughed, ate too much, felt insignificant, and put in last place.

I know I have value. Sometimes I just beg God to show me. I know these kids love and need me. I know I have a purpose. I don't know what my "gifts" fully are yet, but I'll learn. I know I need to keep fighting this fight and that it's ok to cry in secret. Crying isn't a sign of weakness, I know it's not. I'm strong. I can do this. I'm not last. I may have eaten the last row of Oreos, but I am not last.

September 29, 2011
Dutch got on the school bus this morning. He always hangs at the bus stop with the kids, but today he decided to go for it! I quick ran after him, but by then he was walking all the way down the aisle with seats full of kids leaning in for a chance to pet him. He was absolutely *beaming*. His tongue wagging out the side of his mouth, signing autographs as he walked. It was hilarious! It gave my boys some "street cred." Everybody knew his name;

kids were yelling it. He was in heaven, that is until he reached the very back of the bus - with his old age and questionable hips, he had to do a 9-point turn to turn his body around and come back down the aisle, and off the bus. I think if he could talk, that'd be a top five moment in his existence.

September 30, 2011

God has provided! I have seen Him. Danny asked me at dinner if I would like him to concede and do more than just come to church for special occasions. He said he would be more open, set aside his personal thoughts, and just do it. I was so glad to hear him say this! I'm praying he will follow through on these things. All I can do for right now is be grateful for where we are in this moment.

"We know that in everything God works for the good of those who love him. They are the people He called, because that was His plan" Romans 8:28 (NCV Mom's Bible, God's Wisdom for Mothers).

October 4, 2011

I wasn't sure my brain was going to stay in my head last night. I couldn't even lift my head off the bed as I lay there, folded in half. I had to take Excedrin, two horse pills, and my usual prescription to make it go away. My skull still hurts.

I can't be honest and open with him. I am internalizing every single thing. I don't want to poke the bear because the outcome is so over the top that I want to just protect myself, but mostly I want to protect the kids. I do this by keeping quiet and just pushing it down. I am seeing the correlation between stress and my headaches, or not enough sleep (that happens with sick kids or my mind on overdrive.). What am I to do but lift it to the Lord and try ever so hard to let it go? It just keeps happening. It's a cycle. One decent week followed by three to four awful ones.

I go through the motions and keep my eye on the prize. The prize is Jesus; it's salvation. *What are these hard times teaching me, Lord? I am leaning on You. I want to see You in this. It can be so difficult when it feels so bleak. But I know You are here, present in this moment. You want what is best for us... all of us.*

October 6, 2011

I had a good session with my therapist today. She said she thinks I'm an "emotional" person. I think a better word is passionate. Potato, potatoe. I'm really starting to let her in, which helps lift some of the burden off of me. I do enjoy having a place to talk, cry, complain, and sort through all of it. I feel safe with her and don't have to pretend that everything is going well. I can just be me, in that moment, where I'm at.

Danny and I went for a long walk with Dutch out back, and it was great. We talked the whole time. Then, we got some Chinese food for dinner, cream soda, and grape pop. The kids were with Nan and Papa, which is a nice break for Danny and me. It restores some patience. The kids are thrilled, and busy, and I'm able to slow down and take some time to reflect, think, and pray.

Poor Pete has another ruptured eardrum. This kid... He can't have a typical earache; his whole entire ear is messed up. He's such a trooper. I don't want him to struggle his whole life with hearing issues like I have.

October 12, 2011

Tickets for the nature preserve? $9.50. Getting everyone up and ready and lunches packed by 7:40 am? Rushed. Having Pete sit on my lap the whole bus rides back to school after a six-hour field trip? *Priceless.*

Tonight after dinner, Dutch was feeling the underlying stress. While Danny sat in his leather chair watching the Indians game, he started whining at him, then barking. His tail was wagging and hitting the front door a few feet from him. It's like Dutch was telling him to relax. He's so smart and getting bolder in his old age. Maybe I can learn a thing or two from him.

October 16, 2011

Well, I've boarded the train to head home. I cried as Grace and I said our goodbyes and am still on the verge of tears. What a great weekend, just her and me. Sister alone time never happens. She is an amazing human who loves and knows me better than anyone else. I am thankful I can talk openly about Danny and what's been going on at home. She's always been a great listener. It helped having the kids stay with Mom and Dad. I wasn't worried about them one bit. But it's time to get back home...

October 21, 2011
Anna and I had a classic game of airplane going on this morning. I was laying on my back, and she was on my feet flying through the air. Apparently Dutch wanted the attention, so he started pushing buttons on Anna's toy McDonalds cash register. He even ordered a Happy Meal.

November 7, 2011
I took some time to hang at Mom and Dad's house today. I've started advertising on social media about making Christmas ornaments for people. I hope I get some orders! The extra money will help with Christmas, and I love making them.

I've also decided that thirty-four-years old isn't too old for a side ponytail. I like it. I think it's cute. We'll see when I reread this, when I'm eighty, if I agree! I'll probably still be wearing my signature look then...pigtails!

Chapter 19

November 16, 2011

I just downloaded, *He's Always Been Faithful* by Sara Groves onto my iPod. It brings me to my knees. It's the absolute truth.

"Morning by morning I wake up to find, the power and comfort of God's hand in mine.

Season by season I watch Him, amazed. In awe of the mystery of His perfect ways.

All I have needed His hand will provide. He's always been faithful to me."

He has always been, and continues to be faithful and carries me through these times. Even when it all seems so dark, He is the Light that leads me. *Please Lord, continue to help me find my way. I can't do this without You.*

December 20, 2011

Random act of kindness: today I put my hand on her shoulder and told the lady exiting the bathroom in front of me that she had a maxi pad stuck to the bottom of her shoe.

Danny has been questioning his job a lot again lately. What if he decides to quit before he has something else lined up? We don't have much in savings. We've been trying to pay down debt. I did the bills last month after seeing how stressed he's been about finances. It's been an eye-opener to see where our money goes.

Honestly, besides basic kid needs, the occasional sewing or ornament supplies and groceries, I really don't spend money. I never have been a big spender. Eating out and beer are big draws off the ol' paycheck, though. I tried to talk to Danny about how much convenience stores pop up on the checkbook registry, and he got mad at me. He said that he can spend his hard earned money however he wants. I know it didn't help that I bounced a check, but the credit union was understanding and removed the fees. I guess I see it for what it is. I will work to save more when I grocery shop. Coupons do help, and so does paying attention to sales. That's about all I can do.

DK asked me at dinner what those "scars" were on my forehead. Shocked, I turned to Danny. He smiled and confirmed what I thought DK might be referring to...wrinkles. I prefer the term laugh lines. I will admit, I've aged a bit in these recent years, but I didn't realize that much.

December 17, 2011

A mere eleven years ago, this human-like dog was born. He's my buddy, my source of one-sided conversation, and he brings so much joy. He is something else. I wouldn't trade all of his naughty, bizarre antics for anything! Grace says he acts like me. I think he feeds off of me, for sure. When I go out to the clothesline he always follows and has to be able to see me. He's always there for me to chat with. What a silly animal.

Doing the motherly thing, I carried sleeping Anna from her *lean-to* fort and into bed at 10:30 pm last night. She was sleeping so peacefully, but I knew she wouldn't sleep all night. The mess of the unfolded blankets out all over the place stresses Danny out. So I folded them all up and put them away.

First thing this morning, Anna comes to me and taps my arm, hands on her hips, "Mom, you wrecked my fort last night."

My response, "Well excuse me for living!" Oh the things we do for our kids. I took the heat and apologized.

December 19, 2011
Yesterday marked one year that I left with the kids for the first time. It's hard to believe it's been a whole year. I've had so many emotions lately.

Yesterday, I sobbed after church for a woman who lost her husband three months ago in a car accident. She has four small kids, and this is their first Christmas without him. I asked her if I could give her a hug, whispered "Merry Christmas," and went to the car to cry.

When I got home, I felt like I could sob for hours for those times in the past few years when Danny would threaten suicide or actually attempted it. I felt horrible because, what if he actually had? I'm so grateful he is here and how far we've come. Praise God. *I wish he felt that it was You, Lord, who has brought us this far.*

All of the tears and time on my knees in fervent prayer for this man. I pray he will have his heart softened. I've been praying the same for myself lately. I pray that I will return to myself, not this hard, saddened self who feels moody and sometimes struggles to get out of bed in the morning.

January 4, 2012
"How'd it go this afternoon while I was at preschool? Did you miss me?" Anna asked me in her sweet voice.

I responded, "I had a good one. Yep, I did. How about you?"

"No, I didn't miss you at all," she quickly responded. After I stopped laughing, I thanked her for her honesty and told her I didn't miss her either.

January 6, 2012
I've always wanted to be a police officer. Anyone who knows me knows this. There is something about investigating and digging deeper that intrigues me. I love the thrill at getting to the bottom of things. Hey, my job before kids let me do some investigating, so I suppose it's not too far off! It's in me.

I had to jot down this funny thing that happened yesterday: After returning DK's dress shoes, I wanted to make a few more stops. I debated taking the highway, but had some time to kill, so I decided to run to the paint store. I noticed a strange scenario in the car in front of me. I scooted forward in my seat to take a closer look.

There was an elderly woman driving an older Chevy Cavalier, white hair, all bushy, sticking up around her headrest, with a younger male in the passenger seat. He had a knit cap and sunglasses. He was leaning into her seat, uncomfortably, and in her personal space. I grew suspicious.

What was he doing? I decided to follow them. My mind went to robbery. Why was *she* driving him? Why was his hand on her headrest as he leaned towards her? Was he intimidating her? Are they going to the bank where he'll make her empty her account? With so many thoughts, I kept on their tail. She nearly ran a red light in front of me, and I called out, "Don't run the light, lady!" as if she could hear me. She quickly hit her brakes. There we sat at the red light, my fingers tightening over the steering wheel.

Do I dial 9-1-1 and wait to hit *send* to be ready for when he makes a move? Is he holding a gun to her side? I stayed with them. At one point he slid the winter cap off his head to scratch it, and I noticed he was balding. That gave me a better idea of his age.

As we keep going, on goes her blinker. A few seconds later, so does mine. Are they turning into the bank? *Wait.* They are turning into the restaurant driveway right before it. Are they circling around to hit the bank from the rear? They pull into a spot at the restaurant. I wait, fortunately, a car was pulling out, so it gave me the perfect opportunity to not look suspicious as I stalked them. I circled around and out of the restaurant drive. I busted out laughing at myself and my imagination.

The old woman, by then, had walked around to the passenger door. She was helping the man out of the car. He was blind.

January 12, 2012

We talked about money - about how tight it was going to be for a while because of Christmas last month. So how does Danny justify bringing home a new big screen tv and an Xbox? We *just* talked about this. I am not supposed to spend any money except on groceries. When I got upset as he carried it in tonight, he scolded me, telling me to relax and that "he's got this." I'm so upset right now; I just don't understand. He brings this stuff home and I look like the bad guy for not being happy about it. I spent money on thank you notes for the kids to write thank you notes for their Christmas gifts, and he yells at me for my spending. I'm so mad.

January 28, 2012

Danny told me tonight that he's not in the mood for jokes. All of this because I invited Mom and Dad over to see the kids do a little show tomorrow after church. They have been practicing their silly faces while singing, "I'm a Martian," by Marvin the Martian. Danny said they can't come over to our house and that the whole thing is dumb anyway. My heart is breaking because they've practiced so much and giggle the whole time. How do I tell *my own* parents they aren't allowed to come over? Last night he said all I do is joke and sing and that this playful non-sense needs to stop.

Please, please continue to soften his heart, oh Lord. When I try to keep things light, I get shot down. I'm at a loss for words right now.

January 29, 2012

"Holy, holy, holy, I want to see You… to see You high and lifted up, shining in the light of Your Glory…" We sang this at church this morning. I closed my eyes so tight in reverence, trying to focus. Last night was tough, I won't lie.

We had a heated argument over Mom and Dad coming over today for lunch and the kids doing their performance. Danny got anxious about all that would have to be done and what he'd need to do. I was so irritated and felt he was being extremely selfish, making it all about him. Feeling I'd have to cancel plans again because of how he felt, my last words were,

"Whatever, I'll scratch it," and I went to bed. At least acted like I did. I rolled over with my back to him and cried silently as I have so many nights.

So this morning there was minimal eye contact, and only a few words were exchanged. Then he went out to snow blow, and I knew it was going to be a bad day. That was something else he had said last night, "I'm warning you now. Tomorrow isn't going to be pretty."

I stepped out on the porch, and said we need to do something because we can't go all day like this. He said he just needed to get through with the driveway and that he wasn't mad. Whew. I got ready, got the kids ready, and we went to church without him. A few minutes into service, I felt a touch on my back, and it was him. He came to church, and I was thrilled. I saw God's hand. He opened the eyes of my heart, and the sermon opened Danny's. So much so, that he said he felt convicted tonight and hasn't heard a message like that in years. A guest pastor had preached, and it was amazing. Danny talked about volunteering and donating.

Please open the eyes of our hearts, Lord! So we can see you and how to serve. Praise You for this miracle.

Danny fell down the steps this morning. That's what made him stop his anxiety madness and realize it wasn't worth it. He lay there for ten minutes in a heap, and decided it was best to come to church, even if he was late. I told him I was glad he did.

February 9, 2012
I'm thinking of Grandpa Will tonight. I can't hide my tears. They think he has cancer. He is the most gracious and kindest man I know. He is one of few men I know that has lived life with the best of intentions towards others. He's such a selfless example of a God-fearing, kind, smiling, singing, tight hugging, wonderful man. I love you, Grandpa!

The boys want to share a bedroom again. Maybe Pete's room can become an office or a playroom. *Thank You Lord for the softening you are doing in Danny's heart.*

Also, *this*: "Jesus has a big lap." Spoken from the heart of a 4-year-old.

February 10, 2012

I've been peed on, retched on, whined at, coughed on, farted on, spilled on, snotted on, told "It's not fair," cleaned up every mess known to man, pounced on, dumped on, and cried on. And that's just today, by noon. Ah, the things they don't warn you about motherhood.

Even though I don't like the month of February, I need to keep focus. These yucky, dirty snow months will be gone soon and spring will come. Hopefully getting outside will help Danny too. It seems like this has been a long stretch of him being down. I can't seem to find how to help. I encourage, match where he is, give him space, ask him, but he won't let me in. And I can't force it. I just need to wait for something to click, and he will come back.

February 18, 2012

I guess there is a small part of me that feels bad for stealing the movie-sized box of "Dots" one of the kids won at the school carnival today. So, do I:

a. play dumb and act as though they must have been lost?
b. come clean and buy a replacement box?
c. give them the box containing all of the green ones I didn't eat?

I'm going with A.

February 23, 2012

I have this whole going-back-to-work full-time, pressure cooker question working into my mind again and stressing me out. I'm afraid if I say I want to, I'll get overwhelmed and back out. I don't want to let anyone down. I am scared, and need to think and pray about it. I do get excited about having time all day with other adults, but the kids come first.

We could use the extra money to pay down debt. I'd only need to work for another like, nineteen years. How old will the kids be then? And that's when I get nervous and the war within begins.

With my old job, I'd have job security. But working 9 am - 5 pm every day...What will the kids do in the summer? How will I have the energy to cook dinner? Who would help with childcare? And the thought of childcare scares me because I want to be the one with them. *I'm so torn, Lord, please grant me the clarity to make a sound decision. Help me in this journey called life. I want You, Lord to please lift this struggle from my heart and give me clarity for the right decision. I don't want to worry.*

Dan and I have begun rating where we are at with each other on a 1-10 scale. Right now, we both said we're at an eight. That's pretty good.

March 7, 2012

I feel like there must have been a time in my life when I didn't have so much to say? Maybe not? I always do now, that's for sure. I love to make people laugh, to share stories and chat. I don't love the bad headaches like I had today. I took two Codeine to get it under control. I'm not sure if part of it is because Danny has been struggling for a few weeks again?

I'm regretting starting to open up about all that goes on here behind closed doors. Danny has been adamant that it's no one's business and that I'm not going to talk about him to others. I did open up in Mom's group a little about the past year and someone said, "I noticed a disconnect with you and your husband that has continued to ring in my mind."

I felt so tiny. People are noticing and someone even had the gall to say that. *I pray for peace in this and that I'll turn it over to You.*

March 17, 2012

I am stuck here thinking my words single handedly wrecked Danny's mood tonight. One fell swoop, and he's gone. We were talking about tomorrow and the fact that Uncle Nate will be at Mom and Dad's house. Uncle Nate, being a psychiatrist, Danny always feels he's judging or diagnosing him. Simply commenting that he would be there, made Danny go from laughter to piercing silence. *Just that quick the gloves came off.* These times are so hard, and I feel so small. It's like a light switch. I'm sitting on the couch. Do I get up and leave or wait to see if he wants to talk it through? Awkward anger meets crickets, and it is my fault. I pray for God's intervention in Danny's mind!

After assuming the worst, I got the results from my MRI. It looks like my stem/skull/spine area was "crowded." It seems no one can read the results to tell me what I will need to do next. This whole process has been super frustrating. I'm not sure how I will go back to work with this pain all the time. Life feels so heavy, and I know that doesn't help. It's all I can think about, my brain being dorked.

March 23, 2012

I met with the pointy shoe neurologist today in Columbus. Dad took me this time, and he was not impressed. The nurse came in and asked me for my primary doctor information. As I started to relay it to her, she tells me to hang on, tears off a piece of brown paper towel by the sink, grabs a pen, and writes what I say on it. I thought that was real professional.

When she leaves the room, my cell phone starts ringing from inside my purse. Puzzled, I look over at Dad. "Who is calling me right this second? Everyone I need to talk to knows I'm here."

I ruffle through my purse and answer.

"Hi, is this Dr. ....?" I right away recognize it's that very nurse who was *just* in here.

"Umm, no, it's me, the patient, Charlotte. I'm still waiting in the room."

She laughs and says, "I thought this was the doctor's office, oops."

The fact that this office doubles as an OBGYN already had me nervous.

Even with the long drive, unanswered questions, and weird experience, the big bonus was getting to spend the day with Dad.

Chapter 20

April 15, 2012

I see I didn't write in my journal about Easter Sunday and how that upset me. Not that I'm trying to chart every wrong, but I just feel the need to remember some of this stuff in case, some day, I honestly do write a book. We got to church on Easter later than intended. I was feeling the Easter stress of the kids all dressed up and clean, and so on, and I couldn't find shoes to match Anna's dress that Nan got her.

I was a bit of a procrastinator on it, but honestly, I wasn't feeling it. I don't care what we wear to church - matching bonnets and white gloves. At this point, just *going* to church as a family of five is a huge accomplishment. So Anna wore her pink cowgirl boots with her Easter dress, DK wore athletic shorts with a button down shirt, and Pete had on a hoodie. *What gives?*

By the time we got to church, it was so packed that we ended up in the balcony. Danny wasn't happy with that at all. I could tell, so I leaned to him and said, "You can go somewhere else if you aren't comfortable here." I could see the anxiety/anger increasing in him. He reached in his pocket, got his cell phone out, and started watching a golf tournament. I couldn't believe my eyes. I was so mad.

I leaned to him again and said, "Why don't you do that somewhere else." To which he put his left arm around my back, pulled me close, and whispered to me, "I am a grown (cuss) man, and I can do whatever I (cuss) want when I (cuss) want."

I got up immediately, went to the bathroom, and threw up. I was mad. I felt small, embarrassed, and terrified, all at the same time.

Heal My Broken Heart by Daryle Singletary

"The Lord said the blind will see the lame would walk those golden streets
The deaf would hear the angels sing the righteous would be given wings
So I know I will find up there the answer to my nightly prayer
He'll heal my broken heart, put each shattered piece where it belongs"

April 20, 2012
Grandma Gigi died today. I was there, in the room. I don't think it's really set in still. I saw her Monday, the day she was taken to the ER, and she was cracking jokes.

The doctor asked, "What brought you in today?" and without skipping a beat, she said, "My husband."

She was the cute, thin-lipped, wrinkled grandma making everyone smile. By Wednesday, she was bloated in the stomach and there were flowers in her room. The kids got to see her and spend some time. We had supper there at the hospital. Then, one by one, they kissed her on the right cheek and she said, "I love you," and they said they loved her too. I brought them back on Thursday to see her, but she wasn't nearly as sharp. Her face wasn't as colorful, and she was much weaker. Visitors crowded her room in shifts. Grace had come from Frankfort, and cousins came from far off places. The kids got kind of crazy that evening, so we went down to the other waiting area. We ended up at dinner with Grace, Mom, and Dad. We had a good time visiting and telling Grandma Gigi stories.

The next morning, I figured would be her last, so I asked a friend to babysit Anna. I got to the hospital at 10 am and more cousins had arrived. Grandma Gigi was short on breath and unaware, it was a hard sight. Family trickled in to fill up the small hospital room. Just then, Grandma passed. We all stood there crying, one by one walking out of the room. I went over and kissed Grandpa Evan's forehead. He is so dear. Is she really gone? 96 years young.

Into Your arms, Lord Jesus. "Don't let your hearts be troubled. Trust in God, and trust in Me" You believe in God; believe also in Me" John 14:1 (NCV Mom's Bible, God's Wisdom for Mothers).

April 23, 2012

Our barn almost went up in flames tonight. Danny threw a lit cigarette into the mulch, right by the side door of the barn. I happened to look outside, when walking into the kitchen, and saw flames shooting up. I ran out there as fast as I could and put it out. I stomped on it and grabbed the hose. I'm so glad I was able to get to it in time. We have so much stored in the barn and it's very dry. Oh my word, that would have been awful.

April 27, 2012

I feel so tired, like deep in my soul. I want to vedge all day, nap, and do nothing. I just want a quiet day away. Danny has to go into work again this weekend like last weekend. I feel like I haven't had a break in weeks, but he hasn't either, so then I feel selfish. I haven't been sleeping well nor felt like myself for a while now.

And I've come to the realization that we all have people in this life we'd like to punch in the face. It's best to just resist the temptation and pray for them instead.

May 4, 2012

I feel like my normal, jokey self today and it's genuine, even with a bad headache. I like these good days. The "day-to-day" where things run a bit smoother, and I feel like I can stay on top of things. I did have to get an ice pack out tonight to help with my headache. I never know, will heat or cold help? Cold did - so now I have it written down.

I want to live as every day is a gift and not take it for granted, to see things from God's perspective instead of mine, to lean and learn on Him. *I'm sorry for the ways I fall short, oh Lord. I long to wake up every morning and just sit in Your presence. Silently sit and give my day to You.*

Jesus Calling today, *"The secret of being thankful is learning to see everything from My perspective"* (Jesus Calling by Sarah Young). I need to pray and think about this!

May 7, 2012

Yesterday Danny lost his keys. We still haven't found them. I've felt his mood slipping away because of it. When he got home, he told me how he treated our new insurance agent. It was as if he was proud of being an arrogant troublemaker.

"I was very matter of fact. I looked him straight in the eye, no small talk."

I have never met the guy, but his wife is a sweetheart. I'm embarrassed. Why does he do this stuff? I just don't understand. The first time meeting Danny and he acts aggressive and contentious.

He says to me, "I hate dealing with those type of people." His pupils are huge while he's telling me this. They always get that way when he's like, out of body. Another mixed episode, and my heart sank. That thunder I've been feeling returned, and the fighting to keep within myself is gone. Now I feel sunk. Oh, here he comes, here we go. I'd better brace myself.

My face hurts. I just want to go to bed. I even took my heavy migraine medicine. But Danny isn't going to pick up the kids from his folks, so I will. I told him how I feel, but it doesn't matter. He doesn't feel like he should have to go.

On the drive home I told the kids, "Mom has a headache and Dad is grumpy."

We talked on the way home about it more, and Pete asked if that meant Dad was in bed. Then Anna, in her sweet little four-year-old voice says, "Daddy is anxiouity though right now too." She's so precious and compassionate. When we got home, the kids were all open arms and hearts to him. DK came into the kitchen and whispered to me, "I think we are helping his mood because he seems to be happy."

He is so tender. Just now I shared with Danny how I felt, fearing his aggression coming on full force. *Thank you Lord that he listened.* I pray for peace in our home. These are the hard day-to-day things that stop me in my tracks and remind me, I need to be grateful.

May 12, 2012

All I feel is tired. Especially since the doctor tripled my headache medicine. Although I can't put my finger on why. I feel lazy, but then get a little boost of normal me, playful and fun, and right back to exhausted again. We started *Jesus Calling for Kids* devotions last night, and I pray it's one we'll stick with.

It models my Jesus Calling, *"Give all of your worries to Him because He cares about you"* 1 Peter 5:78.

May 13, 2012

It's hard for me to maintain *me* with a husband who goes through hard times. Lately, he's considering quitting his job, our only source of income. He is seeking reassurances from me. While I'm happy to listen and help, I can't constantly be put on the spot, put down and *demanded* to be perfect. I can't be everything he needs, not all of the time. I want to feel wanted, not just needed. I am on autopilot doing what needs to be done. What about my needs, desires, and deepest thoughts? I can't share them. I need to be there and expected to hold him up.

I need to just rely on Him, moment-to-moment. *Help me to do this, Loving Father in Heaven.*

Chapter 21

May 22, 2012

Danny is still hanging out with a friend that isn't a good influence. We got into it again about "religious stuff." He thinks it's all phony. I feel like he was trying to bait and challenge me. He tells me I just don't really get it. To me, it's not religion or religious, it's about *faith*. When I said that, he got really mad. I don't feel like I'm wrong or out of line. He knows I've always felt this way. Since I was sixteen, until now, that has not changed. We went to church all while we dated, were engaged, and then once married. I have *not* changed.

The kids and I are still reading *Jesus Calling for Kids,* and it's bothering Danny. I talk to the kids about Jesus and, well, I just wish things with Dan were different.

I stopped in each kids' bedroom and asked them tonight what they wish was different.

Pete's room came first and he said, "I wish there were no bad guys, that people were nicer, and that once ya started something you wouldn't quit in the middle."

DK wished, "The mean kids and people were just nicer." We talked about kids in his class he's been feeling that way about.

Then I worked my way to Anna's room and she said she wished, "Trees didn't have bumps on them." Then begged for me to read the *Word and Song Bible* with her. So we did. She graduated from preschool today - I still can't believe it. In all, a good day, from a mom's perspective at least.

May 23, 2012

Danny keeps coming up with titles to chapters for friends in his life. It isn't making any sense to me. He's calling everyone a fox and saying people are trying to "outfox" him. I don't get it. Then he was telling a story about a tom and a rooster. It got really disturbing and I had that gut feeling, "Ok, here we go. Brace yourself."

Now Danny is saying how much better he is than his friends. I asked him if he thought life was a competition, and he said no, but that he *got better before his friends all did.* I'm so frustrated with his fixation on this strange subject. I pray he will stop this aggressive starting/control seeking/I'm-a-bigger-man attitude.

May 24, 2012

I'm praying that Danny will turn to the Lord and seek a relationship with Him. *Lord, guide us in these circumstances.* I opened my NCV Mom's Bible, God's Wisdom for Mothers to Nehemiah 2:4 tonight, *"We can cry out for help and begin with prayer for strength to build a family that pleases the Lord."* That is what my heart wants more than anything.

I've recently realized I'm most happy when I'm helping or encouraging someone else. I love to serve. Maybe not be the #1, but more so, the #2 person in charge. Then I can help but not have all of the responsibility. Random thought, but true. Is that my "love language?"

May 26, 2012

We had a really good talk this morning. It was the only thing I could think about, so I knew I had to call him. We talked about my feelings of his "arrogance" about things lately and the underlying aggression. He admitted it's been a hard few weeks. He is going to meet with his therapist again, and I'm so glad. We rated where we were this time, and we both said a three out of ten. Not so good, but honest.

Tonight we talked, mostly him, and I just listened. We need that more. He needs to communicate and also play an active role. We talked about that, too. *Please guide us, Lord. Dan asked me not to give up hope, that there is still hope for him.*

DK had a huge day. He had an in-park homerun at baseball! He's so excited. I love seeing him confident and knowing he can do it. He's such an amazing human. I know he's mine, but he just really is a great kid.

May 30, 2012

My heart is breaking inside of me. We had the discussion tonight. We had to be truthful and honest. Dutch is going to get worse, and we can't have him peeing in the house. He can't help it, and his face says it all. I've shed so many aching tears today, my body quivering. How will I cope with him gone? My best loyal companion who's been with me from the beginning. He's seen me through all of these hard times, loved me, and literally stood between me and Danny. He's always up against my knees, barking or whining at Dan when he feels his anxiety.

He's slept by me, snored, winked, snorted, sneezed, breathed, *loved* me for me. I'll miss him so bad. He's my baby. I had to catch his pee in a pan today, and that is how we learned of his kidney function. It's going downhill. We agreed to give him two more weeks and see if he improves at all. I'm praying like mad he will but also know he's eleven-years-old. We can't pour all kinds of money into him, but I'm just not ready to say goodbye. The thought is heartbreaking. How can I say goodbye? Not yet. I won't yet. We have two weeks.

June 1, 2012

There is an elephant on my chest. I am, beyond words hurt. I can't even breath.

He's gone. And I didn't even get a chance to say goodbye.

My precious Dutch is gone. I can't inhale all the way without starting to shutter. I long for him, one more kiss atop his head, a rub of his soft ears, or the patch of extra fur at the nape of his neck. He's lonely out there tonight and it's dark. What just happened. *What?*

I haven't sought the Lord as I should today, I've been in this denial, trying to grasp why, how Danny could put her down without even telling me. I want him back, to say my final goodbye. But I didn't get to. He was already buried when I pulled in the driveway.

I was on the way home from Peter's field trip with Anna when I came up over the hill and saw Danny's car in the driveway. *Wait, what is going on?* His car door was open, and I could see an unfamiliar blanket on the seat.

He couldn't have. But he did. He took Dutch, had him euthanized, and buried without my consent or knowing. I am broken. I don't even remember putting the truck in park. I ran in the rain to the backyard where Danny met me halfway up the hill.

"He's gone, it's all done," he said, and I dropped to my knees like you see in the movies.

I was beyond hysterical. My dog; he was *my* dog. I just folded in half. I kept looking out the back door to see him lying on the top step enjoying the scenery. Then, I touch the glass and stare as tears run down my cheeks. *Dutch.* He's always been here: by the clothesline, truck, laundry room, burn barrel, kids' rooms as we say goodnight, bathroom, sleeping on Danny's side of the bed when he's not home. He has been with me through it all. Now he's gone.

June 6, 2012
We went to Springfield today. Mom, Anna and I picked up Brutus. She is sweet as can be. We think she's a year and a half old but haven't talked to cousin Dave yet to see. She's already following me around. When I stepped into the backyard with Brut to show her the ropes, it was like bricks piled on my chest and tears filled my eyes. I stood at the entrance to Dutch's trail where he's buried, and my heart just sank. I miss him *so* bad. Brutus will never replace him, but she'll add to our family. *Thank you Lord for this help in healing, she's a lover in the form of a yellow lab.*

123

After everyone was in bed, I found myself lying flat on my stomach, palms raised to Heaven and face in the ground. In full reverence, in *awe* of how He has carried us this far. *You have Lord, You. I am weary and grieving, please continue to carry us, Oh God. My heart is so heavy. I lift this Unto You. Help me make sense of it all.*

June 7, 2012

I am still so sad, grieving Dutch, and I cried more again today. Danny is frustrated with me for not listening to him lately. And we disagree on stuff with Brutus. I just feel so weary; I will get there. At one point he said he thinks my main thing is I'm always on my phone. I feel like it's an outlet, that's for sure. I do use it a lot. I guess I need to be more aware. I wish I would have been able to say goodbye to Dutch one last time, but I suppose even that wouldn't have been enough. And with all of this heaviness, Happy Birthday to me.

Chapter 22

June 9, 2012
"Look at other people through lenses of Love, see them from My perspective"
(*Jesus Calling* by Sarah Young).

I have fallen so short. My patience is so short; I feel really bad. *Help me, Oh Lord, to refocus on You. To see and start over. To stop being selfish, to love and take each day as a gift. I'm trying to be more aware of my time on my phone. I need to be more present. Danny pointed it out, and I need to think on it, although I know I'm not on mine as much as he is. But that's not me, and I need to work on that.*

June 10, 2012
I'm missing Dutch still. I don't bring it up, or show it to Danny, because he thinks I need to move past it. He's heading to Boston for a few days. I hope I'm present with the kids and know what they need while he is gone again.

When Danny gets home, we need to somehow reconnect. He's been upset with me for how sad I am about Dutch. He even told me, "You were so dramatic in the rain when you came up the hill and saw that he was already gone." He even laughed explaining how dramatic I was. That really hurt. I just can't *believe* it. How is any of this funny? That cuts so deep. How could he possibly think making fun of me for this is acceptable?

June 13, 2012

Danny is home now, and he's off kilter. He said being in Boston was hard for him and that I have to be careful around him. He asked if I'll go, instead of him, with the boys to the Indians game. I pray he'll go because it's so important to the boys. They don't want me, they want time with him. I need to pray for his mind and sobriety.

"He has shown you, O mortal, what is good. And what does the Lord require of you? To act justly and to love mercy and to walk humbly with your God" Micah 6:8 (NIV Proverbs 31.org devotional).

This is what I want to strive for. I do. I want to. I need to get back into counseling. I need to find a way to deal with all of this, with humility and grace. *Please have mercy on us, Lord, as we struggle to find how to live in these moments. I feel so defeated.*

June 29, 2012

I've been thinking lately about when I was pregnant for Pete, and DK was just a little guy. I recall one night, staring out the front window upstairs into the night sky, thanking the Lord for everything - a baby and another growing inside of me. I wondered, and remember vividly, if something bad would come because we had been doing so well. I prayed that nothing bad would happen, but also knew if it did, the Lord would get us through.

And He has, despite all of this. All of this hurt and disappointment for what I had hoped life would be like. Not perfection, I'm far from perfect, but a loving Godly home, with our share of bumps that we would weather together. I just never thought it would be like this.

June 30, 2012

I hosted DK's birthday party here today. There was lots of boys and lots of fun for DK. He was smiling, laughing, and having a great time. The unfortunate part was calling the fire department because of the naughty dog. Brutus went into the crawlspace and wouldn't come out for anything. It was 90 degrees out, so I knew, in that small crawl space, it had to be over 100 degrees.

An hour went by and we tried *everything*. So I called and asked for someone to come get her out. Within minutes, three volunteer firemen show up. One walks up to me and asks, "What's the dog's name?"

I tell him and he repeats, "Brutus?"

She came *right* out. I felt like the biggest idiot! He laughed and the boys all thought it was hysterical. Neat.

They leave, and not two minutes later, she's back in there! I called Danny, who was already on his way home, and while getting Brutus out, he found a groundhog was cornered in the crawlspace. Danny shot it with a .22 and tossed it across the street in the woods. Next time Brut got let out, there she goes, darting across traffic.

What a day. And I was worried about entertaining six nine-year-olds...

July 13, 2012

Sometimes I wonder if I'm a super moody person or if it's just my circumstances? I need time to refocus, I think. It's hard to balance everything. I'm trying to be everything to everyone and I know I'm not doing well at it but am not sure what else to do. I'm treading water right now, one moment at time.

I am feeling like everyone comes to me for stuff, whether it be help emotionally, physically, mentally. Is this all just what being a mom is? I think it's a taller order with all we deal with, and honestly, for Danny.

July 19, 2012

After my discussion with Anna about her blatant disobedience, I plopped back down to some peace during quiet time. That is until I heard the sounds of the boys using Anna's newly sanded and painted bedroom floor as a basketball court - shoes squeaking, the whole nine yards. Where is the Excedrin?

July 25, 2012

Dan posted an anti-religious, antagonizing rant on social media tonight to admittedly, "get a rise out of people." These things leave me sad and unsettled. It's not the least bit representative of me or what I believe. Of course he started this with a friend of *mine*.

He was in a mood on the phone with me earlier, and it hit me hard. I ended up crying for the longest time. I need to be here for our kids and how can I work with my headaches? I'm the consistent parent. I'm not a bad mom, despite his rants trying to convince me otherwise.

I feel like I'm, somehow, in the way. I need to move, literally, out of Danny's way...or else. I never like feeling this way, but I do.

August 8, 2012

It struck me today when a friend thanked me for being *vulnerable*. I was raw honest. And if nothing else, I want to be genuine, never fake, always simply put, because me is *me*. I've gotten so used to pretending everything is fine, like people expect. If I were to be totally honest sometime, what would people think of me? Probably that I don't care enough for Danny, that I don't understand. I'm trying; I am.

I'm drowning, though, and it always seems to be about him. I've gone to appointments with him where I've been told what he is dealing with is no different than someone with diabetes. I'm not discounting diabetes at all, but it's *not* the same thing. I left that appointment feeling like the doctor didn't hear me. Danny doesn't want to hear me, he just wants me to encourage and be here for him. When is it ok for *me* to feel what *I* feel? How can I express my feelings? I can't, I'm just stuck here and seemingly in the way.

Oh Lord, all of this is so deep rooted, real, and raw; to the very core. Guide us in what is to come, Oh Lord. When I cry out to You, I know You hear me. How can I keep at this? How can I stop losing myself, Lord, and yet stay on the level. I feel so trapped and afraid.

August 13, 2012

Danny is getting really snippy and short with me. He has had a lot going on, but I've been trying my best to hold him up. It's so exhausting when he's like this. Suffering produces patience, which produces character, which produces perseverance, which produces hope...right? Something like that.

Please help us to be the parents we need to be right now. I pray for strength, for energy, for our daily patience and ability to balance the emotions of all that we have learned recently. Mostly about Danny's family history and things we weren't aware of. It's heavy.

I'm here to hold it all up, bounce the bad off of, and help level out the teeter-totter Danny is on. All while making sure the house meets his cleanliness standards, handle discipline and disappointment. This bag gets so heavy. He doesn't see me. He only sees what he feels I'm not doing enough of.

The relationship with Danny's folks has been complicated for years. Danny's stepdad is on life support now, and it doesn't look good. These are hard times. *There are so many emotions and much happening that you know, Lord. Please keep Danny's mind at ease and able to grieve and process it all. All of this is a lot.*

Third Day, *I Need a Miracle*

"Well no matter who you are and no matter what you've done
There will come a time when you can't make it on your own
And in your hour of desperation, know you're not the only one
Praying Lord above, I need a miracle, I need a miracle."

Chapter 23

August 14, 2012

I feel like he's angry; angry about all that's been going on, and I get it, he has good reason to be. This is so hard. He is refusing to attend his step-brother's funeral service. He passed away this week after a car accident. This timing is awful, with all that's happening with his stepdad. Even with the tumultuous relationship they've had, he was still his father figure.

I don't want to go to the memorial alone - facing the "where's Danny" questions from *his* family. He keeps saying I am forcing him to go. I most certainly am not. In my family, when someone passes away, no matter what, you go. It's not for the one who passed but for those left behind to pick up the pieces. And, this is his family. He needs to go, if for nothing else, his mom. He will regret it if he doesn't. I'm praying and have been scratching my head trying to think of why he feels this way. But I end up at the same conclusion. He's making it about him. What about his (step) brother and nephews?

We are at this place where it feels like we can't get along. Back in the day, we could at least make light of this madness and tease to help each other to help cope. But now we are at odds every ten minutes. He is so angry and resentful towards me.

August 17, 2012

I keep wrestling with my thoughts, my absolute deepest thoughts, wanting this to all be over. I want this drawn-out sickness to be reconciled for all of us. Will Danny and I ever have peace? I feel weary. I feel guilty. I feel Satan is trying to get ahold of me. I long for renewal and ability to start healing.

In Jesus Calling today, *"Accept each day just as it comes to you. Do not waste your time and energy wishing for a different set of circumstances."* I'm trying Lord, I need to wait on You.

August 23, 2012
Deep thoughts by Pete earlier today...

Pete: "You and I are a lot alike Mom, but I'm funnier."
Me: "Pete, I used to be funny, but I have too much ridiculousness going on to be funny."
Pete: "Just let loose and be yourself, Mom. Be funny again."

Wise kid.

August 27, 2012
Danny's step-dad passed away today. There is so much loss for him in such a short period of time. It's been unfathomable, but Danny has handled it the best he can. He's had some hard decisions to make, and he thought through them clearly. I'm proud of him. These weeks have been filled with hurt. I'm learning pieces from the past that I had no idea about. I pray we can move forward, that Dan will be honest with his emotions, and open to counsel. This week has shown just how fragile life is. Maybe he will be more gentle and kind. Maybe he will even realize, as a dad himself, that these days are important and won't last forever.

September 2, 2012
I've been having this visual lately of the Lord holding my right hand. When I tighten my right fist and close my eyes, I can feel Him truly holding my hand. He has me. He knows me. He knows our situation. *Please show us how to keep up at this rate of disconnect, Lord God. I don't know how to keep living in this situation.*

September 4, 2012

So far this morning we've had a traffic jam in the bathroom. Pete barfed because DK didn't clean up his toothpaste, excitement ensued over a tractor passing by, and lights and sirens at the neighbors' kept the kids glued to the window. It's the first day of school and this all happened before the bus even came!

Once I got my photo op with the kids climbing the bus steps, I hopped in the truck to follow it to Anna's school. When she got off the bus and headed into the college sized building, she gave me a big hug and said, "Have a good day Mom!"

She happily skipped on into school and I didn't turn to walk away until the door closed behind her. While walking back to the truck, and constantly looking back over my shoulder, I watched other parents do the same.

I plopped into the driver's seat and watched as all of the other parents get back into their cars with babies and younger kids. They don't know what this feels like yet. Only a few simple tears filled my eyes thinking about them growing up. They are growing up. My baby is in school.

September 7, 2012

I want life, peace, and God's will for me. It was so encouraging to hear my friend yesterday tell me to pray about what God *has* for me. Not just pray about it, but spend some serious time in prayer, seeking His will. I long for that. What is *Your* will for me Lord?

Brutus is done with her hunting training, and it turns out, she's an amazing hunter! Danny is in his glory. He can take her along on his adventures and wear her out. She's naughty at home and needs a hobby! I swear she eats everything - the inside of backpacks, contact lenses, trash, baked goods on the counter, *everything*. I'm honestly happy for Danny. Hopefully this will bring him some peace and purpose.

September 20, 2012

When I stopped at school today to drop something off to Pete, some kid in his class blurts, "Pete? Is that your mom? She's the stop sign!"

Now that I am officially trained by police, this gal right here is a certified crossing guard. Who knew! I first get on the PTA and then hear they need a crossing guard. I'm so excited to work at school! It's a good foot-in-the-door for down the road. I'll be on the same hours and schedule as the kids. I haven't had a job outside of home since DK was born. This is a win-win.

"Each of My children is a unique blend of temperament, giftedness, and life experiences" (Jesus Calling by Sarah Young).

I like this line from my devotions today. We are. Each of my kiddos, unique. They are their own people. I'm so grateful to be their mom. I pray I can show a good example and shine, despite the darkness. I will work to find happiness in the little moments.

Find JOY in the Lord and let it shine...

Chapter 24

September 30, 2012

I had a feeling when I mentioned plans for Thanksgiving that it would turn into a big deal. It turns out it is a *trigger* for Dan. While washing dishes before church, I said I'd like to spend Thanksgiving with family. Grandpa Will isn't doing well and this may be his last. Mom, Dad, Grace, and Joe are going to be with our extended family, so that got me wanting to go visit, too.

He shut down. He got awkward - at first, about driving, then the distance, then the cost of gas and mileage we'd put on our truck. Then came the vacant silence. I could hear crickets. He couldn't express his thoughts. I played cool and said it wasn't a big deal and a decision didn't have to be made right then. Fast forward to church and how he got lippy with my friend when she merely asked him about his goatee. I feel like I have to apologize to her because I know she felt awkward. I had told her just the other day that I missed her and here he acts so combative toward her. It makes me feel sad, and he is ticked.

October 2, 2011

Before school today, I asked the boys if they brushed the *barnacles* off their teeth. I think I've seen too much SpongeBob.

I feel like we went from having a dog that reads encyclopedias, and works a side job as a mechanic, to one whose teeth are weapons of mass destruction. Brutus!

This new crossing guard gig is hilarious, too. Today I got honked at by a tow truck driver. And as I stood all proud in the middle of the street, with my stop sign raised above my head, traffic came to a halt while a cat casually crossed the road. It was following her 4th grader. Oh the looks and smiles! I've never been a cat fan, but this one was pure genius.

October 7, 2012
The upstairs bathroom toilet leaked through the floor and onto the unfinished master bathroom right below it. The kids apparently flushed a few times when the toilet was clogged. I was down here when heard dripping. I went to look, and water was quickly trickling down from the light fixture. I ran upstairs and the floor was soaked. I couldn't grab enough towels to stop it. And the worst part of it all, a piece of poop came through the fixture and landed on my curling iron.

October 8, 2012
Pete was casually swaying on the tire swing out back when the rope finally gave way. Naturally, Pete had to come tell me with the tire still around his waist.

A spunky, cute seventh grade girl just said to me, "You look like your name is Jennifer."

Earlier today when I had a group of kids, who usually give me attitude in the crosswalk, smile as they walked by. I was stumped until I got in my truck and saw the leaf stuck in my hair just above my forehead. Well played, little hooligans, well played.

October 10, 2012
Danny has barely made any of Pete's football games because he's been out hunting. Mom and Dad have come every single time. Dad even went to a game far away that Pete didn't make because of his ruptured eardrum. He wanted to tell Pete all about how his team did and what the competition looked like. He is amazing. He is one special Papa.

October 17, 2012
Today I sealed the upstairs floor after sanding it down and painting it. What a job! I also swept the house, burned trash in the burn barrel, and helped with recess duty at school. Recess duty is no joke - two bloody noses, one kid who ran to me thinking I was his mommy, and I saw the principal do a cartwheel.

I have total respect for this principal. He's amazing! Dad loves him, too. They know each other from all of the times Papa picks up the kids and the field trips he's attended with the boys. It's nice to have a backup when it comes to field trips on space travel or shipwrecks. I have found 3D movies give me an instant migraine, so Papa chaperones those as well. Dad and Principal L. are both top notch.

October 18, 2012
Pete has another ruptured eardrum. This is like his fourteenth one! This poor kid is seriously so tough. I fear he will go deaf. Having some permanent hearing loss myself, I worry about him. It seems people joke saying, "Sorry I didn't hear you, I'm deaf," which is no joke. I was so grateful for my corrective surgery that restored my hearing a few years ago. Being deaf is a very lonely feeling. I need to continue to pray for his ears to heal.

Apparently Anna got too warm in her dress at school, so she opted to wear her tank top and tights instead. I can't make this stuff up. I'm saving this note for her wedding someday. Then this evening, Anna barged in and asked where the black umbrella is. "I don't know, I can't remember right now. To which she responds, "Well, you bought it, so it's your responsibility!"

"Are you kidding me? You are five years old!" I thought.

October 23, 2012
"Miss Gatlin, you there?" I hear on my radio while standing at my crossing corner.
"Yes, I am," I responded.
Then I hear Anna's sweet little voice over the radio say, "I love you, Mama."

If hearts smile, mine showed all of its teeth just then. She's been having a hard time with riding a bus to a different school for Young 5's every day. I'm so thankful to work here, though. I feel so connected and right where I want to be.

October 28, 2012

Grace did something amazing for me. She knows I stand at my crossing corner and that my winter coat is old and tighter than it used to be. I can use it for a few more years, but she insisted that she was going to get me a new, long winter coat. I even got to pick it out. It was so generous. She even ordered me boots for when the weather changes. I hardly spend money, and never on myself, and here she is spending all of these dollars on me. I'm touched, excited, and humbled. I will be a new woman!

November 2, 2012

I got to help Dad take the boat dock out today. He even borrowed waders from a neighbor this year. We have done this in jeans and sweatshirts waist deep before. Even though he provided waders, he failed to mention the pair I wore had a teeny hole in the leg. It wasn't until we were all the way in the deep that my legs filled with freezing lake water, making my legs weigh a thousand pounds each. If anyone else would have done this, I'd be mad. But this cracked him up, and that's how we roll.

November 11, 2012

Danny headed west again for the big hunting opener. He's been so removed again lately that it is becoming much easier when he's not home. We have our routine, day-to-day. Dinner is typically the four of us anyway. Now I can make easier meals and the kids don't care, or we'll go over to Mom and Dad's house. I understand that hunting is something he enjoys, and I don't want to take that from him, but it's just hard that it's so often. There's muzzle loading, crossbow, and rifle seasons. Yet, I can't go away for a night, let alone a weekend, without feeling overly-indulgent and selfish.

It's such a double standard and makes me mad. Oh well, such is life. These kids are the priority, so I will grin and make the best of it. I downloaded this song today. It honestly is what I long for. I just want to feel wanted.

Wanted by Hunter Hayes
"You know I'd fall apart without you; don't know how you do what you do 'Cause everything that don't make sense about me, makes sense when I'm with you.
Like everything that's green, girl, I need you; But it's more than one and one makes two
Put aside the math and logic of it, You gotta know you're wanted too."

November 12, 2012
I'm feeling alone, and with my headaches, I just want to scream. We have had a decent few weeks, though, even good I'd say. At one point I was so shocked and wondered who Danny was. "What can I do to help you tonight?" he asked.

I was shocked. He even offered to help pick up one of the kids from their activities. He also said, "I'll take Anna duty tonight." I'm amazed.

Even so, it has been a whirlwind. Last Monday night, Danny told me some disturbing things from his past. I'm having a hard time making sense of it, and I'm wondering if it's even true. That night brought more emotions than I can name. I went to bed feeling numb.

The next morning, I stared at myself in the mirror and wondered *why this* and *why now*. How could he have kept this from me and why is he telling me these awful things from his past now? I can't even come up with words. He seems so empty, and I'm going through the motions to get by.

November 14, 2012
PART 1 of my day: My heart came out of my eye socket as I watched Brutus tear across our busy road, chasing a fat kitty she found hiding in the infamous crawl space. I screamed, chased, whistled, and panicked. I reached Danny on the phone, so he turned around and came home. He was able to get Brutus back and keep her from going back into the crawl space.

PART 2: I got a dripping bloody nose on our way to school.

PART 3: As DK walked across the street into school, demonstrating what *jaywalking* is, and telling me he could be ticketed for it, a cop drives by.

PART 4: When I went to drop book fair money off to Anna, I got so distracted that I put my visitor sticker on my hair instead of my shirt. Ouch.

PART 5: When I got home and let Brutus out, *guess* what she did...

November 19, 2012

I was only gone for sixteen minutes. That's it. Danny was acting strange when I left, but Anna was already asleep, and Pete was watching tv. I can trust Dan at home with two of the kids while I run out for under twenty minutes. At least I *thought* so.

My heart dropped after Pete came to me tonight and told me how strange his dad was acting while I was gone. Pete ended up sitting on Danny's lap watching tv, and he kept telling Pete to punch him. He was serious. He wanted Pete to punch him, hard, in the face.

Pete thought the first time that Danny was teasing, but he said he knew his dad wasn't. He didn't do it because he told me it was really strange, and he would *never* do that. Pete is seven-years-old! Then after all three kids were asleep in bed, Danny hit me with another blow. He crushed up prescription pills and snorted them tonight.

I am sick, disgusted. I can't even come up with words right now. I could tear this piece of paper into a thousand shreds. I am *yanked*.

November 28, 2012

Pete tried to fake sick today. With a straight face he said to me, "I read a book about Justin Bieber and it honestly gave me a fever."

Later, I walked into the family room to see Anna writing her and the boys' names with black sharpie on the white trim I just painted. I nearly went crazy and shouted her name. She slowly turned to me, with her bottom lip quivering, and proceeded to show me the piece of scotch tape she was writing on.

November 20, 2012

As the day's tick by, he's having more serious mood swings. I have been trying not to react with his ups and downs. He's mostly upset that we spent Thanksgiving with my family. It was a battle just getting him to go. Once we were there, it was excruciating dealing with his mood in front of others. It overshadowed the whole trip. I just want some joy and to just have a good time with family for Thanksgiving.

The car ride was filled with teeth-pulling silence - him knocking his right fist on the steering wheel repeatedly, which I know means frustration. Seeing him do that took me back to when he was angry a few years ago and punched the visor on our truck. He hit it so hard that the windshield cracked. He admitted to experiencing rage and anger, but he would be fine for a few minutes, then right back down at the bottom. It was hard on all of us. DK spoke up from the backseat, "Dad, you ok? Because you don't seem like it. You know how at the hotel, about you being quiet in the room? You're like that again."

"I understand Bud, but I'm fine." I waited and then said, "That took a lot of courage, DK, to say that. I'm proud of you."

Of course the day before's quiet led to me crying after seeing my grandparents showing their age. Danny went off on the hotel staff for giving us a smoking room. The cost of the rollaway brought about a rage at the guest service counter too. I'm scared. I'm embarrassed. This is a small town. These folks that work here know my family.

There's so much to process and feel that I need to handle. I don't want my family or kids to be upset. I also want to cherish this time because we don't get to see this side of the family often, and I love every minute with them. I used to spend weeks in the summertime here. I feel so much happiness here. *Don't wreck it, please don't wreck it.*

I've suffered another headache all day. How can I do it all? We need to work through everything. It's just so hard. I want him to see it, all of it. *Oh Lord, show me what to do here, how to move forward with so much on my mind, for our kids. Please provide for us.*

December 2, 2012

I don't know which way to turn with my head without feeling pain. I honestly have these 10-day-long, awful, lingering headaches. No medicine takes it away except Excedrin, but the neurologist told me it can cause rebound headaches. I can't win with this. It's so discouraging. I get tired of saying, "I have a headache," because people don't hear it anymore. I don't expect sympathy, I'm just frustrated. So I grin and fake, until I am alone. Then I just close my eyes and wince from the pain.

December 13, 2012

My mission has been made clear. That guy in the blue Pontiac, who won't wave back at me - like every other person who drives by my crossing corner in the mornings - *will* wave at some point. I have another six months to get him to acknowledge me and wave back.

This cat crosses every day behind his fourth grader. Maybe sometime it will be timed just right, and he'll see it. Who wouldn't at least crack a smile watching a twelve-pound tiger kitty wait for the clear to cross from a crossing guard? I swear he's human. He will not cross until my stop sign is raised above my head. Classic.

December 15, 2012

I had a hysterectomy yesterday. Mom says I will be so glad I did, but right now, I'm beyond wiped. I'm actually a bit more sore than I was prepared for. I'm glad it's behind me now. They said to plan on a two-week recovery, and I should be good to go. This next two weeks of Christmas break should be enough, I hope. I'm pretty sure everything is done and ready for Christmas, and if not, well then we'll go without this year. Grace got me some comfy pajamas, and I may just park myself on the couch so I can avoid the stairs.

December 24, 2012

It's fun when you laugh so hard you can't even breathe. All of us laughing at the same time is the best. Tonight while I was reading, *Twas the Night Before Christmas,* by Clement Clarke Moore to the kids, I turned the page to where it says, "The moon, on the breast of the new fallen snow, gave luster of midday to objects below..."

As I read the words, "The moon, on the..." Pete chimes in "BLEEP!" in an effort to cover up that I said the word *breast.* Hysterics broke out, and our hilarious faces were all caught on camera. Best photo ever.

December 27, 2012

I'm having a hard time and feeling super small again. Danny has been upset with me for the past week because I haven't been able to clean up the house. I'm exhausted just being awake and in conversation. My body is taking longer than I expected to heal from surgery. It has kicked my tail. So tonight he called his mom to see if she'll come over to clean our house. I'm a combination of embarrassed, sad that I feel like I'm not good enough to meet "his standards of clean," and frustrated. She came with her gloves and bucket and cleaned the house up and down. I kept apologizing from the couch to her. She acted like she didn't mind, but honestly, I did. *Why couldn't Danny have done it?*

Chapter 25

January 4, 2013

Today is our fourteenth wedding anniversary. It's been a while since those good ol' days. He said after dinner, "I can't wait to be married to you another fourteen!" I smiled, but on the inside thought, "*How* am I going to stay married to you for another fourteen years?" I can't, I just can't. Although if I don't, I am breaking the vows we made on this very day. I'm so afraid to get out. How can I? Where will that leave me? What would that do to the kids? Can I do it? How would he react? I'm scared and just don't know how. I do know one thing: I can't keep doing this.

January 7, 2013

I managed to get back to my crossing guard corner this morning. It seemed like the walk to get there today was three miles long. I parked the car closer so I don't have to walk so much. Also, as interesting and flattered as I was about a possible full time job that fell into my lap, I decided I just can't do it yet. I spent a lot of time, while recovering in bed, thinking and praying about it. It would be amazing for me, but my heart is pulling me back and saying, "Not yet."

February 3, 2013

Last night was surreal. We're going to need naps after that all-nighter!

Yesterday DK was at a robotics gig, working with his group on their project. I got a call from one of the moms saying that he wasn't feeling good. So I went and picked him up a little early. He said his stomach really hurt, and he was feverish. We got home and he went right up to take a nap. That was my first clue. He never does that anymore. I checked on him a few times, then he woke up. Burning up, this pain just wouldn't go away. I just felt in my gut that I needed to take him to get it checked. I'm so glad I did.

Once at the medical center, they immediately sent us on down to the children's hospital. It all happened so fast. I called Danny on the way. DK was set up in a room, and all sorts of tests were run. Low and behold, it's his appendix! What are the chances we are doing this again?

Just as the clock struck midnight, he was rolled into surgery, an appendectomy. Dan and I waited in the empty waiting room. It felt like all night. Danny eventually went home after we knew DK was going to be ok, and I set up to sleep on the plastic chair next to his hospital bed. He got as many red and blue slushies as his heart desired. He never even once cried. We got released this morning. What a twenty-four hours! Now two out of three of my kids are without their appendix. Wild!

February 5, 2013
Frankie's cat came out this morning and was met with some new paparazzi. So naturally, he showed off a little and did a loop around my feet before crossing all the way. This cat is the rarest I've ever seen.

Danny has been on a downward slope. I feel like we are just two ships passing in the night. We don't really talk about life, our marriage, or the kids. Instead, we get by with the basics. I don't want to provoke him or to anger him, but he doesn't want to let me in. I'm just taking it all one day at a time, but I'm not sure how much longer I can keep at this. He's so removed, more than ever before.

A song I just downloaded on my iPod. I feel the lyrics. *Blue Sky* by Emily West (feat. Keith Urban):

"...wipe off those sad eyes 'cause I've got some tears of my own. Weatherman says it's gonna rain tonight. The kind of storm where the basement floods and you lose the lights. Should have thought of that before, 'Cause I'm not your blue sky anymore."

February 13, 2013
So far today (and it's only 8:23 am) I've had to tell Brutus *not* to go toilet-bobbing for poop, and managed to spill pomegranate juice on my jeans and prized Ugg boots. I also got a call that Grandpa Will has been admitted to the hospital.

February 19, 2013
I went out to the front porch to find a diaper box. Puzzled, I opened it and found that cousin Rae sent me her Ugg boots - two pair! I sat right down on the porch, slid a pair on, and cried my eyes out. She heard mine got wrecked with poma-gross juice and sent me hers. We have the same size feet, and where she lives, they are no longer needed in the winter. I am so touched by her kindness. There is no way I'd be able to replace mine, not with Danny's tight budget. As it is, my pair that got wrecked were four-years-old anyway.

February 24, 2013
The house is still, quiet, and dark. As I came into our room, I rammed my knee into an open dresser drawer. I shut it, then my shin hit the drawer below it that was left open. I unknowingly stepped on Brut and stammered over her to retrieve a disoriented Pete from sleeping on my side of the bed. Each time I woke him up, he pulled the covers back over himself and rolled over. Quietly cracking up, I finally got him up, hobbled over the dog again, and he thought the bathroom was his bed. I got him up the ladder to the top. When he came back down without a word, he went to the bathroom and fell asleep standing up. Tripping over himself. I managed to help him back up to his bunk. It was the funniest three minute, silent snickering of my life.

February 28, 2013
What a few days! I'm starting to feel stronger, but yesterday I couldn't even get out of bed. This flu-type bug began about two days ago. I told Danny I was extremely weak, but he didn't realize how bad it was until he got

home from work, and I hadn't moved an inch. Anna was sitting with me, and, fortunately, the boys had been self-sufficient all day. Danny decided I'd better go get checked out. My head was killing me. I had no idea how I would even get to the top of the stairs, let alone down them and in the truck. It took a while, but I managed to get there after several breaks to sit down.

We went to the ER, and I'm honestly glad we did. They sat me in a wheelchair and got my vitals. The nurse took my blood pressure three times. Another nurse came in and said, "Are you sure?" to which the nurse replied, "Yes, I've taken it three times." My blood pressure was 70/40.

Then came a whirlwind of tests. They did a spinal tap, thinking it may be meningitis, the flu, or possibly a stroke. Let's just say, it was not my best day. I got admitted after that, and here I am. I had electrodes on my head because my blood pressure showed me as dead. I'm already tired of getting poked. I do appreciate that the doctors and nurses don't mind body odor, three-foot-long leg hair, and stale breath.

March 1, 2013

I had to pee really bad, so rather than the fanfare to get help, I figured I'd just go for it. As I stood up, an alarm goes off. My hospital bed has an alarm. In runs a trendy male nurse wondering what's going on, catching me like a kid with my hand in the cookie jar. Seeing my *fall risk* bracelet, he then observed me as I tried to pee. I have this thing, though. It's called stage fright.

The doctors haven't said exactly what I have going on. They referred to it as a migraine *crisis*. Nothing is helping with my headache, I even have a morphine pump. The neurologist hasn't been in to see me yet, and I'm getting anxious for the amount of time I'm away from home. Dan hasn't been up to see me much, and I'm concerned about the kids. Mom and Dad are out of town with Grace and Joe, so I'm having to rely on others to help with the kids. I'm spending a lot of my time sleeping. The lights and sounds are not my friends.

I have decided the best kind of hospital stay is when you have a baby. Sure you're tired and sore, but you get to bring a prize home. The only prize I get with this hospital stay is a big bill in the mail. Oh, and light blue, grippy socks.

March 4, 2013

I have had a lot of time to think while I'm laying here. I've been thinking back to a few months ago when I was here for my hysterectomy. In the back of my mind, I thought to myself then, I wonder how Danny will handle all of this while I'm down and out. That was a planned procedure, so there was warning. Not that it was a test, but in a way, it was very telling. Instead of feeling appreciated, as I feel I've been missing for years now, I was made to feel that I didn't heal fast enough to keep the house clean for him.

And now, he hasn't been up to see me much. He doesn't have my parents to fall back on to help with rides and the kid's needs. I get that. But maybe bring the kids up to see me - or don't have a tone that makes me feel like I'm some kind of inconvenience. I guess, deep down, I wanted him to say, "Wow, you sure do run our household and I *appreciate* you."

I know, that's a stretch, but instead of any of that, it's been clearly the opposite, which makes my headache worse. I can't do this. I have needs, too. For years this has been about him, but what about me? Mental illness or not, it's how you treat others that you love that matters. I don't think he even loves me. That's how I feel - used and abused. I can't keep living in this marriage. I know it will be hard, but I need to find my self-worth, to get back to the basics of what life is all about. I need to be true to who *Charly* is.

March 5, 2013

I finally got released! I had to beg for it, and honestly, it probably wasn't the best decision I've made, but I have to be home. I'm so weak and utterly exhausted. I am out of sick days, and my corner won't cross itself. That, and, I need to be home.

My latest song, *I Don't Feel Like Loving You Today* by Gretchen Wilson.

"I don't feel like loving you today. And I've got sixteen hours left to go.
I might tell you that I'm leavin' even though you know I'll stay,
Cause I don't feel like loving you today. But you know I will anyway,
Even though we make it hard sometimes. I'll wind up forgiving you and probably loving
you for the rest of my life. But I don't feel like loving you today."

March 6, 2013
When you go back to work and aren't sure if it was the right decision, but a kindergartner runs up to you, and without a word, wraps her arms around you and hugs you so tight -that right there, was worth it. Now I'm going to go home and take a thirty-nine-hour nap.

March 10, 2013
"Only My Life in you can empower you to face this endless flow of problems with good cheer" (Jesus Calling by Sarah Young).

I feel like this is my source!

And also this, *"Rest in My Presence, receiving Joy that no one can take away from you"* (Jesus Calling by Sarah Young).

I need this! I'm trying to keep my head up and endure this endless flow of problems. The root is the hardest. I'm trying to keep my eyes focused on Jesus and His grace. I want this *joy* restored that no one can take from me, but I feel it has been taken. I feel awful that this situation has the power to hurt me like this. When I'm at my folks, and Google ways of abuse, I see I have been in an abusive marriage - emotional, financial, verbal - these somehow seem less than physical, but they are *real*. I am damaged. I am lonely and know I feel these conflicting feeling about myself because of how Danny has made me feel. It's like a game to manipulate me and then mock me. I can't imagine how this is ok in his mind. I know he can't help the mental illness piece, I *know* this. But the other ways, I believe in our hearts, we can. I don't want to keep doing this. I want to get well. But how much worse will it have to get? What would happen if I said, *I'm done?* I'm scared. There's so much unknown. How would I, when would I, where do I even start?

March 14, 2013

We have official word, Grandpa Will is going downhill fast. It breaks my heart, but he loves Jesus, and is ready to go Home. Danny says he can't go with us, so Grace will join the kids and I on the trip to say our goodbyes. Grace is flying here in the morning. We'll grab her at the airport and then go see Grandma Ruth and Grandpa Will. We'll stay at the stinky motel there in town so we are out of the way and have some space for the kids to be squirrely. It's going to be a hard trip. It will be heart-wrenching to say, "See you later."

March 17, 2013

These past two days have been tough. We spent as much time with him as we could. He's under hospice now, and I know it won't be long. At times, I just stared at him sleeping. My mind flooded with memories. I longed to hear him laugh. He has the *best* laugh. So when he was awake and coherent, I cracked a joke about being *"appetite over apple cart,"* and he gave the best belly laugh. I had to leave the room to cry my eyes out. *Thank You, Lord, for I can still hear it in my ears as I write this.*

There were lots of tears shed, laughs shared, sometimes the two combined. Love is an amazing gift, but it hurts, too. I shared a little with Grandpa Will when it was just him and me, about how I just don't know what to do in my marriage. He told me, "Char, yeah, you deserve to be happy, and those kids too…" He always called me "Char." I know he knew what I meant without getting into any details.

Grandpa Will is so selfless. He insisted that I try his oxygen in my nose to see if it helped my headaches. I just pretended like I was on a soap opera. We got a good laugh. Grandpa never met a stranger, never spoke a harsh word, and always had joy and a smile. He would read the newspaper and quickly wrinkle it to scare you if you weren't looking at him. He would have us kids gather around and say, "If you tap me before I count to five, I'll give you a million dollars… 1,2,3,4,5" (so fast there was no way). I didn't do it. I really thought I'd get a million dollars at least one of the times though.

March 23, 2013
Precious Grandpa Will, with his infectious smile, is in Heaven now.

Anna said to me earlier, "So his body is still here, but his wholeness is in Heaven, right?"

Yes, that's right. We'll head back tomorrow. I'm having a hard time with losing Grandpa Will, and Danny says he can't take any more time off work to come for the funeral. I'm so angry with him, so mad. He knew Grandpa well, but can't take time to be with us in my time of grief.

March 26, 2013
I've never seen so many people coming to visit at a funeral home. It just shows the kind of man he was. The room was packed when they showed Grandpa's video montage. Grace and I had to stand around the corner and react to cousin Sylvie and Amanda's faces. They would giggle, and we'd giggle. It would quickly change to crying, and we just sobbed watching them, knowing the photos told Grandpa Will's story. When the video was over, Grace and I walked up to them and told them how we reacted to them. We all cried and hugged so tight.

What an emotional week, makeup running and all over the place. It's heartbreaking. He was so loved. His heart was as big as the sky.

March 29, 2013
I've had a ten-day headache, but that's the least of my concerns at the moment. I was helping write out thank you cards at Grandma Ruth's when Dad told me he'd take the kids back to the motel to get ready for bed. Anna has been sick, and it seems Pete caught the bug too. Having a break from mom duty was a treat, until Dad called from the motel and needed us to come right away. World War III just occurred in his motel room.

Anna fell asleep and Pete was sitting next to her dozing off on the bed. Apparently Anna farted and, let's just say, it was *loaded*. She blew out her pajama pants. Papa clicked into clean-up mode as Pete projectile vomited on the bed. He stands up to run to the bathroom while cupping his mouth.

Darting for the toilet, Pete starts pooping his pants, leaving a trail on the carpet in his wake.

Hearing of the happenings, I could just picture Dad trying to catch as much as he could, while in utter shock. Let's just say, the motel employees wrapped the room in yellow caution tape and called it a crime scene. The smell alone was enough to choke a donkey. I'm not sure they will ever allow us back here again.

April 3, 2013
As the days come and go, I'm not sure I can stay in my marriage much longer. I feel like we live separate lives. He doesn't want to see or hear my grief, and I feel like I should be able to share it with my husband. I'm merely walking a straight line when it comes to him. I can't be myself. I'm not allowed. I hate this. I am trapped, and I can't get out. I don't even have a job, so how *can* I get out?

April 9, 2013
"Dear Lord, thank you for the day, thank you for everything, Amen," in precious Anna's voice. She lit up after we opened our eyes. She volunteered to pray at the end of devotions tonight, which was way out of her comfort zone. She's so cute.

We take turns now, praying out loud. I don't want the kids to be as old as I was when I became comfortable praying in front of others. I tell them to just pray what is on their hearts in that moment. It's made for some precious words and the occasional giggle. I love it.

April 11, 2013
"I enjoy a strong, biting non-stop wind, trash bowling at me, police, power company, and road crew trucks lining the streets leading to understandably curious parents, along with an out-of place-man walking by," said no crossing guard ever.

I've been doing more research and trying harder to understand all of this. I just know in my heart that being diagnosed with a mental illness does not define you. And if managed correctly, it doesn't have to look like this.

It just doesn't. I have tried, prayed on my knees sobbing for help in this. I know the likelihood of one of our children dealing with mental illness is great. And that's ok. It doesn't have to look like this. It doesn't have to be covered with substance abuse, belittling, or condescending others. It doesn't have to be a bad thing that causes shame and pain to those closest to you. We can work through this, I know we can. I just feel Danny won't, he doesn't see it or think it's a problem. He sees himself as the victim. Rather than taking a step back, and seeing this life for what it is, he has punished and pushed me so far away. I can't keep this up. It doesn't have to be this way, I know it doesn't.

April 29, 2013
Seriously, of all of the students in Pete's second grade class, he had to be the one that walked in on the toilet spraying water like a sprinkler. Just as I walked into school this morning, after working at my crossing corner, I passed his teacher muttering, "Major bathroom issues, your son," as she ran out the door to find the custodian.

We keep going through the motions of life every day. He's living his, and we're living ours. People have stopped asking, so I don't have to make excuses anymore when it's just four of us. He doesn't even come to teacher conferences. I'm the only parent that the school knows. I know the kids see other dad's helping coach baseball and always being around. That's hard for them to see, and I notice it too. I'm grateful we have Papa. One of the moms at school thought Dad was my husband. We got a good chuckle out of that one. In all ways though, he is kind of like their dad. He fills in the blanks and has never once let them down.

April 30, 2013
Anna is so cute playing t-ball. I know part of it is just for the t-shirt and trophy, but she is awfully cute out there, giving it all she's got. Papa has been to every single game and practice for all three, even when the wind is whipping, or it's sleeting. He is my hero. His cape is the red folding chair he keeps in his truck for events such as this one.

May 2, 2013

I just had a heart attack. It's bedtime, and Brutus wouldn't go out the front door to go potty. After trying to coax her out, I turned the front porch light on, and there, coiled up on the mat, is a huge snake! Brut backed up, and I screamed. I called to Danny up the stairs to have him come help me. He yelled something down about doing it myself. I yelled up again that there was a snake on the porch, so he finally came down to check it out. He grabbed a rake and chased the little, ugly, legless monster off the porch and into the woods.

I'm never going outside again.

May 3, 2013

I got to help in a kindergarten classroom. I'd love to get a job like this next year! We did paper mache, and it made a huge mess, but the kids are so cute. It's worth it. While cleaning up the mess, I overheard rumblings of a kid in a different class throwing chairs. I figured I'd go take a look and see how I could help. It ended up just being him and me in the room. I was talking him down from throwing things. He thought taking out his frustration was better suited for me, so I had to put him into a safety hold until he calmed down. I kept trying to talk softly and quietly that he was going to be fine, all while he's trying to bite and head-butt me. I got into a position where his head would hit my shoulder, and he finally gave up the fight. Once more help arrived, and he was calm, I told him I'd see him later and headed on down the hall.

This afternoon didn't quite go as expected, and when I got home I found Brut had eaten what was left of the cherry pie. We should have renamed her Rascal.

Also, I have decided that from now on, I will approach the front porch with a pitch fork, baseball bat, .22, shovel, and helmet all while wearing waist high waders.

May 6, 2013

I had to write this down. I am so incredibly proud of DK! The score was 8-9, he's last up with bases loaded, and two outs. Bless his heart, he struck out. He held it together through all of the well wishes and, "That's ok," until he saw me. It sure made this mama feel special that he buried his head in me. I hope I'm always that person for him.

For the other two crazies, Pete put out a warrant for Anna's arrest earlier today, for riding her bike too fast. I'm guessing he caught her, because on the back of her arm, in brown Sharpie, it says, "I caught you!"

The best thing of all happened today. That man in the blue Pontiac that passes my crossing corner twice a day, waved back.

May 8, 2013

I decided it's time to join so I did. I am now an official member of our church softball team. Being active, outside, and meeting new people sounds like just what I need. This will give me a chance to wear mismatched knee socks and pigtails regularly. I won't be playing catcher or even attempt to pitch. If all three kids can be doing baseball, I will too. Every single night during the week someone has a game, and I love it.

May 14, 2013

At our PTA meeting tonight, as the principal said something nice about each of us on the board, he used the word *calm* in describing me. For some reason, the room broke into hysterics.

I love our school and this whole community! We feel like such a part of it. It's great for the kids to feel a part of it all, too. People know us and we know them.

May 20, 2013

Today:

#1. Between my allergies and the mosquitoes, I was mistaken for doing the Macarena at my crossing corner.

#2. A kindergartener couldn't remember my name, so decided he'd call me "Mrs. Fun."

#3. DK's mean classmates' name-calling from last Friday turned into the principal meeting with both third grade classes.

Chapter 26

May 25, 2013

I'm glad summertime weather is upon us as we've been so busy with baseball and church softball. Dad has helped tremendously with running all over the place. Danny comes when he can, but he's been struggling. If I can do it all on my own, I just do. It's not worth trying to make sure everyone is covered and then last minute not show up, making the kids more stressed. If I need help, it's Papa to the rescue.

Being at school as much as I am, I hope the kids know they are loved. It's a blessing to be right there, and the staff has been so kind. I feel like I know almost every kid by name. It's great when I can pick-up extra hours here and there. Maybe next year I could get a paraprofessional job in a classroom, then I'd still have summers off. I'll have to see what opens up.

May 31, 2013

I rush to grab a sandwich. Anna is crying because I didn't surprise her with something new to try. We pull in fast so DK and Anna can get to their baseball fields in time. Pete and I are lingering behind, and I ask him if he'd be willing to sign a contract stating he'll come home for the holidays when he grows up. He happily agreed, and took off running to join the other two. There I walk alone with hands full of dinner trash and a water bottle. As I approach the trash can and stick the water bottle between my legs to open the trash lid, I apparently squeezed a little too hard, and now it looks like I peed my pants.

June 1, 2013

I was yawning and thought to myself, *why*. It's probably because Anna was sleepwalking again. She was so out of it that I had to tell her four times to wipe after going potty. In her delirious state, she yanked the entire toilet paper roll off the holder, and went for it.

I'm wanting to hold Danny up as he's struggling, but he doesn't want to let me in. What am I to do? I feel so empty in my marriage. *Lord, what shall I do?* I know divorce is frowned upon in the bible. I'm struggling with that piece. I talked to some friends today and they helped me have some peace, I guess. Lord knows how hard I've tried and what we've gone through. He has remained faithful and has provided safety and well-being for us throughout. I just don't feel safe anymore.

June 3, 2013

When you have a field trip with your son and he tells his buddy he already has a partner, then turns and grabs your arm...I do believe my head filled with helium and left my neck in that moment. *Be still my heart.* This dream job I've been blessed with, and wanted as long as I can remember, is harder than I thought. It's trying, patience-thinning, and exhausting, but being a *MOM* is the greatest gift. I wouldn't trade one minute of this time for all of the money in the world.

6.5.13

While talking to the kids about middle school and how big of a jump it is from elementary, I told them I made it out ok. This, to which Pete responds, "Mom, did you know there is a book about you called *I Survived Middle School: 1910?*"

Today was the staff volleyball game where we got to play the fifth graders. I left with a pitted shirt, refreshed trash talking skills, and a smile that still includes all of my teeth.

June 13, 2013

The boys went out behind the barn in an attempt to help with my softball fielding skills. This met with a near sprained ankle in flip flops, Brutus getting into the (unlit) burn barrel, and Anna competing for my full attention. A bucket of baseballs is now forever lost, and I didn't learn anything I didn't already know. I will never tell them that, though.

Earlier while sitting on the porch playing, *I'm thinking of something starting with the letter…* I interrupted Anna and said, "I'm thinking of something starting with the letter I, IDIOT," just as a crotch rocket sped by our house at ninety-eight miles per hour.

I keep up appearances and maintain my smile. The kids do too, but they feel it all. I can't protect them if we stay. That has been my main job. I can take it, but *them*? No way. They need to be safe, secure, feel loved, and not uneasy in their own home.

Help Me, Lord, I come before You with the rawest of emotions. How do I proceed? How can we do this? I know we can't anymore. He is escalating to the point where I don't know what he is capable of. Please intervene, Lord. Please help us!

June 27, 2013
Once I gathered my thoughts, I managed, "When you grow up and have a brand new car, I'm gonna climb in and spill some red staining Powerade and laugh! We'll see then how funny you think it is!"

We just got this truck. It's my *dream* truck. A black GMC Sierra pickup (just wiped the drool off of my chin, again). And it's mine to drive! I'm so excited. We got Danny's Explorer not too long ago, and he said we can swing both car payments, so I'm *beaming*. I've always wanted a pickup truck, and this one is beyond my wildest dreams. The back window even goes up and down. We can easily pull the trailer, and well, I'm loving it!

Danny has been struggling more and more, and we're growing more distant. I feel like my soul purpose is to help hold him up and be Mom, nothing else. I don't trust leaving the kids with him alone anymore. I'm trying my best to manage my thoughts and emotions. But I just don't know if I can keep doing this. I feel like I can't do it. There is more to life, there has to be.

July 1, 2013
Today we celebrated DK's tenth birthday. *How in the world?!* Double digits. He's so smart and compassionate. He has such a big heart for a young kid. Ten - I can't believe it.

I woke up with such a bad headache that my face hurts. I feel bad it's this way for DK's day. I took some medicine and will just pace myself. I can't let it stop me from helping DK feel special today.

An older couple stopped by the house and told us that where our garage was built used to a garden filled with asparagus. And where Dutch is buried in the back, there used to be grapevines. I love that people stop by and reminisce about this place. It makes me smile. Oh, and it was the milkman who found the old lady dead (heart attack) on our front porch! Mystery solved.

July 2, 2013
"Pray about everything then, leave outcomes up to Me. Do not fear My will, for through it I accomplish what is best for you. Take a deep breath..." (Jesus Calling by Sarah Young).

Deep breath. How will I find a full time job? How is there enough time in a day? Should I write my book? Will I be ok with all three kids back in school full time this fall? I'm scared about it all. I need to let go of my fear and unknowns, and just wait on Him...

July 10, 2013
Today, Anna cried because of the waves while we were on Nan and Papa's boat. DK cried because he didn't get permission to punch Pete back. I'm wondering, does Calgon, from the 1980's commercials about bubble bath, *really* take you away? Because I could go for some of that right now.

We had dinner with Mom and Dad and got home by bedtime. Danny was home and in bed already. This seems to be the usual routine these days. I totally understand that he needs to keep a strict routine to help him feel better, but we have no time spent as a family anymore. I guess it's been gone for a long, long time.

July 12, 2013

We got home from our camping trip a few days ago. I guess I had in my mind what I thought it would be like. Fall Creek is my most favorite place to camp since we went with my folks back in our newlywed days. Dad has a lot of memories camping here with his dad. He even came here to camp with his dog when he was in college. It's a far drive, but the peace, minimalism, and disconnect with technology is worth it. I want to move there. It's like a step back in time.

Mom and Dad weren't going to join us this time. Dad wanted to respect our family time. As we got closer, Danny's mood has been more unpredictable. Dad changed his mind. He wanted to make sure the kids and I were safe. I'm grateful Mom was able to talk him into it. We made a plan to play it as a surprise for Pete's birthday. That's how I sold it to Danny, anyway. Mom and Dad came up a few days after us and surprised Pete with a BB gun. With them, came a sense of peace. I felt like I couldn't fully breathe until they got there.

On Pete's ninth birthday, Danny didn't feel like leaving the campground, or the trailer for that matter. I was having flashbacks to the other time he refused to leave the trailer. Mom wasn't feeling the best, so Dad and I took the three kids into town for the day. We bowled, went to an arcade, and let Pete choose the lunch spot. It was so fun, and also sad at the same time.

The whole trip, I tried making it all about us and our family. I kept taking family pictures as if everything was normal. In reality, the kids and I spent more time with Mom and Dad than Danny. He was fine with them joining us. He wasn't mad they were there. He is pulling farther away, more removed than ever. My heart hurts, and I think I know what I have to do. I'm hiding behind this smile. Sometimes I can feel my top lip quiver when I smile. I want what's best for our kids, for me, but I have no idea how to get there. I'm not a wife or even a partner anymore. I'm just an easy target. As we pulled out of the campground, I knew it, deep down, this was our last camping trip as a family of five.

July 27, 2013

"I never let go of your hand... Hope lifts your perspective from your weary feet to the glorious view you can see from the high road. I am training you to hold in your heart a dual focus: My continual Presence and the hope of heaven!" (Jesus Calling by Sarah Young).

Amen! Thank you Lord for the power You show and me having these thoughts earlier today. I sometimes make a fist knowing you are holding my hand. The visual is a great reminder of the truth! You are here with me, Lord, right now. I praise Your name.

August 1, 2013

After a short interrogation, it has been determined it was Zacchaeus who's been shoving his dirty socks behind the couch cushions.

These kids! They crack me up, and are aging me prematurely. It seems everything in life has been aging me these days. While driving to meet Danny for dinner, I managed to run out of gas. Sure, this truck has an actual working gas gauge, but I wanted to see how far the *low fuel* light got me. Apparently, it's pretty accurate. I had to sit and wait forty-five minutes for Danny to come give me a hand. Life lesson #94: new car gas gauges don't lie.

August 7, 2013

Since we bought this house, we've talked about moving the kitchen to the front of the house and having a more open floor plan. So, this morning when Danny took a sledgehammer to the plaster wall separating the kitchen and dining room, I got excited. I think my excitement was overridden by working out so much anxiety, pain, and fear. I went after that plaster and lath like I had never done a project before. The kids played outside while I opened windows, put on a mask, and went for it...all day long, like I was obsessed. Once I started, I had to finish it. I cried secret tears while slamming the wall, dust all over the place including my face. The sledgehammer was soon replaced by a crowbar.

All of the layers of that tough old farmhouse, they were me. I had to work through it all, down to the studs.

August 11, 2013

Danny hasn't been up for much since Grace has been in town. She came along with us horseback riding today. We had been trying to find a place while camping, but couldn't, so I promised the kids we'd go once we got home. Of course, I had the biggest, most stubborn horse. It bucked, tried to bite my feet eighteen times, ate greenery the entire ride (despite my wrist breaking pulls), and, well, Fancy wasn't living up to her name. Her glare was met with mine. But we did it, and both lived to tell the story.

August 15, 2013

"When things go wrong, you tend to react as if you're being punished. Instead of this negative response, try to view difficulties as blessings in disguise. Make Me your Refuge by pouring out your heart to Me, trusting in Me at all times" (Jesus Calling by Sarah Young).

We are heading for Frankfort today. Grace, Dad, and the boys (it was supposed to be Danny too, but he opted out) are going to a baseball game. Mom and I will take Anna shopping, and she's so excited. I want to get her a doll for her birthday, but they are pretty expensive. We'll have to see.

August 16, 2013

My heart is in my throat. Danny and I chatted earlier on the phone, and he was super short with me. I'm also really feeling like now is the time. Last week I went with him to discuss electric shock therapy with a new doctor. The doctor thought it was a good next step in Danny's journey with his mental health, and we have talked about it a lot lately. I've felt so strongly in my heart that if he does this and is off of work, he needs someone to take care of him. I *have* to stay. What would that show the kids if I left him in that desperate time of need?

Danny just told me he isn't going to go that route right now. I had to excuse myself from everyone watching TV at Grace and Joe's apartment so I could go for a walk. I was outside, looking up to the sky, and shaking, praying out: *Lord, PLEASE, is this time? Can I do this? Please, Lord, carry me right now. I feel in my heart and mind that it's time. Guide the next steps, Dear Lord.*

Grace appeared next to me and saw my tears. I told her, *it's time*. It's time to get out of my marriage.

Grace and I went to pick up pizzas while Mom and Dad stayed back with the kids. That's when I made the call, and left a message for my therapist. She's met with Danny and I twice now for marriage counseling.

"Tomorrow at our session, I'm going to tell Dan that I want a divorce. I don't want you to be surprised when I say those words."

August 17, 2013
I'm an absolute mess. I told Mom and Dad last night too, that it's time. I rode in the front seat all the way home and cried the *entire* time. I'm grieving my marriage, but I have been grieving for years now. I'm afraid of what will come. I just don't know. But I don't feel like we're safe anymore. Mom offered to feed the kids and watch them when I headed to counseling. As for Dad, he got in their car and followed me.

I went in to the counseling office waiting room with my heart beating so loud I'm sure the guy in the chair next to me heard it. I'm thinking, "Please (therapist), please call me back to your office before Danny gets here." But just then, Danny walked in. I was making small talk, all while feeling terrified that he could see right through me. It seemed like three hours before we were called back into her office. I started crying the minute we sat down. She asked if I had something I wanted to tell him.

I composed myself, took two deep breaths and said, "I think it's time to get a divorce."

The therapist quickly chimed in and said, "Why don't you start with a trial separation?"

While I shook my head yes, I knew in my heart I was *done*. Danny, sitting back with a smug look on his face, turns to me and says, "Yeah, I was going to suggest that, too."

Yeah right. Either way, I said the words with a witness present. For the remainder of our session, I have no idea what was even said, except that we will tell the kids the news together. Fear came over me as we left her office and walked out to the parking lot. By that time, most cars were cleared out. But, off in the distance, Dad was parked, making sure I was safe and that Dan didn't hurt me.

We drove home separately and were both in tears as we got home. The kids knew I was crying on the drive home from Frankfort earlier. They knew something was up. Danny and I were respectful towards each other while telling the kids. Sitting in the kitchen, we told them we are going to start living in different places, that we're our best when we are not together. They will always come first and get to spend time with both of us. I don't think I will ever forget the range of emotions I felt this day, for as long as I live.

For now, during this *trial* separation, Danny is going to stay in our trailer on the other side of the barn. This is no trial. I am ready to be done.

August 20, 2013
Anna was *furious* last night at bedtime. "Why do I have to do everything!? I have to put my bike away, bring my doll back in off the porch, and I'm not allowed to say bad words!"

Despite these hard days right now, the kids bring so much joy. I'm so thankful for the gift of laughter.

August 21, 2013
I don't enjoy this loneliness at night, that's for sure. In this quiet house, I'm afraid to turn off the light because my mind will only race. When does life begin? When you are a little kid standing there at the mailbox in Gobles, looking up at the sky wondering, who am I? I guess you ask yourself the same question when you grow up, too, when you are faced with these types of decisions.

I felt frustrated tonight at the lack of space. Knowing it's hard for him, I've had time to think this through and prepare my heart for the past two years. He emails three times a day, and when he doesn't get a response, he texts me to call him right away like I used to. I told him I have other things going on and won't just drop everything. I want him to be well, but I can't carry his suffering right now. I can't deal with his work issues, anxieties, or carry his weight. When I'm not, I feel lighter, and my patience comes more easily.

August 23, 2013

I'm feeling heavy-hearted today, mostly because I just drove right passed the house without stopping knowing he was coming home. I don't even want to see him. I can hardly push the gas pedal down. I'm so heavy-hearted and debilitated. I know it was the right thing to leave though, he needs to see my truth here. As harsh as it is, I am *done*.

August 24, 2013

This morning Dad went with me back to the house because I was sure I was going to find Dan dead.

I stayed at their house overnight with the kids since I didn't trust where Danny's head was. He's been staying in the trailer and has been so *dark* and unpredictable. He wasn't answering any of my texts or calls this morning, and I had a feeling deep in my gut. I went upstairs to ask Dad if he would come with me, that I had a bad feeling about what was going on at home.

We rode over together, and as we pulled in the driveway, I noticed the front door was wide open. My heart sank. I thought for sure he was hanging somewhere upstairs. Dad went with me, and we checked the whole house, calling out his name with no answer.

Then I thought to go check the trailer. It took several knocks before I heard movement from within. He answered the door coming from complete darkness. The trailer was all closed up, blinds drawn. *Whew, he is alive.*

August 26, 2013

Today is Miss Anna's sixth birthday. I know going out for lunch will be awkward with Danny there, but it's important to have a united front. We stayed overnight again at Mom and Dad's last night. Anna got the doll she's been wanting and was so excited.

Thank You Lord for getting us here, to this point. We are safe and able to celebrate Anna today. These weeks have been awful, but You have been here in the storm, and I am thankful for Your protection and provision. I'm struggling to find words or peace and have no idea what comes next. Jesus, right here, we need You.

September 27, 2013

August 27, 2013
We're having Anna's birthday party at the park nearby so kids can eat and swim in the lake and I don't have to worry about the house. It's embarrassing to have people over with walls missing and floors torn up. What will happen with the house? I'm not sure if Danny will let me stay or if he will want to. It has so much potential. And, of course, Dutch is buried in the yard. I think I'll just take all of my emotions out on that ugly, pink unicorn piñata for Anna's party.

September 3, 2013
It's the first day of school for these crazy kids. DK is in fourth grade, Pete is a third grader, and Miss Anna-Banana is a kindergartner. Oh, how the time flies. Anna is excited to finally be at the boys' school, and I'm excited for them all to be in one place.

I zipped my lip up in my sweatshirt earlier. Life lesson #825, do not lean forward and zip up while not paying attention.

September 5, 2013
I did it. Today was *the* day, the day I've wondered if I'd have the courage, the day I knew in my gut would come, but never knew how I would get here.

It is official. I filed for *divorce*.

Thank you Lord for Dad going with me and helping me answer all of the questions and finding the strength to walk into that office. I have no idea what comes next. I'm terrified. But I know, despite the rumblings in my gut and headache, that this is what I need to do. I pray for forgiveness in this, as this is not what I ever intended when I got married. Ever. I fall so short, Lord. Please give me strength to put one foot in front of the other.

How will Danny react when he gets the papers? I can't worry about that right now. It's done.

Chapter 27

September 11, 2013
I thought that, because this is Danny's parenting time with the kids, he would handle situations. Here I am, staying with Mom and Dad because of our arrangement to have the kids stay consistent. We will come and go, depending on parenting time. Danny calls to tell me DK tripped while waiting for the school bus and needs stitches. He was bringing DK to me to take care of it rather than taking him to urgent care right away.

I know I'm *Mom*, but Dad can do some things, too...right!? As furious as I was, I know DK wanted me there anyways, and the cut on his knee was stitches worthy. I was there to hold his hand and keep his mind occupied. I'll take it.

September 12, 2013
Being at a different crossing guard corner this school year, I'm going to mourn the loss of my cat crossing encounters. But this morning, I did find a new friend; an old German Shepherd was staring at me through his bay window, blinking heavily as if ready for a nap or wanting me to pet him. I think we'll be good friends.

I'm grateful for these blessings that seem so simple. They are reminders that despite this whole
heap of unknowns that You are holding me up. Please hold me close, Lord God!

September 14, 2013
I feel like I could throw up. He got home right when I did again. I dropped the kids at his mom's for an overnight. Last night they were with my folks. I fear he'll hold it against me, that two nights in a row they weren't with me, but I coordinated sitters for my time, so what's it to him? It makes me nervous. He makes me nervous being right there. It's like I'm suffocating.

September 15, 2013
Danny came, with a few friends, to get *his* furniture out of the house. We talked about most of it ahead of time, but as it ended up, he left us with barely anything. We were left with one chair in the family room, the dining room table and chairs, and the kids' beds. He took our $1300 king bed and bedframe, my desk, the family couch, and more. The house is so empty. I have been watching for garage sales with furniture and things. We have a $40 loveseat that I bought that smells like cats, but it's something to sit on. We'll be ok. It's only stuff. There are no curtains, walls are knocked out, and the flooring has been removed to the subfloor. Construction began and was never completed, so seven projects are half finished and at a standstill. Now we have no furniture.

September 18, 2013
I was just overcome with emotions while looking over at the empty spot next to me in bed. I feel bad for how I handled the kids before bedtime. Tears are rolling down my cheeks. How will I do this alone? This space is becoming so real. Danny is moving away; he got an apartment downtown.

That security of having him here, as much of a hindrance as it's been, will be gone. He will be gone; not here anymore. We won't run into him. He will live somewhere else. I'm surprised it's hitting me like this, considering everything he has put me through. It's part of the grieving process, I guess. Nothing has been easy about getting to this point, none of it. But I had to get out, not just for me, but the kids cannot be raised thinking that is how a husband treats a wife.

September 23, 2013
I got whistled at standing at my crossing guard corner this morning.

DK just told me I'm brave.

From eye roll to tear-filled eyes, here I go.

September 27, 2013
Brutus being home all the time, instead of out in the woods with Danny, has led to a naughty pup, big time. Sure, she's cute, but wrecking things is getting expensive. Just a bit ago, as I was calling her from some secret mission she was on in the backwoods, she bowled me down, right on my bottom. I should have calculated her speed, and my being in the way, because I felt like I broke three toes and my wrist. There I sat. It took me a few minutes to get back up.

September 30, 2013
This corner gig is heating up. Today this guy drove by, turned his car around, and the next thing I know, he's handing me a folded piece of paper while asking, "Can I give you my number?" *Umm, that would be a no. No, thank you.*

It was kind of funny because I had still been wearing my wedding ring. I'm not sure if I should keep it on until the divorce is final or take it off now because I know we're done.

I decided to take it off tonight. It was surprisingly harder than I thought it would be. It's been on my finger for over fifteen years. I just stared at my left hand and pulled it over my knuckles. Off it came, just a thick white circle around my ring finger remained. Now both of my hands are plain. My left thumb keeps involuntarily feeling around where my ring would be out of habit. This is going to take some getting used to.

October 10, 2013
I was helping change the sheets on the top bunk just now, and the boys and I were in hysterics. Pete managed to hand me five missing t-shirts, a box of Kleenex, a Model-T, Miguel Cabrera's baseball bat, two throw pillows, a hairbrush handle, and home plate. This was all before we even got the old sheets off the bed.

I'm feeling overwhelmed with everything that needs to still be decided. I'm glad some things are done with, but this whole process is hard. Danny keeps texting me and demanding to talk to the kids. I have told him he is able to anytime, but when I talk to the kids, and they genuinely don't want to, I tell Danny that as well. I'm trying my best to be transparent. Danny thinks I'm trying to control. I'm not, but I want what is best for these three kids. End of story.

October 11, 2013
When I went to his apartment last night, I noticed his large pupils. It scared me that the kids were going to be spending the weekend with him like that. What can I do? Was it because I found his new place based on Pete's directions? He wouldn't tell me where he lived, but I have every right to know. He knew I was coming. I've learned that's his "ready-to-pounce" look.

I left reluctantly, drove down the street, and got a medium Coke from the drive-thru before parking for about an hour. I just wanted to be close to make sure. I haven't heard anything from the kids. Someone at church gave me a prepaid cell phone, so I sent it with DK in case he needs me. He hid it in his pillow case, but I do think it gave comfort to him knowing he had it in case.

It's me again, Lord, standing in the need of prayer. Please keep them safe. I pray a hedge of protection around these gifts, these kids. If they need me, they are able to call. My hands are tied here. I pray Danny will be gentle with his words and actions.

October 12, 2013
Dad and I were looking over all of the financial statements, credit cards, bank account usage, etc, Dad said, "What's Match.com?" I mocked him thinking he was teasing me, but he said, "No, seriously, what is that? There's a $119 charge from that website on your bank account." There was also another charge from a drive-thru liquor store. *What in the world?*

I need to locate the past six months' bank statements, as well as half our savings, because he's literally draining the whole thing out. It's down to

170

$1,500. He's using credit cards to write checks to himself numerous times. What else don't I know? I honestly don't know how this could be. I know I'm doing the right thing by getting out. What can I do with literally nothing? How will we live?

October 14, 2013
Today, while standing at my corner, I had to go to the bathroom so bad. I wasn't sure how I'd make it thirty minutes. I start walking back to school, with a bathroom in sight, when I turn back and see a little second grader on her bike ready to cross. I ran to her, and thankfully, I didn't pee my pants. Job security.

I found out from DK that Danny may have taken the prepaid cell phone. DK never took it out of his pillow case, and it's gone. I suppose it could have fell out. Either way, I'm speechless and furious.

October 16, 2013
Just as I stepped out of the shower today, a grayish black, furry beast ran under the bathroom door. I let out an explicative and leapt back. After almost slipped on soaking wet tile, I collected myself and bravely opened the door to find Anna riding the broom. That was the furry animal? *Whew.* Cardiac arrest diverted.

I made a call to Dan's employer today. I have had this sinking suspicion that he is going to get his hands on the entire 401k. With the divorce, I get half of that. He already used my retirement account from my old employer to pay off some debt. I am kicking myself for that. He is the one who likes nice things, so basically it's his debt. His boss called me back after a few hours and said that Danny had in fact tried to get the 401k.

Are you serious!? His boss knew nothing about our divorce. I'm so dumbfounded. He also informed me that the company has decided to let Dan go. Shaking my head, I'm...I don't even know what I am...

All of these things happening right at the same time is so much, Lord. But You continue to get us up every morning. I know, somehow, this will all work out. I have no idea how, but You do, Dear Lord. We need calm, and I need to have peace so I can embrace my kids. I need to be strong. I need to put one foot in front of the other.

October 20, 2013

Anna just told me through her tears that she's going to wake up mad tomorrow. I told her that I will too then. We high-fived, and she grumpily stumbled off to bed. Hey, I'll take it. At least she's keepin' it real.

October 22, 2013

I did what I've wanted to do for years. We got professional photos taken of me and the kids. Danny never would get them with our whole family. He kept saying it wasn't the right time, maybe *next* summer, or I *need to lose weight* first. I am usually the one behind the camera to capture photos. It was time to be on the other side. Grace helped me think through the color scheme, and she even came to town to take me to the mall to buy outfits. She takes great, candid shots. They turned out beautiful. We all look so happy and natural. I'm going to make Christmas ornaments of these photos. This is a big deal.

October 24, 2013

I took off this morning without taking the two pills I had set on the dresser. I bet ten bucks that Brutus won't have a migraine later.

I've been trying to take life in stride. Every day is a struggle, yet I knew it would be. I still want to laugh and make others laugh. I have said a hundred times, if the kids and I end up in a cardboard box, we'll be fine. At least we'll be safe. Although, this is more than I anticipated. I honestly feel that way. I just don't know what Danny is capable of.

I did learn some things today, though. I'm not really surprised, but I am shocked. Does that even make sense? I called Danny on my way to the playgroup this morning. I had to know, Dan to Charlotte, what was he doing? The money he is supposed to be leaving in the bank for the kids and me is gone. The money he's supposed to leave me for groceries isn't there; it's all gone.

I blatantly asked, "Why are you doing this?"

He responded with, "It's what you *get* for filing for divorce. You think you have control? You don't. Let's see you pay your own bills."

He told me he will no longer make our mortgage payment, my (brand new) truck payment, cable, propane, utilities, electric bill, any of it. He said that he didn't have to, that this was my lesson to learn, my payback. *Oh, and the trailer?* "Plan on that getting repossessed." He said he's not paying on that anymore either.

How in the world can someone be so cruel? This isn't about just me. If it were, that would still incredibly selfish. We have three children. *We* have three children, and this hurts them too, but he doesn't care at all. That cardboard box scenario isn't too far off, I guess. How can he do this? How could anyone do this to their family?

I pulled the truck over into a neighborhood, put it in park, and pull down my visor mirror. "Breathe Charly... We'll make it. I need to get a job. We will be ok. More bumps, but God has got this. He has never left us without. Just breathe…"

Chapter 28

October 30, 2013

According to Anna, Pete is going to defend our property by sleeping out on the front porch all night.

According to Pete, Nerf gun in hand, he says, "You'll find me with this upstairs if you hear anything strange in the night."

According to DK, "I'll be in bed reading, *The Indian in the Cupboard.*"

According to me, "It's bedtime. We'll just leave the porch lights on to make sure no one smashes our pumpkins this year."

October 31, 2013

Dressed as a hot dog, because I'm a crossing guard at an elementary school on Halloween, a police officer pulls up to take my statement. Hilarious.

Next, the creeper guy that's asked for my number, rolls down his window to say "hi." I've figured out that he drives four different vehicles, all of which license plates I have memorized. I have some friends that work at the local police department, and they know I want him to leave me alone. So this morning, hot dog costume and all, the police officer gets out of his cruiser to see if my creeper has been by. Just then, he passes and waves!

I go, "There he is!" and the cop hops in his car, lights him up, and warns him to leave me alone.

The guy said, "Well she flirts with me every day. She waves at me."

To which the officer responded, "Dude, she's a crossing guard. She waves at everybody."

November 7, 2013
I'm just so thankful and humbled by those who support and love us through tough times; who pray and encourage us by thumbs up as we drive by; who frequently send "thinking of you" texts, messages, and check-ins. My eye liner was gone before by 8:23 am today.

Funny thing. My creeper still drives by, but now, won't make eye contact. Although, I did see him slowly lift a certain finger at me as he turned the corner.

November 10, 2013
I had to hide out with the kids at a local hole-in-the-wall pizza joint tonight. Since we have been in talks with our attorneys about parenting time, Thursday is supposed to be Danny's night with the kids. He's been grilling me all day via text and email. He's not in his right mind. I can't send the kids with him, I just can't. So I took the kids to this small restaurant in town where he wouldn't find us. It's raining out. Once the pizza got to our table, and each kid grabbed a slice, I stepped out in the rain to call my attorney. I told him I couldn't have the kids go with Danny when he's like this. He told me to stay put, that it would be fine. We stayed there for a while, waiting for time to pass.

November 19, 2013
I was honestly excited about starting this bible study, but nervous too. Who will watch the kids? I should go. I *need* to go. I'm glad my beautiful friend, whose story is so similar, is encouraging me to go. It's for those going through, or have been through, divorce. I need that. I need care. Men and women were both there. It seems like a nice group.

We got to laughing tonight. We all have a lot in common. This is just what the doctor ordered - laughter and honesty, with other adults who get it.

November 21, 2013
Last night the boys were bringing down laundry. I told them to make sure it was all dirty and not just random novelties they can't find a place for in their rooms. As I loaded the washing machine, I found Monopoly money, a Florida Marlins pennant, jeans they've never worn, a shirt three sizes too small, a football trophy from 2010, and a stethoscope.

November 22, 2013
After giving the boys the "you need to be more responsible" spiel, DK says to me, "That was a nice four-minute speech, Mom."

It wasn't until we got to our destination that the boys realized they forgot something and were yanked. I snickered to myself. My point was made.

November 26, 2013
Today I made a big-girl-pants, practical decision (with Dad's help). Before the bad credit hits, I got a minivan. It was hard to swallow initially, but it'll grow on me. I will miss my truck. That thing is a *rock*star, but I am a mom, so a minivan fits. Not a soccer mom, I'm a baseball mom.

November 29, 2013
I figured out why the previous owner turned in my bunk minivan. The horn sounds like a whoopee cushion that ate bad lunch meat. I mean come on, I have a reputation to protect.

On our way home from visiting family for Thanksgiving today, we stopped so I could buy a bed. Yet, said bed didn't fit inside my new van, so I had to tie it to the top with cheap grade twine. Not feeling so trusting, Mom, Anna and I found a nearby hardware store where I picked up some bungee cords. The sight of me and four bungees, in the loading zone, over a mattress, when my patience had already been spent was *neat,* I'm sure. I hoped and prayed they'd hold. We made numerous stops with the hazards flashing on the expressway, and my speed maxing out at 40 mph. I got a stiff neck from gawking at the side passenger mirror. We got off the expressway and waited patiently in an outlet mall parking lot. I couldn't trust it anymore, so we sat and waited for Dad to come save the day (which turned to night, by now) with his pickup truck. Have I mentioned how much I miss my truck?

December 4, 2013

I do love Brut. She's a sweet, sweet dog, but I don't know how much more of her *destructo* behavior I can take! She eats socks, candy, Christmas stockings, pistachio shells, trash, toilet bowl bobbing, hogs the bed, ate a tube of Desitin (yeah, for diaper rash), toothbrushes, pumpkins, lunch boxes, the inside of Anna's nice new winter jacket, cash, full loaves of bread, orange peels, and I know there is something I'm forgetting. I've asked Danny to take her because I know they are best buds, but he can't. I can't keep coming home to crazy antics on top of everything else. *Oye, BRUT!*

December 15, 2013

After a long search to find Brutus a new address, she left today. I tried, I know I did, but this isn't the best scenario for her. She's great with the kids and all, but she needs more than I can possibly give. My friend's folks took her on (good thing they've had labs before, who were naughty, because I was 100% honest with all that she's done around here). If the situation were different, and she could run and hunt and get the exercise she needs, I would have kept her. I don't even know where the kids and I will live in a few months. When will the bank come kick us out with the foreclosure notice? It takes a bit I know, but they have been calling. So many creditors call me. I don't answer my phone if I don't recognize the number anymore.

With Brut re-homed, I do feel a huge weight lifted. She's in a good home. I'm glad for that. I can sleep easier knowing there will be a few less messes around here.

December 20, 2013

There are no words. I left school in a heap of emotions today. The whole staff did a collection and gave us over $400 in grocery gift cards to help with Christmas. The tears are rolling right now. I am so grateful. I feel loved and encouraged. I'm so humbled that they would do this for us. Wow.

Unfortunately, we had to hide out at the pizza place again tonight. Danny was furious with me, and I couldn't allow myself to send the kids with him. I called my lawyer, and he said to stay put. Again. I feel destroyed. This hostility. I just don't know where his head is at and can't risk it.

Lincoln Brewster's song, *The Power of Your Name* is bringing me peace tonight.

"Surely life wasn't made to regret, and the lost were not made to forget
Surely faith without action is dead, let Your Kingdom come
Lord break this heart, And I will live to carry Your compassion"

December 22, 2013
Now this is relaxing. I found this round oak table for $15. Here it sits, covered in a 1000-pieces of a Christmas scenery. I get so lost in it, and time flies when I'm doing a puzzle like this. The lights glowing and blinking on our Christmas tree are the only lighting I need. DK and Pete made tacos for dinner, followed by brownies. Cooking and baking are huge skills I want all three of these kids to learn. I'm proud of them. It was all delicious. I'm thankful for feeling relaxed. I love that something this simple can take my mind off all of the stress I've been feeling: just the basics of finding corner pieces and using my eyes to scan the table to find what I need next. This right here...if only life were this simple.

Someone left a card on our porch, earlier this afternoon, when we weren't home. Inside was $100 bill and an unsigned card with an encouraging cover. I'm so grateful. *Directly from You, Lord God!*

December 25, 2013
We spent Christmas at Mom and Dad's this year, and it felt magical, like it should. Surrounded by laughter and love. It was perfect. Danny only took the kids for about five hours yesterday, so that was a blessing. The more time the better! It makes for more time for our usual traditions.

Mom and Dad fed us, and they even had batteries on hand for the toys and stuff! Grace and Joe stayed too, so it felt like Christmas should. For this, I am grateful.

December 30, 2013
The year 2013 has been a noteworthy one, to say the least. It's been filled with Brut's antics, a trip to our favorite camping spot, being hospitalized for migraines, hilarious crossing guard moments, stitches, strangers' (and people known to me) incredible kindness, losing Grandpa Will, so many precious moments with my kids, and the ugly - filing for divorce. God has been good to us, and I pray He will continue to watch over us in this upcoming year!

January 7, 2014
It was bedtime until the UPS man made a late night delivery! Pete has been wetting his pants over when this would come - the air hockey table he bought with this Toys R Us gift card. At least they can't sneak play. That sound is hard to miss, especially the plastic clangin', (*high quality item, Clark*), when a goal is scored.

January 8, 2014
I received a full time job offer today. I left saying I would take it. I'm scared to death! Dad says he knows I can do it. I'm nervous about heading into this new chapter, for the kids, for my time... to be away from school.

The kids' principal could tell I was on the verge of tears, so he invited me into the conference room, and I just straight up ugly cried and told him I'm so scared. He told me, "Look at all you've done, I know you, you can *do this*!" What an amazing man. The school has been so gracious to me and my three. So, let's see if I can!? I need to try to sleep. My mind is in 1,034 places.

"God will carry you through every storm and give you the strength to make it" (GodVine devotionals by Proverbs 31 Ministries).

January 11, 2014
She walked with her tasks in mind, had me get on the scale, asked what medications I take, etc. She glanced to the top of the page and noticed I was there for a pre-employment physical. As she put the blood pressure cuff on my arm, I told her, "I'm a single mom, I'm nervous about going back to work..." Her entire face changed. She dropped everything and

embraced me in a hug! She is a single mom, too, and she talked with me about her life and promised me that things will all be alright. When I left that medical center yesterday, she told me I need to call her to let her know how everything goes for me. What a cool experience! *What a blessing, Lord! You continue to provide people in my path who are encouraging me. It's going to be just fine.*

January 19, 2014
I decided to go to the women's retreat this weekend at the last minute. I used to go every year with my dear friend, but this year I went solo. I got bunked with someone I've never met, (hey, I saved a buck on the room) who scared the living' daylights out of me! I slept with one eye open for fear she may knife me. I may be exaggerating, but she did dart glares at me while listening to a speaker and wouldn't even speak to me. "Crazy-single-white-female" stuff...Ha!

But also? The most amazing thing happened. I got to hang out with a friend I don't get to see nearly enough. I should have roomed with her! Today, as we got ready to leave, she told me how her and her husband had been saving to tithe for church and were in the process of finding a new church home. I listened as she told me all about it, but was floored when she said, "So we prayed about it and decided to give this to you." *Say what?* She handed me a white envelope and told me to put it away for now so no one would know. My eyes filled with tears, and I hugged her not knowing what to say.

Want to talk about *huge* tears? When I packed up and said my goodbyes, I pulled over to grab some gum out of my purse and saw that white envelope. Curiosity got the best of me, and I figured I'd go ahead and open it. Even a dollar would have been too much. I am just so humbled. Then I start counting, I'm crying so hard at this point, I can't even see what is in front of me. *Lord God, You are good. You provide always in ALL ways. This is such an amazing, generous gift.*

I shared with Mom and Dad when I went to grab the kids from them. They cried, too. I didn't tell the kids; this is big people stuff. We are going to be alright. The Lord has continued to provide hand over fist. *Gracious Lord, we Thank You.*

January 20, 2014
Dear God, I don't like the problems I face, and at times, I wish I didn't have to go through the troubles ahead of me. Remind me that your strength is mine, that your grace is enough, and that I will survive every challenge. Amen. (Daily Devotions inspired by 90 Minutes in Heaven by Don Piper and Cecil Murphey). So applicable!

January 22, 2014
Anna and I secretly hit McDonalds after dropping the boys at youth group. DK interrogated me after he found out. Looks like this mama will be putting $5 in the naughty jar.

January 25, 2014
I have been having a hard time in the cash flow department. I've been finding random things left behind by Danny, or things we can live without, and selling them. From tools that were like new and left, pretty dishes I don't need, throw pillows that I once loved, curtains, my clothes, pots and pans that we never use; anything that will sell so we have money to put gas in my van. I sold a power tool the other day online to someone who drove forty-nine miles to come pick it up.

Unbeknownst to me, it wasn't even Danny's (like he had said it was). He had borrowed it from a family friend two years ago and never returned it. Once I found out, I had to get ahold of this guy and have him bring it back. I was mortified. I paid him back his money and gas money for his time. I know these things are meant to hurt me and somehow, embarrassing me is rewarding for Danny. I need to keep moving forward. I need to let these intentional hurts go. But it's so hard. He keeps at it. I know there are people who live much harder lives than we do, and that humbles me. This life we've been living, the recurrence of ridicule and hurt, is not what I intended for the kids. I just hope and pray I can show my kids a home with love and happiness and break free of these chains. We won't have much, but we have Jesus and each other, and that's plenty.

February 1, 2014

I wasn't cut out for that job. It was too much stress, and I couldn't do it. I was terrified and nervous to mess up. I feel like I let Dad down because he thought I could do it. I've had so many people encouraging me, but I felt so terrified deep down. I had to walk out. It's not for me. I will admit, I ran to McDonalds and ate my feelings.

Lord, please help me to find my way to a full time job. I know it isn't this one, I'm not built to handle other people's emergencies over the phone. I'd rather give them a hug.

February 4, 2014

The past two days have been insanely frustrating and complicated, sprinkled with big people decisions. So, with all my wacky-ness, when someone pulled into my driveway today? Yes, I hid - next to my stove with a bag of cheese puffs.

February 5, 2014

Best one liners today:

Anna: "Why do they still have their gingerbread men up? It's not even ginger!"

Pete: "Who gets the tacos for lunch tomorrow? Going once, going twice? Sold, to the dude in the Indians shirt!" He was the only one that saw the one package of tacos so no one else even had a shot.

DK, after telling the kids when they grow up and are dating, they won't want to hear my advice: "Yeah, but I really do wanna hear it now."

February 7, 2014

With the onset of a migraine, I climbed into bed in my pajamas while Anna was playing the Kindle she got for Christmas. Next thing I know; Anna is bringing me a (cutely saturated) warm washcloth for my forehead. DK then went and got the devotions to read in my place. Anna sat here, rubbing my forearm, and Pete gave me a huge hug. I feel so blessed. We are going to be OK.

In these moments of great compassion and empathy, I know if we had not been through what we have, these amazing qualities wouldn't be what they are today. I need to cling to hope and that there are lessons in all of this. We aren't being punished, we are being taught. Lessons only life can teach, real, true pain and suffering. These lessons only God can teach us.

February 9, 2014

These past six months have brought a lot of tears. Today is no different as I watched out my bedroom window. They are here to repossess our camping trailer. Lots of memories going through my mind as I watch them trying to hook it up. I had become pretty good at that myself, at least I like to think so. I knew this would happen, but seeing it has me here with lots of Kleenex. Sitting on my bed, I'm trying to hide my tears from the kids. Seven years' worth of memories, good and bad, being pulled and taken away for good, by some dude with a cigarette hanging out of his mouth.

I didn't think they'd come in the wintertime. The whole thing caught me off guard. Just another worldly possession being taken away. I know it's not something I can keep, but it's so hard to watch. We've had it since before Anna was even born. I feel like a fool.

I've had to cut out cable for the TV and internet. If I need a signal, I drive to where they have free Wi-Fi. I can't afford the trash service, so we are recycling everything. Anything we can't recycle, we take to various places and toss it in their trash cans. I also can't afford propane anymore to heat the house, so I hope we don't run out. I'm keeping the house at a lower temp, and we're dressing warmer. It's hard because this house already loses a lot of heat, but with so many walls exposed, it's even colder inside. I don't have any extra money for salt for the water softener either, and I hope it won't break. I hope it holds up until we have to leave. After all these years, I finally get why Dad has always gone around and turned unnecessary lights off. If I can drop this electric bill, that'd be so amazing. I read up that by unplugging anything you aren't using; you can save money. It's worth a shot! Every single penny counts right now.

February 10, 2014

Today, three boxes of Wheaties fell on me at the grocery store, my driver door buttons are all on vacation, and I've dropped every single thing I've picked up. I slid sideways into a snowbank in my own driveway, I blamed my weight at my doctor's office today on my shoes, and I cried in front of a woman who probably thinks I'm nuts, but that's because I have skin cancer on my neck. I wonder what else today has in store.

February 11, 2014
My devotions today put it so simply...

1. *The steadfast love of the Lord never ceases.*
2. *His mercies never come to an end.*
3. *They are new every morning.*
4. *Great is thy faithfulness.*
5. *The Lord is my portion.*

(Live Loved: Experiencing God's Presence in Everyday Life by Max Lucado)

February 17, 2014
Lord, at times I feel like I'm drowning with all of these unknowns and what I see as pressures. I need to find a job, but what? I can't deal with fluorescent lights, or too much stress, because both cause an instant headache. I want to be the best mom I can, but I know I fall so short.

My beautiful bible study pal says, "Grace. Allow yourself grace..."

I long to do right by my kids. I long for them to know why I do what I do and to see me and respect me someday. Where will we live? How will I make ends meet? How will Danny continue in their lives? Can I get away from his control? He still has an emotional hold on me, and I need to move on from it.

It's all my fault the way he makes me feel. He makes me feel like I was an awful wife, a bad human, like I didn't do enough. I didn't honor our vows. He keeps saying that. When I wanted a break, I was made to feel selfish. He told me I was lazy and that I didn't have his permission to stop working full time. That was the cycle, over and over again. All of it, my fault.

Help me, Lord, to see Your truth in my life, and to guide me and my kids. Protect us, provide for us and what we need when we need it. Where will we be a year from now?

"Father, you created us, and you know everything there is to know about us. You know how discouraged we get at times and how we want to give up the struggles we face. Sometimes it seems as if we have more struggles than strength. We are tempted to quit. When that happens, Lord, remind us to endure for one more day, to be patient one more time, to serve without reward for one more season, Amen." (Live Loved devotional by Max Lucado).

February 24, 2014
Today, a perfect stranger gave me a pair of free winter boots for Anna. Hers had cracked on the bottom. This woman, unbeknownst to me, also gave us a pair of matching gloves. *God* provides. Wow, we are so touched.

February 25, 2014
The motor in my driver door isn't working! So for anything I would roll the window down for, I have to open the door. Being downtown to meet with my attorney, I got so embarrassed at the line of twelve cars waiting behind me in line as I tried to pay for parking. I had to open the door, step out, and slide the ticket in (the wrong way the first time).

I had to run to the credit union, pull up farther than the expanding drawer at the teller window, only to have the sheet of paper with my notes blow out, never to be found. I circled the parking lot twice.

Then, picking up a migraine prescription, I had to step out of the van at the drive up window. That lady thought I was gonna rob her. "No worries, I just can't roll down my window." Someday this will all be funny, but not so much today.

February 26, 2014
This was my second time seeing the dermatologist, and I am scheduled to have a minor surgery on my neck next week. I just have to say, these nurses and doctors have been incredibly kind and encouraging to me. I tell ya, you share a little of your "story" and make heartfelt eye contact, you

get words like, "You are a strong woman." These words have made me feel encouraged. My last dermatologist (twelve years ago), called to say, "You have cancer" and hung up. What a difference. I also know I have to have this done before Dan's insurance coverage is gone when the divorce is final.

Speaking of insurance, I'm trying to make sure the kids and I get covered under Medicaid. This process is grueling. I know it shouldn't be easy, but I am college educated and capable. Why do they make it so hard for me? I need to make sure we are covered. Danny is supposed to keep the kids insured, but until he has a steady job, I just can't rely on that. I'm also trying to get food assistance. I may as well give them my left arm to make that happen. I'm not making any of this up, people, I can't afford food! It's humbling, but I never thought I would be here. We are safe, though. We will be fine.

March 4, 2014

There are eleven stitches up the right side of my neck, but the skin cancer is gone. I'm good to go. Dad brought me and sat with me while they did a biopsy, and now we're going to get some lunch. Time with him is the best! And just the two of us is rare these days! We went to a local favorite diner for old times' sake. He's been my rock my whole life, but with all of this divorce and financial stuff now, too. I don't know how I'd do it without him!

March 7, 2014

The kids and I had one last spin in the Sierra. I decided we would just take it to the dealership, Dad followed behind in his truck. When we found my salesman, I handed him the keys and said, "I am doing a voluntary repossession. I don't need you to come track me down, here you go."

I hadn't been driving it for months anyway. It was parked next to the garage. I know it was the right thing to do. I don't want to wait for them to come take it away like we experienced with the trailer. That was heartbreaking.

Since Danny stopped payment on it months ago, I knew they'd be coming soon. The $600 payment was ridiculous, anyway, but Danny said we could swing it. Not so much. Someday I'll have another truck. I will.

March 9, 2014
One of the greatest achievements of a mom is asking her ten-year-old son to hop out and move his basketball so it doesn't get run over, only then to honk the horn and scare the absolute melons out of him.

I have to laugh when I can these days. There are so many ups and downs these past ten plus years. Nothing like a good belly laugh.

March 12, 2014
Today has been so bittersweet. *I am officially divorced.* Hard to believe.

I was pulling out of school when I got the call from my attorney. I had to pull over and collect my thoughts. I found myself looking into the rearview mirror, doing some self-talk.

"Well Charly, it's over. You did it. It's time to heal. It's time..."

This process has been so stressful. I knew it wouldn't be easy, but wow. There were very few ups and a lot of downs. I'm so glad it's over. I know, in my heart, this was the right thing. I had to let go of all of the pain. I had to get out. *We* had to get out. Bitter, bitter stuff, but then, so sweet. I'm actually single again. That's a strange, yet liberating thought.

March 15, 2014
Something I never thought I'd have to do, I did today. I had to file for bankruptcy. Before we got married, I had perfect credit. I had the first money in our joint bank account, and never had a late payment or balance on a credit card. I know when you get married you have debt. Of course, we had some debt. The retirement savings that Danny took from would have still been growing if it was left alone. Danny used that to pay down debt. Great. I thought we had gotten ourselves out of a lot of the debt. I knew we still had some.

In these past six months with all of this stress, looking over bank accounts, credit card statements and all? I am blown away with the nearly $62,000 in debt we are in. Sixty-two thousand dollars? And I have to say "we" because despite most of it being name brand expensive golf clubs, expensive tools, hunting equipment, expensive steak dinners, booze, dating websites and all, it's still in *my* name. I didn't know. I had *no* idea. It's not my stuff! And I have not benefited from any of it. But unless I filed bankruptcy, I'd owe nearly $31,000. *I don't have a job.* Getting the child/spousal support has been excruciating - all of it has been. This is not my fault. I'm just, ABSOLUTELY furious.

It will take me forever before I can get on my feet. How will we get a place to live? My credit is gone. I can't get a credit card to help pay for clothing for the kids or life in general. He left me with nothing. Literally. This isn't a game; this is real life. All of it...gone.

Positive note: I do like our bankruptcy lawyer, he's a good guy. He's been really helpful up to this point. Dad hasn't been feeling very good but insisted on coming with me to the appointment to file for Chapter 11. So we made a deal. After the appointment, he'd go get checked out at the hospital. But, typical Dad, he didn't want to wait around the Emergency Room, so we went on home.

March 17, 2014
Today was a pretty typical Monday, or so it seemed. Kids had school and I was Googling houses for rent in the area. We drove quite a ways north of town and passed a cute house. The kids and I decided we didn't want to be that far out of town. We headed back towards home but stopped first for a gallon of milk. That's when I got the call.

I had to pull over. Mom took Dad down to the ER to check for pneumonia. After some scans and wait time, they got the news. Dad has Stage 4 lung cancer.

Wait, what? What we thought was pneumonia or a bad cold *was lung cancer?* I think deep down, he had a feeling. That's why he didn't want to get checked sooner. I don't know that I heard much else right then. The tears fell like rain. I collected my thoughts, wiped each eye, and told the kids who were sitting with quiet anticipation in the backseat.

"Guys, Papa has cancer again."

My heart broke into a million pieces.

"Put your hope in Me, and My unfailing Love will rest upon you. Some of My children have forgotten how to hope. They have been disappointed so many times that they don't want to risk being let down again. So they forge ahead stoically-living mechanically. Other people put their hope in problem solving, medical treatments, the stock market, the lottery, and so on. But I challenge you to place your hope fully in Me" (Jesus Today: Experience Hope Through His Presence by Sarah Young).

March 19, 2014

I wish I had a recording of tonight's bedtime routine. Lying here, relatively helpless, I listened as Anna called out, "Goodnight everyone!" before turning out the hall light. DK responded with a boastful deep voice, "Goooood night!" Anna, yanked he didn't use his normal voice, marched into the boys' room. Ten minutes later, they are still disputing from their respective rooms, across the dark house, how you are supposed to say goodnight like Mom. Priceless.

Lord Almighty, I am having a hard time putting together my thoughts, my prayers to You. You know me in the depths of my heart. I am not sure why at this point, why this is so. You have gifted me with an incredible, earthly father. One who has been my best friend my whole life that I can remember. I need You, Lord, You to hold me, hold us up. I pray You would heal him, if it Your Will. That You would guide these decisions for treatment and all. Please Lord, PLEASE have mercy on us.

Chapter 29

March 21, 2014

I had one of those memorable things happen while watching Anna, so little in the dark staircase, telling me she hopes Papa's cancer is gone by next year. Actually, that it's gone by this fall. She wishes he didn't have it at all. She told me she prays while she's at school. Awe, just six-years-old.

Pete had water come out of his nose and mouth because he thought something funny coming out of the bathroom tonight. I cried telling DK of how I talk to Papa every day and I can't imagine not doing that. These are hard, hard times.

Praying, hoping, trusting God to heal him. *What comes next? Please Lord, heal him. We're clinging to hope...*

March 22, 2014

Dad gave me the courage to file for divorce. He helped me wallpaper this very room I'm sitting in, twice. He and I have our inside jokes, our nicknames. He has always been the one who gives me advice, talks me through doing my taxes and discipline for the kids. He taught me how to drive, mow grass, laugh at life, and drink coffee. He is where I get my "thick" legs and long toes from. He taught me how to budget and what's most important is the *time* you spend with those you love, not money. He's shown that in how he lives. I'm geared the exact same way.

He is my sounding board, my confidant, my humor, and the one person who truly gets me. He told me in Arizona, one time, that we are the same, except, I wear a bra. I want to make him proud of me. I want to live my life how he and I see it. *Why Lord, why now? Why him? It could be anyone else, so, why him?*

I am really struggling with how I could live a day here without him. I keep flashing to his funeral in my mind and the tears pouring out. I don't want to, but my mind can't help but go there. How can I be all that my own kids need right now when their whole world is upside down, too? How can I give them the mom I long to be with these thoughts?

So I tell myself that I need to trust God. He is in control. Then, I waiver and plead with Him to keep Dad here, for me, for my kids!!! *Please Lord, please keep him here. Help me to cope. Help me to be a strong mom. Help Lord, HELP.*

March 30, 2014

Today, Dan was trying to talk to me about not having any clean dishes, and having to wait an hour for the dishwasher and about his lack of space in his apartment because of all his furniture. He knows full well he broke the dishwasher at home years ago, making me do dishes by hand. And the fact that he left us without furniture. He's just trying to get a rise. I don't know why he feels this is all fun and games. I guess, shame on me for getting upset.

Praying for answers in the coming week for Dad. I'm scared, wanting and yearning for good news. *Please Lord, I pray he won't get a "timeframe" or anything like that. Heal him. Make him healthy on the inside. My heart is in my stomach, constantly in wait.*

April 1, 2014

After my quick job interview last week for a daycare center, I found out I got hired. Finally, I have a job, albeit part time! I can pick up more shifts as I go. The biggest perk is that I can bring all three kids with me to work. I am so thankful. I can't call on Mom and Dad right now to babysit, and

DK isn't old enough to stay home with his bro and sis. This is honestly the best case scenario.

If Danny would be made to pay what he owes in arrears for child and spousal support, then I think we'd be just fine with part-time pay. I'm going to keep looking for full time, though. I know I need full time. But over the summer and all, this will be good. I'm super excited! This will be good! For now, we will make it work.

April 2, 2014

Lately, I've been letting Danny in a little more. He claims to care about Dad and me, and he even hugged me on Sunday. Our conversations have been fine. Tonight I filled him in on Dad's biopsy today, and then the topic of child support came up. He got a letter stating he did not pay me spousal support in February and only paid half to me in March.

He wasn't really happy and he told me to write a letter saying he had paid me. I said I wouldn't. He was angry, wondering why they would even question if he paid me or not. I told him they have my bank account information, and maybe they saw it there. He proceeded to tell me he just didn't understand because he's done all that he can and has paid me. I brought up that through February and March, the amounts were incorrect, that he didn't put the correct amounts in the bank, so I had to go back repeatedly to check and see if I had money in my account.

They even know me by name at the bank because I have to go in there so much. Danny would put in $31 here and $15 there. The court saw that the amounts were not accurate, and yet he's calling *me* to write a letter on his behalf. *Are you kidding?*

He said, "I can't believe you right now. I can't believe what you are saying to me! I have done everything in my power to get you your money every time." Then it was silent, but I could hear him rumbling about me under his breath, so I hung up on him. I was shaking but managed to put up my right hand and smack it with my left. "Way to go Charly, way to go." My own high-five.

April 8, 2014

I had my last appointment with my therapist today. Now that I am on Medicaid, I can't afford seeing her anymore. It's a bummer. I've surely grown fond of her and learned to trust enough to open up. She typically just sits and listens while I cry the whole time. I've moved past feeling embarrassed or apologizing for it. Today she told me she's proud of me, that I'm strong, and I will be just fine. She also told me that I definitely have PTSD. She encouraged me to find another therapist that will accept my insurance. I'll work on that. It just took so long to get to this point with her.

Anyways, I always thought Post Traumatic Stress Disorder was only for folks in the military? But as she explained it, it isn't. And it fits some of my reactions to seemingly simple things. The abuse I endured? It was traumatic. My tears and fears? I have PTSD. Wow.

April 14, 2014

I thought it'd be a great idea just to get away, get outta dodge for a few nights over spring break. I think I left my patience at the bank, where I also forgot to get my debit card out of the ATM.

I drove a few hours east, all excited, only to check into the hotel and not have my debit card. All I had on me was some cash. I could have croaked on the spot, but we managed all weekend. It was a waterpark/hotel deal, so Anna was happy as a fish. The boys too, but they wore tired of it quicker. We ate out, and I lost my patience a few times because sharing a hotel room with three kids is not overly relaxing. They fought over who slept where, what to eat, what to watch on TV. Whoever slept with me kicked me all night. I had to endure snoring Anna and early riser DK, but alas, we did it. Not that we'll do that again, but we did it.

Mom and Dad headed to Cleveland Clinic yesterday with UB and Aunt Gene. Dad tried calling me last night and texting me with no response. He got nervous, so he called his neighbor to come look for me. That neighbor drove up and down our road searching for me. My phone was simply charging and on vibrate. Here he is, so sick and still did all that for me? Again, this man is my hero.

April 18, 2014

We wanted to camp tonight. We even drove out to a campground close by, but they are still closed for the season. What were we to do but set up in our backyard, only to find we are missing stakes and the poles are dorked. With a side caving in, we came inside to eat some supper. All of a sudden I hear, "Mom! The tent blew away!" Ah, oh well. It's the thought that counts.

April 20, 2014

It's Easter today. This year, the truth about Easter is hitting me really hard. I have never done the Easter baskets and eggs with our kids. Danny's mom does it, so I guess part of me felt it would be redundant. As kids, we always had Easter baskets, matching dresses, photo ops; it was a huge deal. Maybe there is a part of me that's just rebelling against those traditions?

But what Easter *really* means? I am so humbled. And Good Friday is sobering. Jesus died on that cross for me, for all of us. He died for *our* sins and transgressions. He did that for us? To really think that through makes me so grateful and literally brings me to my knees. He did that for us. Easter isn't about dresses, bonnets, and peanut butter eggs (although delicious); it's about what Jesus has done for us. It's that simple and that complicated. *Praise Him. He is Risen indeed.*

April 23, 2014

I started authoring Dad's CancerCare page today. This way we can keep family and friends updated on how he's doing and track his cancer journey. I hope this is a helpful tool and a way to reach others.

He has been in the hospital since Monday morning and looks forward to being discharged tomorrow. He's having some heavy chemo they call, "ICE." When they went to Cleveland Clinic last week, they were told to follow this protocol. We want to make sure they do it right this time! The first two times Dad went rounds with lung cancer, were very frustrating and unnecessary. We found out the first time that the chemo they used was outdated. How can a doctor even make that mistake? Then twenty months later, the cancer was back. Both times then it was contained at Stage 1.

Now, It's all over his body. *Stage 4.* Hard to even say those words without my voice quivering.

April 25, 2014
Mom told me she's waiting for the in-home nurse to come and show her how to care for Dad's picc line in his right arm. That's where they give him the *juice,* as he calls it, instead of a port in his chest this time. The kids still get a kick out of his "gunshot wound" scars on his chest (where his ports were the last time). I'm praying Dad gets some of his much needed rest. He's up so much in the night with night sweats and a gut ache. I know he wishes it was a gut ache from late night Velveeta and Triscuit snacking, but that's not the case these days.

April 26, 2014
In all of the running for baseball and soccer to the fields, Papa came to see Anna play soccer today. The *highlight* of the day. He said he'd be there, and he even had a fancy ride in a wheelchair being pushed by Grace and Mom. Grace has been here non-stop. She's so selfless and would be an incredible nurse. She would have loved to have been, but with all of the knee surgeries, lifting is too hard. Either way, what a wonderful gift for all of them being there today. So much love.

"Today will never come again. Be a blessing. Be a friend. Encourage someone. Take time to care. Let your words heal, and not wound" (Life After Love devotional online).

April 27, 2014
I'm glad Dad had a decent day today. He got out of the house earlier, on his own, and tonight, stayed up late chatting with Grace and me. She is going to stay one more night, then head back to Frankfort in the morning. Her heart is here; she's been so helpful.

I'm enjoying the new job; the other ladies are really nice. Some pay more attention to their phones than the kids, but that's every job these days. It's so frustrating. We don't get paid to stand around and chat! We're watching kids! It's not many of them, really only two. The high school kids are amazing, picking up shifts and are fun to work with. It's just pretty obvious who's here for the right reasons. Those seem to be the people I connect with best, people who get it; those who were raised as I was - to "keep my nose clean and do the job I'm getting paid to do." I'm thankful to have a paycheck coming in.

April 30, 2014

I haven't had a chance to talk to Dad these past few days. He's been extremely weak. He went to the hospital for blood work again, and they started loading him up with fluids and platelets. They had to stop because he had a slight fever.

A tremendous blessing for Dad today was the boat dock going in. The boat will go in the lake tomorrow. I'm thinking Dad seeing them both in the water will raise his spirits. His smile remains. He's true to who he is even in these circumstances. I just admire that strength he has. I know it comes from above.

I'm praying that Danny will take his parenting time. It's not just about me needing a break. Sometimes, I want him to be a dad. I know I can't *make* it happen, I just want it. And I don't want to worry about it. Why does this have to be a battle? It's all uphill it seems. He owes me so much in child support and time with the kids. It makes me so angry.

The boys opted to start out in my bed tonight. It was hilarious walking them up to theirs. Pete couldn't walk straight and kept asking me, "Are you sure we need to go where instead?" I kept having him repeat it. First because it made no sense, then because it cracked me up. DK simply followed behind us on the steps with a terrified, sleepy look. Added bonus? My sheets are still warm.

Chapter 30

May 1, 2014

Dad was taken by ambulance in the middle of the night. His fever got super high, and they said to go to the ER. He's been admitted (not committed - he'd like that joke).

I got a chance to talk to him, and his voice sounded stronger than it has in over a week. He's a tad frustrated with the hospital because he doesn't know what is going on. But for me, I *love* to hear him rant about how he doesn't know, "who's on first, who's batting..." because that's who he is. He told me he took a dump this morning, and it reminded him of me. It makes me smile and tear up about how he continues to make light of this whole situation.

This makes the hill I'm climbing with Danny seem so small. *Oh Lord, please keep Dad safe and heal him! Please bring Mom and all of us rest. This has been a hard one to swallow. This is a hard season right now. One foot in front of the next. I am back to taking life one moment at a time.*

May 2, 2014

I talked to Grace a bit ago, and she informed me Dad has a blood clot in his arm near his picc line. My mind instantly went back to seven years ago when he had a clot in his neck and lied to me, or as he saw it, protected me.

He had been to the doctor that day, and then we met for lunch downtown at our usual spot. It was close to his office and just a short walk from my trade school. We liked meeting there. On that occasion, I managed to dump my coffee all over before we ate. Dad still mocks me about that. "Want a little coffee with your creamer?"

I asked him what the doctor said and he said everything was fine When Dad told me what the doctor said, he promised everything was fine. Later that night, I overheard him talking to Mom about it in the kitchen. They found a clot in his neck. I was so mad, so yanked. Looking back now, I know he just didn't want me to worry, but I do anyway, even though know worrying doesn't add a moment to my life, and isn't worth it.

Dad's lost forty pounds in recent weeks. For a guy who's weighed the same forever, forty pounds is a lot. He looks good in the face, though, and his humor is right on cue. When leaving his hospital room today, I looked around at the room and the white board on the wall said his nurses were *Grace* and *Charlotte*. This brought a big smile.

I am constantly amazed at how much better DK, Pete, and Anna are doing with this than me. They are encouraging, loving, and hopeful. I need to model them and their behavior. I wish it was as simple as that.

May the 4th be with you (I like that joke), 2014
Dad has been, and will be, in the hospital for a while. These past few days haven't been good for him. He had that whole blood clot thing. His fever keeps coming back, and he needs platelets. I'm praying for rest for him, a feverless night in the hospital, and the food to taste better than barf. When I saw him today, the first thing I noticed was his upper lip.

I haven't seen that in sixteen years, since his second go round with chemo. He decided to shave off his mustache today because it was falling out. He looks younger! He offered Anna a Sharpie to draw it back on.

May 5, 2014
Dad is hoping to shave his head today. My kids have been telling people how Papa looks so different now without a mustache. I'm sure a bald, non-'stache Papa will bring them a lot of funny jokes. Papa wouldn't have it any other way. I did hear that today wasn't good for him. Mom said he

has the shakes and a rash. They are trying to get to the bottom of it. He is delirious, talking as if he were back at work. My heart is broken. I'm praying he will get past this. He's so strong, so how can he be delirious? It seems impossible; he's always seemed unbreakable. This strong man is weak, so weak. How can this be?

May 6, 2014
Dad had a seizure. Mom called me in the middle of the night. He's being moved to the ICU. He is seizing again. Mom just called. It's really scary. I'm headed down to the hospital as soon as the kids are off to school. I'm dressed in my work uniform; thankful someone is covering my shift.

Oh Lord, please please get him through this. We can't lose him.

May 6, 2014 (later on)
He's incoherent. I walked in, bawled at the site, went into the hallway to gather myself, walked back in and said, "Hey (one of our many nicknames we used on each other)." He opened his eyes a crack and then closed them again. He's been super fidgety, too.

Please Lord. Lord, we need some smiles out of this day. He is resting more comfortably now. His arms and legs had been moving non-stop all day. He's so frustrated but can't communicate. He's very agitated when he feels he needs to use the restroom and keeps trying to get out of bed. Grace and I and other family stood on either side of him to hold him down and talk him through what's going on. Just watching Dad's siblings and our whole family come together to do everything they can, has been so powerful.

Grace packed up her belongings and decided that she is moving in with Mom and Dad. She wants to be here, to be here for doctor's appointments, medication tracking, all of it. She is so amazing. This will be so good for Mom and Dad. She gets things done and with that comes peace in her ability to manage it all.

"We have small troubles for a while now, but they are helping us gain an eternal glory that is much greater than the troubles. We set our eyes not on what we see but on what we cannot see. What we see will last only a short

time, but what we cannot see will last forever" 2 Corinthians 4:16-18 (NIV One Year Bible).

May 7, 2014

Dad had a restful night last night, so that's a blessing. Apparently when they came in to check him and ask his name, one time he answered, "Fred." That there, is a good sign.

Gracious Father in Heaven, You continue to provide for us! Thank you for keeping Dad here a while longer, however that amount of time will be. We are grateful for these victories. Please help me as I continue in this battle with Danny. I pray for enough, for fairness, for calm. For sleep and safety.

May 8, 2014

As I walked into Dad's hospital room tonight, I anticipated an improvement from the texts and emails I received today, but wow, it was way better than expected! Right away, Dad said, "Hi Charly!" and we carried on a conversation. It was the best feeling in the world. Dad was back. I even got a chuckle or two out of him, which is a favorite sight and sound.

They brushed his teeth for him, lubed him up with chapstick, to which he joked about having cherry red lips. I hung out a bit until he dozed off, for which Mom and I looked at each other and smiled. When he stirred awake, he opened his eyes, looking right at me and stuck his tongue out.

He's getting there. Baby steps. This was a huge step back, but boy, the power of prayer! So many folks have been praying him through. It's incredible to see the results of prayer right in front of our eyes. *We pray and seek You, Lord! In these moments, we know You are present.*

May 9, 2014

Seeing Dad today sure brought a smile. He was sitting up in the recliner in his room, attempting to eat "two pieces of burnt bread glued together," aka hospital grilled cheese. Even the applesauce tasted like gravel. So he did what anyone would do, started showing us how, if he put his fingers through his hair, it fell right out. Therefore, he had to put his hair in the applesauce. Just to make Mom and Aunt Gene gag. Hilarious! He just sat back and laughed.

Soon after, the oncology nurse came in and shaved his head; no more hair to get put into food or stuck to his pillow. Well, I can't account for his nose hairs, but he said they are holding strong in there. He's a trooper, I tell ya. He manages to smile and chuckle with his one-liners. I'm so glad his MRI came back CLEAR too!

May 11, 2014
Mom told me this amazing story, and I just had to jot it down. Her and Dad stopped to get gas earlier today, and Mom was having some trouble with the pump. The fella nearby, also pumping gas, told her he had issues, too, but that it eventually worked.

Mom got the pump going, and this man offered to wash the windows on her car. She said sure, and while doing so, he caught sight of Dad in the front passenger seat. He asked if he could pray with them. They then joined hands and prayed. They had ever met this man before, and he said he was from Texas, so they'd probably never see him again.

Incredible Lord. What a gift from You!

Another gift is a friend (whose son is friends with Pete) who offered to counsel the kids and I for free. I am feeling so grateful! The kids could use someone to talk to besides me, who can guide and encourage them. There really aren't any words. Amazing.

May 12, 2014
The kiddos and I stopped over to see Mom, Dad, and Grace around suppertime. Dad was sitting in his recliner with a smile, and we had great conversation. We ate supper together, all of us, and shared laughs, recent baseball stories, and watched the kids play out by the dock. Dad was in excellent spirits, and we all basked in being able to see him, hear him, and spend quality time with him. This was one of the best Mother's Day gifts I've ever gotten.

May 14, 2014
I've had the pleasure of talking to Mom and Dad a few times today, via phone or text, and all is well. Dad is having another weak day, but this is

just what his oncologist at the, "Shiny Moron Building," as Dad calls it, predicted. No matter what though, Dad wanted to see the boys playing baseball. I sent him some videos I had taken just for him. There he sat watching them, over and over, smiling and saying, "It wasn't as good as being there, but a close second."

May 17, 2014

I think we all need to feel wanted, like we matter, to someone; be it our husband, a friend, just someone who gets us, and explains when it doesn't feel right, who comforts us, and knows us so well. We want to feel "gotten." I think I'm being forced to learn even more about myself. I can feel Dad's and my relationship changing. He's changing. I need to deal with it, and it's really hard. I want to cling to his words but then struggle that it isn't the conversations like we've had for thirty-six years. Am I selfish because I feel this way? I feel so alone.

"Be merciful to me, God; be merciful to me because I come to You for protection. Let me hide under the shadow of Your wings until the trouble has passed" Psalm 57:1 (NCV Mom's Bible, God's Wisdom for Mothers).

May 21, 2014

Dad had another good day! We got to see him tonight. He came to Anna's soccer game, sat in the passenger seat of his truck, and caught the game from a front row parking spot. That old saying, "Where there's a will, there is a way - He is living proof.

He goes before the transplant board tomorrow. I'm praying all goes well. There are so many unanswered questions, so much we still don't know yet. How does this work? When will it happen and where? What are the chances it works?

"The Lord himself goes before you and will be with you; he will never leave or forsake you. Do not be afraid; do not be discouraged" Deut 31:8 (NIV One Year Bible).

May 22, 2014

Dad, Dad, Dad... He had a good day and even managed to come cheer the boys on at their baseball game. The fresh air, Dad cheering for the boys, talking to them through the fence of the dugout, and smiling, made the evening memorable, like a dream.

Grace asked if he was glad he didn't take the walker (he was wheelchair bound), and he said had he not had a three-hour meeting before the transplant board, he still may have been able to use the walker. Whatever mode of transportation, we were just glad to see him energized enough to be able to be out.

The way that Dad makes us a priority is incredible. Here he is feeling weak, fighting fevers, and needing sleep, yet he makes it to these games, and Danny doesn't. It's hard for me to reconcile how someone could be ok with missing so much of their own children's lives? This is their passion, their time to learn and shine, and we need to encourage it. I pray Danny's heart will open up, that he will learn and be the dad these kiddos deserve.

May 26, 2014
What a wonderful day! Dad has had another few good ones in a row! Boat rides, visiting with people, being mobile on his own two feet around the house - what a blessing of strength. The kids and I are camping in Mom and Dad's backyard in our new tent I found on clearance for sixty dollars! What do you know, it has all of the stakes and poles too! We got limited sleep but a fun camping experience just the same. If we can't camp with Mom and Dad, we'll camp close by. Crazy kids.

"Do not let your hearts be troubled. Trust in God, and trust in Me" John 14:1 (NCV Mom's Bible, God's Wisdom for Mothers).

May 28, 2014
The kids and I ran up to visit Dad after my church softball game tonight. He lit right up in the hospital room recliner at the sight of the kids' faces. The evening sun was shining in his corner room windows. He had his IV pole sitting there next to him as the chemo kept plugging away. Dad shared that his insurance and hospital are still in discussions as to whether or not to let him have the transplant here in Grand Rapids. Praying they will allow him to stay here, by family and friends to help support him and my mom. This insurance fiasko is such a racket.

May 29, 2014
"... find Me in every situation" (Jesus Calling by Sarah Young).

I need to focus on this, finding *me* in every situation. Wow, *truth*. I'm working on this. I have been feeling so grateful for time with Dad as he fights this fight. I am trying, *Lord, to seek you in every moment*. I'm still struggling with trusting Danny when he has the kids, and when he's constantly belittling me over text or email. I'm trying to stand strong, but I still feel so weak.

I have seen the Lord's Hands in this with Dad. And I am so glad to be out of my marriage. I'm better equipped to let go of what Danny says or does, as much as it hurts, because I am not responsible for him anymore. He doesn't reflect me. I can see Dad staying strong, he's truly finding the Lord in each situation. I need to model his outlook and try my best to rise above all the rest of this stuff...

June 1, 2014
Dad continues to put others first, make people chuckle and encourage them. I respect him with everything I have, and I admire him so much. He continues to be an example, even with all of this garbage going on.

He even made it to Anna's soccer game. He's amazing.

June 2, 2014
Dad has gained nine pounds! That's a really good sign. Like he's always said, he has a lot of time and money invested in his gut. Food is starting to have a taste again. It doesn't all taste like metal. He's still dealing with the insurance people, and it's so stressful. This is not what he needs, like, not at all.

Although, it's so good to see him wide eyed, smiling, and laughing, to chat with him on the phone, and run life's day-to-day thoughts by him like we always have. I had a pretty awesome talk with Anna tonight about prayer and how to pray. We prayed for strength and enough energy to get him through these upcoming days.

Earlier, while trying to get groceries, thinking that our food assistance should be available for the month, my card got declined. I stood in that grocery checkout line with hands full of basic necessities but not enough money of my own to cover what I thought assistance would. I had to leave the groceries there, all of them, right there.

I'm not sure I've ever been quite as humbled and embarrassed as in that very moment.

I know there are lessons, even in these times, Lord. May I lean into You so I can learn. I will have to wait until funds are reloaded on my card and go back for groceries then. We have enough to get us by for a few days.

June 7, 2014
It's my birthday. I'm thirty-seven today. With the past couple of years, I feel more like ninety-six years old. I got Dad laughing about the possible skin cancer on my backside. It is the greatest sight to see Dad, leaning forward, eyes shut tightly, holding his stomach because he's laughing so hard. It's the *best* medicine and gift.

June 11, 2014
Dad continues to amaze us. He was able to come watch baseball and soccer wrap up tonight. He used the walker. I caught him walking next to the walker at one point. I think he wants the kids to see him strong and independent, no matter the cost. I kept thanking him for coming to the kids' games, but I know it means so much more to him than anyone.

He loves being outside, being mobile, and being able to be a part of the action. He looked and sounded really good today. Good days are amazing gifts from the Lord. It's refreshing to have just a glimpse of something normal. It helps me forget this heaviness. *I'm still wondering, Lord, what lessons are you teaching us? Help me to see clearly.*

June 13, 2014
Sounds like Dad's insurance won't let him have the stem cell transplant here. We are all really upset and frustrated about it but need to cling to hope that he'll be fine, even if far away from home. It's not what we were

hoping for. How far away will they have to go? For how long? I just want him to get better so they can come back. Maybe we can go wherever they end up just to visit for like a weekend. We'll have to be healthy though, for his sake. We will miss them like crazy. I feel heavy-hearted when they leave for Arizona. This is less than ideal, for all of us.

June 15, 2014

I'm so thankful that on this Father's Day we got to spend the day on the boat with Mom and Dad. He didn't even need the walker today!

Dad has never been a fan of any day celebrating him. But we are, maybe not through gifts, but time. Just having time is the best gift we could have right now. It surely puts a lot in perspective.

June 17, 2014

Dad had some bone marrow extracted today from his hip. He's tough, but it hurt so bad. It sounds like he'll have to travel a long way to have the bone marrow transplant. It's so hard to think of him leaving and being that far away, having to find a place to stay for all of that time. I am grateful that this clinic won't be as far as some of the alternatives.

June 18, 2014

I think I usually write the most about Dad at bedtime because I can't fall asleep thinking of him. We had a great visit today, sharing laughs. The kids got Dad chuckling over an impression of a mannequin. We talked about everything under the sun, and he admitted he wishes he was coming along camping with us. We told him he is in spirit and that we'll "blow up his phone" with pictures and tell all of where we are.

There aren't many camping trips for the kids and me that haven't included Mom and Dad. For goodness sake, they drove twelve hours last year to surprise Pete on his ninth birthday when we were camping! They've also kept Anna with them so we could camp easier, just the four of us, when she was a baby. I tell ya what, we look forward to camping next year with Dad! We will go again, we just need him healthy and able.

Chapter 31

June 19, 2014

The kiddos and I are ready to head camping! The van is loaded to the max; I can't see out the back window. Praying we'll be safe and have fun!

June 22, 2014

We are home and *that* was memorable. Not for all of the right reasons... These are the lessons I picked up on this time around, my first time taking the kids tent camping, alone, far from home:

1. Falling off a bike doesn't feel like it did twenty-five years ago. My entire left side feels like someone took a baseball bat to it.
2. People you meet at a campground are nice people.
3. Kids who have a pyro for a mom will most likely dink with the fire pit too.
4. Walking twelve campsites to the bathroom was fun, until the fourth day. Then it's nice to have one right up the stairs, minus dead bugs and a tp holder that falls on your right shoulder because the cleaning lady had just changed the rolls but didn't close the Georgia Pacific toilet paper holder all the way.
5. Rain the morning you leave, in a tent, makes for a messy clean-up. This calls for a temporary pack job that awaits the clothesline at home. Only to then have to figure out how to fit it into the mini-sized bag it came in. Kids don't know how not to fight when in a small tent or outside where all the other campers can hear.

6. Being a single mom, taking your kids camping, and getting sick is tough. The kids want to do things like eat, play, and run down sand dunes, so you stay in the minivan and watch, camera lens on full zoom.

7. When your electrical box is opposite your screen tent, you make due and cook your pancakes in the grass fifteen feet away and just smile, because what else can you do in that moment?

8. Bogs are great for wearing on the beach. Especially when your ten-year-old says the water is so cold "you will get hypothernmia."

9. When a family settles in across the road and are all "kumbaya" with each other, mom and dad huggy, kids obeying, you need to realize they aren't you. You are doing this the best you can, you get after your kids and they hear you, and you know what? That's reality.

10. Meltdowns in jammies and sweaty-tent-bedhead are ok. Really.

11. It's ok to be as angry as I was with the kids for picking out a Peanut Butter *Snickers* instead of a Peanut Butter *Twix* at the gas station. It wasn't about the Twix, but they didn't understand that.

I think my handy list covers most of it, except for the other details around the bike incident that I don't want to forget. I left my wallet in the van by accident as we boarded the ferry to the island. I tried not to panic. I have a hundred dollars in my pocket.

We get to the island and decide to rent bikes. It was fun until someone (they each blame each other) stomped on the brakes. I was busy looking off to my right, and didn't see that they had stopped abruptly... I smack the brakes and head over handlebars like a sack of bricks. There was nothing graceful about it at all. Everything went white.

I just sat there. I was embarrassed and sore while a whole slew of folks rode on by. I got my bearings and pulled the bike off to the side of the road, terrified it was damaged because I didn't have money with me to fix it. Fortunately, it was fine, but I wasn't.

We headed into town so I could find a restroom. I ended up on a back stairwell at some place, nearly passing out. I didn't know where I was. Only thing I knew was my kids were waiting for me outside, alone. There happened to be an off-duty paramedic passing me on the steps and asked me if I was alright. He led me to a table and got me a glass of water. I was so worried about the kids, so he went to get them for me and called 9-1-1.

Shockingly, that teeny island has a hospital. I declined treatment (partly because I didn't know if I had Medicaid yet) and just sat until I got my head on straight. It was all sorts of wacky. We didn't do much more on the island except wait for the ferry to get us so we could ride back to the campground. The bugs were everywhere, the kids were trying to be compassionate, but they're kids, and kids can be *dinks*. So, they were dinks, and my patience was shot.

We made the best of it - I yelled too much, and I felt too sick to do much else.

June 28, 2014
I had some great, typical conversations with Dad again today. I'm so glad! We see the world the same way. He gets me, again! As he says, we solved the world's problems. He has a way of making me feel strong and independent; like I can do this, I can take on a new day. Like my Heavenly Father does, he gives me strength to make it another day no matter what is thrown at me. Even if it's hard moments from Danny, or lack of patience with the kids. I am feeling good. I have some bounce in my step again.

"But the people who trust the Lord will become strong again. They will rise up as an eagle in the sky; they will run and not need rest; they will walk and not become tired" Isaiah 40:31 (NCV Mom's Bible, God's Wisdom for Mothers).

July 2, 2014
We had an opportunity to see Mom, Dad, and Grace before they leave for the clinic today. It's DK's birthday and Papa wanted to see the birthday boy. Despite Dad still having a lingering fever, he laughed, he teased and ate at the table with us. It's always good to see and something we take for

granted. He texted a bit ago that they made it to the "dump inn" near the clinic. He said there was a dead body removed from their room, and the Dateline crew was there already. He's hilarious. His appointment is tomorrow morning, and we're anxiously awaiting to hear what comes next.

July 5, 2014
Mom and Dad are back from the clinic and we spent most of the day with them. We watched the fireworks last night, just us. We reminisced about the old 4th of July gatherings they had hosted over the past fifteen to sixteen years. As the fireworks popped and lit up the sky, I just watched Dad's face. In the dark with glimmers of color as the firework show continued. He was so at peace. I felt so thankful to be sitting right next to him, watching his reactions and his smile.

Since we have been back home today, the kids have been fighting, Anna has insisted on being no less than four inches from me. DK asked me, while talking about dialysis, "Isn't that what Viagra is for?" Anna had to come downstairs after bedtime three times to insure light bulbs aren't filled with fire. This mama's job is never done.

July 12, 2014
Mom and Dad were very gracious and helped with the kids tonight while I had to work. They made cheeseburger lasagna. This is a favorite of Dad's, and we grew up with it. It's so fun to watch the kids learn some family recipes.

Dad was so sick but still managed to get on his feet and have the kids each do a job. He has so much patience for spills or "oopsy moves" by the kids. Dad has had a fever, feels puny, and his eyes say it all. The doctor said it would be a few weeks before he's feeling better.

"When you are suffering, your need for me is greater than ever. The more you choose to come near Me, affirming your trust in Me, the more you can find hope in My unfailing Love. You can even learn to be joyful while waiting in My Presence - where Joy abounds. Persevere in trusting Me, and I will eventually lift you up. Meanwhile, cast all your anxiety on Me, knowing that

I care for you affectionately and am watching over you continually" (Jesus Calling).

July 14, 2014
A few things we will surely miss about this house:

- my clothesline
- our awesome barn quilt
- the sound of traffic and birds while taking a nap with the windows open (but who has time for naps anymore? And the traffic, otherwise, *bites*)
- running my hands along the plaster bumpy walls while going down our narrow staircase
- the gigantic pocket door
- looking out the side window in Anna's room where I sat and rocked all three babies to sleep
- Dutch is buried here
- Dad saying every time he comes over and stands on my front porch, "an old lady died out here."

Things I won't miss:

- doors that don't shut all the way
- not having a bedroom or any privacy
- half painted walls and unfinished rooms all throughout the downstairs
- the traffic!
- Jake the snake living under our front porch
- having one bathroom
- the *no* closet thing...

July 21, 2014
Wow...that's the word. Wow. Dad went from sitting in the green recliner all day yesterday to walking down the steps and out onto the boat! We had a day filled with swimming in, as the kids call it, "the deep part." Dad was watching the kids swim with the biggest smile on his face. He would

typically be in the lake with them wrapped in a life jacket, but loved just watching from the captain's seat.

Prayer is carrying us through! Thank You, Lord, for granting Dad strength today that he hasn't had in two consecutive weeks. Such a gift, such amazing moments.

July 24, 2014

I texted Mom today to ask how Dad's blood work went. I got a response soon after saying, "First they tied a rubber band around Dad's upper arm, rubbed a vein with some alcohol, and then stuck a needle in the vein."

I wrote back, "Did Dad tell you to write that?"

To which he wrote "Nope, I wrote it." He never loses his sense of humor through all of this poking and prodding.

He's mentally tough, physically doing the best he can, and *loving* always. We are still waiting to see the specific date he'll head to the clinic for his transplant. When will that be?

July 27, 2014

We went to a pop-up summer carnival with Grace and Joe today. It was honestly nice to have a day where I didn't feel stressed about Danny, what comes next, Dad, or any of it. Afterwards, we stopped to see Mom and Dad and to tell them about our day. There sat Dad, as he always has, ready to hear every detail and share a laugh or expression when we are telling him all about it.

My whole life I've loved sharing with Mom and Dad. They listen so intently and want to know more. I now understand how, as a mom, that's hard to do. But they always have. It's a trait I really want to have with my kids. Be it they care what I'm talking about or not, they always listen. Dad is doing ok. I'm wondering when they will head to the clinic.

July 28, 2014

Found out today they will go to the clinic for his stem cell transplant on August 25th, Anna's seventh birthday. They'll be gone for seven weeks.

Maybe if he's up for it we can go see them on the weekends. That's not that far from here.

Dad watched Grace and Pete *row, row, row* their boat all the way around the lake tonight. Pete's $26 inflatable boat, that he bought with his birthday money, was a hit! Dad sat on the deck and watched with a big smile and would occasionally break into song. It's side-splitting hilarious! He's always done that. He'll hear something that reminds him of a song lyric, and he'll sing the song aloud.

After Grace and Pete got back from their epic floating journey, Dad started singing some old WWII song. I was teasing about how no one else has ever even heard that song before, but then Pete starts singing with him and finishes the verse!

July 29, 2014
We got home from running errands today to find the foreclosure notice taped to the storm door. I knew it'd be soon, but having it posted made my heart sink.

It's time. We need to leave this place.

I'm so grateful for UB and all of his work he's been doing to provide the kids and I with a rental house somewhere. I've called this very place home for thirteen years, the longest I've ever lived in a house. Dutch is buried out back, the grass is worn from the tire swing and where the boys play baseball. I've pulled every weed, moved bushes, spread mulch, mowed this very lawn so many times. It's like running my hands along the plaster; if I were blind, I'd know by the bumps right where I am. Every wall, every ding, every piece of trim I have repainted white. A piece of me is in this very place. Blood, sweat, tears were shed here, a lot of them in secret. We have to go now; we don't have a choice.

"Praising God is at the center of contentment. As we praise Him, we position ourselves toward God's face, not our circumstances" (Glynnis W.).

Chapter 32

August 1, 2014

Those family stickers on the back of cars we see all the time? Mine would be the mom pulling her hair out, two boy stick people punching each other, and a little girl with the words, "Stop it!" coming out of her mouth.

It's super cool that I had food assistance issues again at the store. I even called first to make sure funds were on the card. So, there I stood, with a cart full of groceries and the kids with me. I had to flag down a clerk, who had to basically go on the loudspeaker to tell everyone in a three-mile radius that I was having issues with my card. *Oye vey.* As if just doing the act of grocery shopping isn't stressful enough with three kids...

We finally got it working and my armpits were leaking through my shirt, I'm sure. I'm grateful for the help with buying groceries, but wow. Why in the world does it have to be this difficult!?

August 4, 2014

Last night, I'm sawing logs, and I hear, "Mom?"

"Huh?" I blurt out.

"Mom?"

I open my one eye to see Anna's shadow over me. "You scared the baloney outta me, Anna."

"Mom, what's in your hat?"

I look around the room half asleep and completely confused, and respond, "Nothing…"

"Ok," she says, and goes right back to bed.

August 15, 2014
I drove out to pick the boys up from Camp K today. The mess hall was filled with kids, parents, and bible songs. I was so filled with awe. This week DK and Pete just had, was amazing. They were with friends in a cabin, learning about Jesus, and getting filthy dirty. On our hour plus car ride home, they insisted on stopping to see Papa. I was so afraid DK would be homesick all week, I could hardly think of anything else. He doesn't like being away from home. Someone I work with gave me the idea to make each boy a notebook with pictures, fun stuff, and reminders of home. I knew Pete would be fine, though. He's pretty flexible and goes with the flow. Having each other there was a big help, too.

Their first thought when we got in the van was to go see Papa, so we did. We headed directly there to visit. Just sitting listening to Dad and my boys talk camp, bunk beds, Indians baseball, and all of the candy they ate, made my heart smile.

August 17, 2014
We spent the day at Mom and Dad's today. We watched old home movies, Dad pulled the kids tubing behind the boat, did some swimming, and we ordered Chinese food. It was a pretty great Sunday. We have to take these while we still can before they leave for the transplant and the weather cooperates like this.

In the morning, Dad will attempt for the 2,384th time to get ahold of his doctor to see if they need him to be there sooner for transplant. As much as we don't want him to leave, the sooner he does, the sooner he comes back, and prayerfully healthy. The kids and I got on our knees tonight and prayed for him. I kept thinking, "Where two or more are gathered…"

What will this two-month ordeal be like for Dad and Mom? *Lord, I lift to You, Dad, Mom with all that she faces, too, our whole extended family, for anxiety and stress to be turned over to You, for You have us all in the palm of Your Hands. All of the pain, pokes, prods, procedures, doctors, nurses, where to be when...all of it.*

August 19, 2014
Dad has decided to let go and give it over completely to the Lord. This whole waiting game on when, where, how, and phone tag is done. We're praying for good timing, the right timing.

It's so hard, yet it's comforting to know God is in control. I want it on my timeline, and I know Dad has, too. We all have prayed, but we need to wait. The story of our lives, the lesson we seem to practice: *patience.* I get to where I'm ok with waiting, but then in moments of doubt, those anxiety of just wanting to know comes up again. *Lord, in these fleeting moments, in these trying times, please give us patience to wait and just take life for what it is right now.*

August 20, 2014
I feel like I just floated through today, like my mind wasn't anywhere, just my body was. I think I got by like that at work. I feel emotionally exhausted, just plain tired in my soul. I can hardly hold my head up on my shoulders; it's so heavy. Even sleep isn't refilling my tank. How will I be able to function when I have to work full-time?

It's beyond exhausting. My soul aches. I need help, peace, and good rest.

August 22, 2014
All of this with Dad and Danny, with squeaking by with finances and patience, have brought about constant headaches and exhaustion unlike I've ever known before. Balancing momhood and full time employment seems impossible. I think this is what being "deep in the valley" is.

I'm in this space between the past and our future, my future. This time right now, I just don't know how to do it other than get by in survival mode. My mind won't turn off. I have feelings of thankfulness yet fear of the unknown. I can't sleep a whole night without my mind racing.

Some things are easier than others. There are mountains and valleys. I haven't had a mountain in a while; not a big one at least. I've had to climb, but I haven't had a mountain "high." I haven't had the feeling of elation, silly, hard-to-explain giddiness. I pray someday I will feel on top of a mountain, for me, for Charlotte, that I will be loved and in love. I pray that I will be able to look back at this valley of my life right now and be ever so grateful that I made it.

August 25, 2014

We had an awesome day today. Dad was able to cart himself over to the west side of town to watch the boys play their first double-header as the *smash brothers*, the nickname given by the coach. One of my most favorite things is when the boys are on the same team. They love it too.

Mom came a bit later with Grace and Joe. Uncle Nick and Aunt Dawn came, too, which was a wonderful surprise. The weather was nice, and the boys had a great time. It's so fun to watch them do what they love.

Dad and I had the same thought: there was no where on earth we'd rather be than right there this afternoon. The huge bonus was Dad walking all the way to and from the field without a walker!

They will leave tomorrow for the clinic. It's been so up and down, emotions running high, and just wanting to get this ball rolling. God has provided some special memories and extra time built in this past week. *Lord, please keep them safe as they travel.* I pray for calmed nerves, for both Mom and Dad, good food, helpful and knowledgeable hospital staff, comfort, healing, strength, sleep, for all of it. It's so hard to say goodbye, especially on Anna's seventh birthday. But they will return, Good Lord willing, in October and we'll just keep journeying on. We can hold down the fort until then.

August 26, 2014

We were hit with some pretty heavy news today. I was actually standing in the breakroom at work after DK came to tell me, "Aunt Grace called and texted to call her, and Nan called..." I knew it must not be good news.

Grace told me that Dad isn't going to get the stem cell transplant after all. Shocked, I listened to her. A huge lump formed in the back of my through, but it felt odd, it felt like...*amazing peace*. I then called Dad, and he went over it, too. My voice got quivery with him. I hung up and started to cry in front of co-workers. But then, that same *amazing peace* enveloped me like a hug. And just a few minutes ago, it hit me. It is a peace that passes all understanding, it truly is.

And for this, I am grateful.

I think it's because I had fears saying goodbye to Dad yesterday after having Anna's birthday brunch. I had images that this would be the last time we got to see him, that something was going to happen while they were gone for his transplant. I started to bawl saying goodbye (especially seeing tears in his eyes, way to go DAD!), but then pulled myself together, talked myself out of it, knowing the kids and I love him like no other, and also that we've had so much opportunity to be with him.

And for that, we are grateful.

We have so much coming up. We're moving into our new house, saying goodbye to this old house (isn't that a TV show?), school starting, Peter having tubes put in on Friday, me continuing to hope for a new job (that pays better), and life. I'm praying for what is to come.

August 27, 2014

A couple of thoughts this morning:

1) waking up with praise song in my head is awesome.
2) having that praise song taken over by the Frozen soundtrack is not awesome. No, I do not want to build a snowman.

3) when you have to pee so bad it hurts and think if it's part of your dream that you're on the toilet, you'd better wake up first.

4) leftover birthday cake is not my friend.

5) I got a four-hour time frame for when they'll come pick up an old freezer today, but half of it is when I'll be at work. Do I hope they'll come in the first two hours, or be realistic and realize they won't show until the last three minutes?

August 28, 2014

I've been hitting the packing hard this afternoon. I think I may have even packed my brain somewhere. We are excited to move on Saturday! Dad wants to help - Mom too, it'll be a fun, memorable time once I get out of work at noon to start bringing our stuff over to the new place! I told Dad that his job can be the second driver. That way, we can use my van and his truck.

I got the call that I got the job as a security officer at the high school! Not sure when I'll start but guessing it'll be next week. With the start of school Tuesday, I suppose I'll be standing post somewhere.

I'm just laying here, having a hard time going to sleep, thinking about something Dad said to me today. He told me, "You're an amazing person."

But when he told me, he was all choked up, red around his eyes, and he said I'm amazing. I
started to well up and told Mom and Dad, I get the strength from them (and the Good Lord). My whole life, my dad has been my hero. I want to make him proud, I respect him with everything I am, I strive to be like him.

He said I'm amazing...

He is the one who is.

August 29, 2014

Today was full on B-U-S-Y. Pete got his tubes this morning. The poor soul didn't react so well to the sleepy drugs. He threw up and cried when he came to, then puked twice in the van (good times, good times), and twice at home. I called the ENT doctor for some anti-nausea medicine, and they never called me back.

He was so sick, poor buddy. He took a good nap, and after the upchuck was all out of his system, we got to packing up. Off we go with the first jaunt of our stuff to the new casa!

August 30, 2014

I'm so glad Dad had a good day today. His spirits are up, and he's who he always has been, maintaining his incredible faith, strength, humor, and determination. Praising the Lord for these times, for any and all time we get together. Tears and good conversations have been had. I'm thankful to have some peace in all of this. He's confident and humbled that we get to spend eternity with him when all is said and done. There are just no words.

I'm heading to bed tonight reminiscing. Tonight is our last night sleeping in this old farmhouse. This house. There are so many memories within these walls. All of the work we put into this place - adding a bathroom, fixing up the barn, updating the kitchen, painting, repainting, rearranging from upstairs to down, and so much more. That was the fun stuff.
As time wore on here, the house became an "emotional attachment" more than anything else.

It was a dream to add on. We even had professional plans drawn up to add the house to the garage in order to make more space, enjoy the country living right outside our backdoor.

Then came heartache. Not sudden, but gradual.

First it was the behavior that changed, moods that became more prominent. I remember the night so clearly, talking to Danny at the dining room table (which happens to be where my bed is now). Asking him if he'd be open to seeing someone for counseling, someone who could maybe help. It took weeks to have the courage, but it actually felt like he heard me and saw it himself.

Then the alcohol. It grew and grew. I used to hide it in the empty chicken coop out back behind the house. One day I went in there to check and lost track counting how many bottles were strewn all over. One time, there were seventeen empty glass beer bottles in our camping trailer by 1 pm. I had to confront him at the campground. We cried together and agreed that it was time for some help. I thought maybe we were on the right track.

This was until both the moods and alcohol grew out of control. For every three to four weeks of pure awful, there was one week of good. I would be on my knees praying God would keep him safe. I remember being worried sick not knowing where he was every other night until 9 or 10 pm because his counselor told him to "only drink every other day." The moods were dramatic, frightening, and demonic. Life felt impossible, but I had to be "me" for my kids. I took the kids away from it as much as I could, but as they grew, I couldn't hide it anymore. My body started reacting, in the form of migraines. As much as I tried to maintain, I couldn't. I was afraid; so afraid of what he'd do to me or himself. I had to be done. It took me nearly two years to gain the courage to end it. Dad told me I had to end it. I had to know, though. I had to be at peace as best I could. Finally...I knew.

Now I look in the mirror sometimes and say out loud, "I'm proud of me." I risked losing it all by saying I am done, but it was worth it. And I, in essence, have lost it all. My house is being taken away, my truck was repossessed, so was our camping trailer. Bankruptcy was filed because he used credit in my name. Losing this house was my *consequence* from Danny. This very house where dreams once grew and our babies learned to walk and talk and play... Where we had a tire swing out back and Dutch opened windows and the back door. All of that seemed to disappear in these walls. It became an empty shell, in more ways than one. Danny started taking a wall out, so I, thinking it'd help (and let's be honest, smacking it with a crowbar was great stress reliever), put it down to the studs. There was half-finished laundry, bedrooms, bathroom, kitchen, and den.

That was last August, and it still remains. Drywall and outside walls were gutted and never finished. But after going through all that we have, we've grown thankful for simply a literal roof over our heads.

I have told the kids, "our memories will come along with us in our hearts. Now we get to make some new ones." With some new hope, as we leave this place, pack it all up (man, what a job), we will turn back and remember, smile, maybe shed a few tears (especially for Dutch), but are so happy to be moving on to a new chapter, a new place we can (eventually) call home.

August 31, 2014

The much anticipated move happened today. We moved out of our home. I don't say house because *this* was a home. I'm not sure how long it will be before our new place feels like home. I'm beyond grateful for this new place we are going. It's just an emotional day of goodbyes.

There are so many hands helped us make this day happen. Families from church with trucks and trailers, and Dad's siblings were all here. It made the day special. It's just been super emotional to have to leave. The foreclosure hit me hard. Losing all of it has been tough. I know it's just *stuff,* but it's been my adult life.

UB and Aunt Gene have done more than I can ever thank them for by providing a house for us to go to. It's beautiful, has walls and carpeting, and we each get our own space. There's fresh paint, appliances that work, dry wall, bedding, a dishwasher, deck, all of it.

The best part of the day was that Dad was there with us. He carried in things he shouldn't have, sat on the stool to "supervise" bed frame building, and finally plopped on our couch with Mom to take it all in. The fact that he was able to be here, on this pivotal, up and down day is more than I can ask for. He has a hand in making our new house a home. No matter what, I can always know Dad has been here in this place. When all was said and done, sore backs and all, I sat on my new bedroom floor in folded tears.

September 5, 2014

Dad has had a good week, and he now has a new mission - an early morning alarm clock that comes in the form of three precious kids. He has graciously taken on the role of bus driver, breakfast maker, and ESPN co-watcher with the kids on school mornings.

I'm beyond excited for this new gig, working full-time within the school district. The only issue will be having to be to work by 6:30 am and all that crazy morning stress with three kids who prefer to sleep. We did it today, though. We drove the 8 minutes it takes to get to Mom and Dad's from our house. I was excited and nervous, so I didn't sleep again last night. I pull into their driveway in the dark to see, shining in the headlights, Dad, sitting on his Toyota Tacoma tailgate with his "sippy cup" of coffee in hand and a big wave with his other one. He doesn't do a corny wave, just a big wave, across the air, in the shape of a rainbow. The kids and I like to tease about how different people wave and what a "good wave" should be. They like Papa's as much as I do. He had this huge smile on his face. So did I until I backed out of the driveway. Then I cried, ugly face cried, the entire way to the high school.

"...straining toward what is ahead, I press on toward the goal to win the prize for which God has called me heavenward in Christ Jesus" Phil 3:13-14 (NIV One Year Bible).

September 11, 2014
Dad and I got a chance to talk on the phone today which was great. He's my favorite voice on the other end. He and I have pretty much talked on the phone every day since I can remember, sometimes five to six times a day. He always listens, advises, and laughs with me. I'm so grateful for his constant voice of reason and teasing. In this past year, he's rode the ride with me. He has been with me every single step of the way.

September 15, 2014
Dad brought the boys home from baseball practice. It seems they made a special little stop on the way home for a bite to eat. He even let the boys order off the *big* people menu.

Dad claims he is feeling really good lately. He looks pretty good, but you can see in his eyes, he's whipped. Just the hours he keeps playing Papa and taxi/school bus driver alone, is exhausting. He is a miracle, an amazing human being, our hero. His humor, drive, and selflessness are 100%.

September 16, 2014

Dad came to our house today to help with the kids at the crack of dawn. Why? Because he wants to make life easier for me. He is truly something else.

He could hardly make it up the six steps from the landing, but there he was, always putting everyone else first. No matter the time, or the need, he was there. Our hearts are so full that we have this gift of time with him. We know it's fleeting. I cry every single day on my way to work.

September 17, 2014

He's sixty-four today. We had this conversation earlier about how I'm the age he was when his dad died, thirty-seven. Anna is seven, which was Dad's favorite age for us kids. I can remember him getting home from work to our house in Plymouth, me sitting on their bed while Dad talked and changed clothes inside their walk-in closet. When he was in his comfy clothes (out of the suit and tie) he told me, "How about you stay seven? You can't get any older than this." I innocently agreed. I'd stay seven.

This man, my federal agent dad, the one who brought home machine guns, arrested bad guys, solved cases, had such huge responsibility to serve and protect people. Watching him open a birthday card picked out and written in by your eleven-year-old son and he starts to cry brings me to a full on cry. Quickly, I fan the face, talk myself out of it, make a joke, and change the topic. I asked Dad to wait to read my birthday card until later. It'd be *go time* otherwise. Neither of us could have gotten through it.

Of course, Pete's card said something about Papa not being old until the fat lady sings, then when the card opened all you heard was an opera-type voice yelping repeatedly. Anna gave him one with a fat dude on the front and a precious seven-year-old-misspelled note inside. So cute.

I'm very thankful to spend this evening with our extended family. I'm praying Dad will remain strong on his feet, for the pain in his knees and hips. I'm so grateful for the gift of time and for family, love, and all that God provides each moment. Even if we don't see it until hindsight, we know He is here in the details, and we need to keep trusting Him.

September 18, 2014

We are in our new house. It's beautiful and feels much bigger than I thought it would now that we're settling in, which is super fun. We're still finding places for little things and have boxes of Anna's toys to find places for. DK ended up moving into Pete's bedroom about a week ago because they were pulling bedding into each other's rooms anyways each night. They are buds, best buds. They can't fool me. DK's room is used as a Lego mania while Pete's is the sleeping quarters.

Getting up for school is a different ballgame. We are tired. It's more like walking around with toothpicks to keep our eyes open. My alarm goes off at 5:15am. I must admit, today I felt like a rebel when I hit my snooze button. It felt so good! I've been trying to get to work by 6:30 am, but realize my hours are really 7 - 3 pm. My boss and another co-worker are there at the absolute break of day, so I want to be in "in crowd," too. However, neither of them are single moms with three kids to have up, ready, and dropped off at Nan and Papa's on their way to work each morning. They are both fifty-something-year-old, retired sheriff's deputies. So today, I allowed myself some grace, and I figured if I'm pushin' 6:45 am, it'll be alright.

Work is good. It's interesting as all get out. My boss told me on my very first day that no two days would be the same. He wasn't kidding. I've had my eyes opened wide. I've learned that high school kids are can be straight up troublemakers.

There's dramatic break-ups and make-ups, kids throwing fits and include anything they can find to throw; refusing to get up out of chairs/desks, lying, locker jams, principal office visits, interviewing naughty kids, theft in locker rooms, skipping class, etc. is just what a typical Monday looks like. I'm only three weeks in and already fourteen years older.

September 19, 2014

A few pointers I've picked up on since starting work at the high school:

- Just because you can grow a mustache, doesn't mean you should.

- Leggings or jeggings (some are called) are "in." Apparently, even if they are sheer. To me, those are called nylons and require a skirt over top, but hey, I'm an "old lady."
- Standing in one place for an hour and a half makes my feet and knees sore. I try to shift my weight from my left to right, but it still gets kind of old come lunchtime, standing there making sure kids are doing what they should.
- I can never seem to pick the right key the first time.
- Every day after third lunch, I see Peter walk by me, only it's the spitting image of him in six years.
- The locker room wing for a tornado drill smells like a massive arm pit that hasn't been shaved or deodorized since 1994.

I downloaded this song recently, after hearing it on the radio, and crying my eyeballs out. "The House That Built Me" by Miranda Lambert:

"I thought if I could touch this place or feel it. This brokenness inside me might start healing. Out here it's like I'm someone else, I thought that maybe I could find myself. If I could just come in I swear I'll leave, won't take nothing but a memory from the house that built me."

And the part about, "My favorite dog is buried in the yard." *I'm cooked.* It's all over (tears). This is my song.

September 22, 2014
There he came again, to our house at 6:11 am, limping up the stairs and into the family room with his "sippy cup." The kids are all still asleep, and off to work I go. I forget for a few minutes how sick he is, then I realize it on my early morning trek to work and just bawl the whole time. I always try to stop crying a few minutes before I walk into work so no one notices. I've stopped wearing mascara for this very reason. Unless I can guarantee a non-crying experience, I won't wear eye makeup. And these days, I can't remember the last time I wore any.

When we got home from school today, I thought it'd be therapeutic to get outside. So we rode bikes. It felt good to get the ol' blue, floral cruiser out again. But if that's what riding bikes is like by the new digs? I'm out. We passed four snakes on the road, and I about fell off my bike having a heart attack every time. So much for quality family time!

September 23, 2014

I bought a new extension cord at the store yesterday, so just as the kids were going to bed, I was trying to hook, or shall I say, rehook everything all up behind the TV. I guess I got a little carried away because Anna came out of her bedroom in her strawberry jammies and said, "Umm, Mom? You're talking to yourself is getting kinda creepy." I was answering my own questions. I think I got it figured out, though. It's just another one of those things that would be handy to have a husband, but I gave myself a silent high-five for doing it myself.

Here we are, ready to head into a new week. At least I think we're ready. I'm trying a new lunch menu which included chopping up some actual veggies today. I'm hoping the kids will be fans. I'm thankful for another weekend-long of time with Dad. The kids got to spend a lot of time over there Saturday while I grocery shopped, and then today, with baseball being rained out, and football on tv, there was more Papa/DK/Pete time. *Priceless.* Dad didn't look like he felt too good either day, though. That part is concerning and a good reminder that he isn't "fine." I'm hoping he can stick in here and keep on having good days.

September 24, 2014

The neighbor's dog just peed on my van... again. That's neat.

Work was good, nothing major went down. There was lots of surveillance tape viewing. When the kids and I got home from work/school, I got chicken in the oven and hopped on the mower. Pete, bless his heart, offered to make the "sides" for supper. I didn't quite get the lawn all the way done when Pete waved his arms from the deck saying dinner was almost ready. DK set the table, we all sat down, and had a nice supper. I had Anna do the dishes and back out to mow I went.

I just came in after finishing up, put the sheets back on my bed (they've been off for two days with laundry backups), and now I can relax. I feel accomplished. Homework and lunch packing happened in between there.

There were hangnails to check out, scooter-viewing from the window (that Anna insisted on - after all, it was with her new friend), crumb-sweeping, toilet-paper-roll-replacing, lint-tray-cleaning, and homework-initiating, too.

September 25, 2014

He'll fight through and be here at my house at zero-dark-thirty to help with the kids because he's such an incredible man. Seriously. Never in my life has anyone ever cared for, or done for me, what he does. His love language and mine seem to be the same, so he knows the gift of time. It's what fills his bucket, gets his mind off the *big C*. For me, it literally grips my heart that he does this for me, for us, and that he loves us enough to spend whatever time he can being an active part of our lives while he can. I'm sobbing.

I'm just...I'm so touched and full. I know these days will be a memory someday and that makes me cry harder. How could I possibly do this without him? He's so brave and patient.

September 26, 2014

I had to jot this down. Dad told me on the phone, "On our way to school this morning, the kids wanted me to tell them a story. So I made one up about the boat breaking away from the dock last night." But they said, 'No, no, tell us a true one about your police days.'"

Then Anna asked me, "Did you know Abraham Lincoln?

The boys quickly said, "No Anna, Papa isn't that old."

Then Dad told me, "I love this time with the kids. I love every minute I can get it, I love being their driver."

September 28, 2014

I would feel awful if Dad caught my cold. Oh, I pray he doesn't! He's been coming over to supervise UB hanging up window blinds in our new house. They look so nice and give us privacy! To think, not too long ago, at our old house, the blinds were taken down, and I was left without any window coverings right inside the front door.

I have to keep my cold to myself. I've been wearing a mask around Dad. He told me I look better with it on.

Chapter 33

September 30, 2014

Papa took the boys to baseball practice, fed them, and brought them home. As he pulled away tonight from the house, I stood in the driveway and said out loud, "he is my hero." I think that about sums it up. HERO. He pushes through it all for those he loves. He'll be back here by 6:15 am tomorrow morning to feed the kids, make sure they have their homework ready, and take them to school.

Danny hasn't taken the kids in three weeks, and Thursdays are his parenting time with the kids. He hasn't had them on his parenting weekends in a while, either. I have a hard time keeping track. I need to go back and document each time for court, though.

How could someone not want to see their precious kids? Especially these kids? They are deserving of so much, and they get it with my dad. I pray they soak it all in as long as they can with Papa here on Earth. I pray that they see the incredible example of a godly man Dad is for them when they grow up.

I caught myself starting to cry at work yesterday, thinking of the fact that my dad won't get to see my kids graduate from high school. There I sat at the high school entrance "watching" the front door, tears started to well up. I had to talk myself out of it while a big lump formed in my throat. He'll be there, in spirit, though. I'm more proud of them than anything.

For my kids have been through an awful lot in their young years already, they will in these short years here ahead. I pray for a good, loving, treat-them-like-his-own sort of man to come into our lives that will love all of us and come alongside us in this journey called life. We'll just have to see what the Lord has in store for us, in His timing...

October 1, 2014
"But you need to wear leggings with that 'cause it's too short..." I just said to Anna. *Yeesh, already?*

I'm tired. Pooped. I've been tired all day. Watery eyes, runny nose, I know I'm getting a cold. I'm terrified I'll pass it along to Dad. I've been popping allergy capsules like candy today hoping to get on top of it. I'll have to keep my distance. I just hope it doesn't go from me, to the kids, to Papa. We can't afford any of that! No way!

Another interesting day at work. I didn't get punched, although I did get scolded a few times. I'm learning as I go, just need another few lessons, I suppose. I ran into a higher-up on my way to the van this afternoon and, he's so sincere, he asked how I was doing. I said I had a few "tongue-lashings today." He wondered how bad of a chewin' I got? I told him, "Just softly."

He said, "Anyone gives you trouble, you come to me, 'cause you're doing awesome."

That right there made me leave with a smile. Whether or not I am doing awesome, he made me feel awesome.

Since I'm on an awesome-feeling roll, my kids are also awesome. DK asked if he could talk to me tonight right before bed, just us. Figuring it was something really serious, I got pretty curious. We waited until we thought Anna and Pete cleared out. DK wanted to tell me about signing up to be a "buddy" to one of the new kids in the building. By new kids, I mean a child with special needs. I just sat and listened with a light beaming from my eye holes, nostrils, and mouth. I'm so proud of this fine young 11-year-old. What a heart of compassion.

My ora of light gets interrupted when we hear Peter cough from the steps below us. DK rolls his eyes and says, "Pete, are you listening?"

Pete appears with a halfcocked puzzled look on his face, admits it, and chimes in that he, too, signed up for the same buddy program.

The lights started shining through my face-openings again, bouncing now off both my boys. I'm one *proud* mama.

October 5, 2014

They want to put another port in Dad's chest. He hasn't had one in quite some time and never has good luck with them. I can't even imagine the discomfort of a little screen, put under your skin, that they poke through. It makes me cringe. I'm praying it won't get infected like others have.

He's been feeling so puny. Earlier when I stopped by to visit, he and I got talking about Heaven. We were equally choked up saying how we know that one day we'll get to spend eternity together again. Then he told me to knock it off because he was watching football, and being teary-eyed and watching football don't go together. He's the one who can make me laugh and cry at the same time.

When we got the boys to their baseball field, the other team didn't show, so it's a forfeit; we won. We decided that we'd make it fun and the parents played the kids. I enjoyed watching many of the dads and a couple moms get in there, competitive, but laughing at themselves. It was great. I didn't get out there, perhaps should have, but enjoyed watching from behind the fence. After the brief friendly game, Uncle K took all three kids on a ride on his trike motorcycle. Anna was beaming.

We then went to Nan and Papa's, the boys (mostly Pete) teased about me dating Derek Jeter! DK found online that he's already *taken* so we conceded and ate some sloppy joes. Then we went for a nice, long boat ride. The kids got to stick their feet in the lake and drive the boat. You couldn't have had a prettier afternoon. We went on home to pack lunches, read devotions, and listen to Anna's constant nightly chatter before bed.

Funsies for me! I got to go to the Homecoming dance! I didn't even have to have a date. Working at it felt pretty cool. I was the only female security officer, so I had to check on some things the male officers can't. I do love my job - connecting with these kids, being able to get after them, and still love on them at the same time, it is rewarding. I finally have all of my pockets in my cargo pants filled. I know exactly what is in what pocket. I'm glad I get to work with such great men every day. We are getting to know each other more and more. Not knowing from one day to the next what may happen is so fun.

October 6, 2014

I didn't get a chance to see Dad today but the kids did. He gave them a ride to school in his truck, as a matter of fact. Mom has been the one meeting us in the driveway with a big wave as we pull in, so Dad can sleep in. Then, once the kids get inside the house, he hoists out of bed and hangs out with them while they eat their bowl of cereal.

Working at the high school, I'm learning stories about these kids, and I can't help but have a heart for them. One kid sleeps in his truck, depending on what's going on at home on any given day. Another girl got called to the office because of something we later found out, her sister did, not her. I had to walk her through the crowded hallways, in her gym clothes, while everyone else, already dismissed from class, stared at her walking with me, the security chick. I apologize for embarrassing her in front of everyone, to which she said, "Oh, I don't care what they all think." Her head is on straight.

Another girl, who catches my eye daily because of her unique style (she wears platform seventies heels every single day), walked into school this morning bawling. I stopped her, put my hand on her left shoulder and asked what was wrong. She proceeded to tell me her mom made her get out of the car and walk the rest of the way to school because her sister is an epileptic and her mom is so stressed she just needed some space. *What?*

Here are these kids, coming from so many walks (and shoes) of life. Some are rich, some are poor, and some just needing love. Some just need a place to sleep. What an eye-opener this job is. At the end of that day, it surely makes my eyes easy to close.

"We have small troubles for a while now, but they are helping us gain an eternal glory that is much greater than the troubles. We set our eyes not on what we see but on what we cannot see. What we see will last only a short time, but what we cannot see will last forever" 2 Cor 4:17-18.

October 7, 2014
Man, I've been battling tears on and off like a faucet, today.

I held it together pretty well all day until I heard again how bad the teacher at the kids' school is doing. She's battled cancer three times, and in this past month, has just gone downhill, quickly. Now she's in her final days. But she knows where she's going, she is faithful and strong. What a testimony. She has been steadfast in her faith. That's when I get weepy.

I know my dad is, too, and I'm so thankful. I get so caught up in this mixture of being in awe of all that God has done for us, for what He will do for us, but then in the selfishness of not having the loved one here on earth while the rest of us are still here. So, trying to talk to the kids about the teacher, resulted in me thinking about Dad, and I had to stop talking in five to ten second intervals to gulp, breathe, then try again.

DK stopped me. "Mooooooom..." he'd say.

Then, I'd pull it together.

"It's not about the teacher, DK, it's about Papa."

Because honestly, this is the stuff I talk to Dad about...my feelings. Once he's gone, I can't talk to him about it. Then I cry about that! Ugh. Now comes the faucet again!

Dan texted me tonight and cancelled on the kids again for tomorrow. This time he had a classic excuse. "I can't afford to feed the kids tomorrow night. I just can't. I have nothing in the fridge or freezer, and I can't buy any food." What about me feeding the kids? It's not optional; it's necessary. He's still so behind on paying me any child support.

He just went deer hunting last weekend when he could have had his makeup weekend with the kids, and huh, got a deer. Last I checked, ammo costs money. Doesn't gas to drive places, too? And to process a deer? Then he texted me later, "It's also the gas to drive the kids home." At this point all I can do is shake my head.

DK says to me, "Mom, I need some paper and a pen." So when we got inside, he took some stationary and went down to his and Pete's room. Pete and Anna sat upstairs with me. He comes up and asks for Danny's address. I told him and he grabbed a stamp out of my purse, went out in the dark, and put it in the mailbox. Mailbox arm up. He wanted that sent tonight.

At bedtime I whispered if he wanted to talk about anything, that he could tell me anything. He sat and shared that he just felt he needed to write his dad and tell him he wished he'd spend more time with him and be the fun dad he knows he can be. That he doesn't understand why he doesn't take his parenting time (big people words, huh?) and that this wasn't coming from Mom or anyone else, but from me, DK, so that he wouldn't get all mad. I told DK that took an enormous amount of courage, and I'm so proud of him. Wow, what a kid.

Then Pete farted, and we all laughed. I tried to read devotions, Anna kept doing gymnastics (which I've tried to tell her 39,302 times not to do during devotions, and Pete farted again). DK started imitating Anna's gymnastics' moves. I stopped reading and said it's time for bed. *Whew.* What a day.

October 9, 2014

My daughter wins the award for the biggest bedtime staller. I think this was honestly the thirteenth time she re-opened her door to tell me she loves me. This time she also had another reason: so that her fart didn't smell in her room, only in the hallway. That's a good reason, I suppose.

It's been a long week. I caught myself rubbing my eyeballs at the supper table tonight, and Pete stopped me to ask if I had a headache. Nope, (I didn't tell Pete this) it's just that Danny had his hand in making it that way with his long texts that ranted and raved. I must admit, I have tried to erase their content from my brain. Not that any of it speaks truth, but why now, would he go into all of this? And why can't I just file that motion for full custody?

Oh I'm so tempted.

But the kids aren't there yet, so I'm not going to do it. Since he's moving in with his aunt next month, and they still see her, it's tricky. So, I'll leave it be. At least when they go over, they will be "supervised" visits now. The rants from him, three loooooooooooooooooong texts that spoke of me hiding behind my God, that I'm a life wrecker, an awful human, a controlling (cuss), how I didn't give our marriage a chance, a liar, etc., then the next morning telling me that he still loves me.

I had *oh so many words* to say back; the first being, "If this is what you say to someone you love, I wonder what you say to someone you despise?" But I haven't responded with one single word. This makes him even more mad which makes me kind of laugh (I know, probably super mean), but I've lived this for too many years, and I've talked myself out of numerous fights. I've looked myself in the mirror, gathered my thoughts and would go back into a situation with a smile. So *this* time there are no words. I need to just keep moving forward. He is not worth my effort or time. My dad is. My kids are. Sleep is. So that's that.

Ugh, and so why have I had a headache this week? Hmmmmm....

October 11, 2014
I'm not exactly sure how you can be tired after not doing much of anything, but it happens. I guess in the past few days I've done a few things...

There were three fight incidents at school. I must admit, it's thrilling to go running and get in on the action. I think I walked fifteen miles around school yesterday, then had to drop the kids off to Danny. That wasn't so easy. He wanted to "talk" for a few minutes, and I agreed. We sat on the porch at his aunt's, and we were between the glass sliders of where his aunt was making dinner. Anna was putting barrettes all over Grandpa P's mustache and eyebrows, and the boys were outside playing whiffle ball. Danny proceeded to tell me he still loves me, about his money woes, etc etc.

My big thing was to make sure he was going to be cool with DK after receiving the letter he wrote earlier in the week, the one about spending more time with them. I hope and pray Danny handled it right with DK and will maybe open his eyes. Who am I kidding? This is the same guy who told me he's still struggling with having to get a divorce. It's been over a year since we lived on the same property; it's over.

I spent last evening having dinner with Mom, Dad, UB, and Aunt Gene. Today I dinked around at home, worked on my budget, and watched some mindless TV. UB came over to show me how to work a trimmer/weed whacker. Then I spent the evening at Mom and Dad's again. We had an emotional conversation tonight but always good talks to have. I love Mom and Dad more than words could ever possibly begin to say. And I'm so thankful for time with them, especially with Dad right now.

He is my best friend.

To think of not having him to text or call on a whim, absolutely breaks my heart. We talked again tonight, of how we have comfort in knowing that this time on earth is temporary. That we will all be together again in Glory. As much as this all hurts so bad, and we can't imagine the pain that lies ahead, what God has for us in eternity will outweigh it all. We cling to that. We must.

On that note, perhaps it's easy to see why this lady is tired, emotionally and physically.

October 12, 2014
Last night I sat with Mom, Dad, UB, and AG and we talked about all sorts of things. One of the things that came up was Dad's grandpa, Finley. Dad used the words "moral compass" to describe him. That's how the family

viewed him. I've thought on those two words ever since and I told Dad tonight, that's what HE has been to me, to my kids, our moral compass.

"Joy emerges from the ashes of adversity through your trust and thankfulness" (Jesus Calling by Sarah Young).

October 14, 2014
The kids and I just got home. I'm exhausted and putting on my pajamas. All of a sudden I hear it, nails on a chalkboard.

So, I start yelling, "Pete, if you want to continue to live here, *turn* that off!"

Laughing hysterically, he cranks the volume on his Netflix find, "Caillou."

October 16, 2014
I just sat there, big ol' smile, I'm sure, across my face, watching my boys play "rock, paper, scissors" for the odd numbered chicken wing. We went to the steakhouse for supper, a rare treat anymore. We used to do more stuff like that when we had more money and when we had more time. Now it's a very special treat. DK won the hand with *rock* but before either of them ate a thing, they both bowed their heads to pray quietly to themselves. Mama beamed. I'm proud of *me* boys (pirate voice).

Now, here I sit in my bathrobe and jammies, half covered in my bedding and ready for some sleep. I've been rather tired this week come, oh 7 o'clock. It might not help that I've had DK or Anna climb into bed with me two nights this week. DK just came in to tell me about his stomach pains again. We talked about how he can maybe start to prevent this rather than rely on Tums. The poor kid has a weak stomach.

Work has been busy. It seems my path to the office is getting quite worn. I'm really enjoying it, though, that they trust me enough to call me when the stuff hits the fan, when they need kids retrieved from classrooms, or have an anonymous tip and need something discreet. When there was a hit and run in the parking lot and need an accident report, I helped out. I like being in the action, in the know. It "fills my bucket" as Anna would say.

We are having family pictures taken tomorrow evening, so we've been looking forward to that. I've had a hard time deciding what to have us wear and coordinating our outfits. So we'll see (and hope) it all comes together!

October 17, 2014
We were able to find a time to get some family photos taken today by a friend of mine, same friend who took pictures right after the divorce, too. It was, in a way, a sign that we can do this, the four of us. The weather wasn't the best but that didn't matter. If we didn't get them done now, what if Dad wouldn't have been feeling up to it later? The time didn't work for Philip and family. I wish they would have been a part of it. I can't wait to see the finished pictures. Afterwards, we went out for pie a la mode.

Dad's port went in the other day. So far so good. He says it's really tender around the spot, but he's tough. I'm praying for peace and that Dad will regain some strength lost, that he'll overall feel peace in his heart and mind for the upcoming days.

"Being joyful isn't what makes you grateful, being grateful is what makes you joyful." -Unknown

October 19, 2014
Just as I came around the corner, I saw Pete at the table with the sugar canister from the countertop. He got the one cup scooper emptied onto his bowl of Wheaties. I give the ol' "HEY!" which makes him adjust in his seat. In his guilt-stricken, nervous mind, he then proceeds to try to put the sugar back into the canister. It's too bad half his bowl of cereal went in too. I shut my eyes, slowly bowed my head, and walked away.

October 20, 2014
"Anticipate coming face to face with impossibilities: situations totally beyond your ability to handle. This awareness of your inadequacy is not something you should try to evade. It is precisely where I want you - the best place to encounter Me in My Glory and Power."

When you see armies of problems marching toward you, cry out to Me! Allow Me to fight for you. Watch Me working on your behalf, as you rest in the shadow of My Almighty Presence" (Jesus Calling by Sarah Young).

October 21, 2014
Anna is conked here on the bed next to me. She's had a long day. I feel her pain!

Dad is ready for chemo tomorrow. He'll be trying out that new port. It was really cool today...Dad came to check out where I work and got a chance to sit and have a cup of coffee with my boss. They've been meaning to catch up for quite some time (they go way back) and I must say, I sure was proud to have my dad come walking into my workplace. Being in a security uniform, I had to maintain my tough girl face, but on the inside I was ugly crying grateful tears.

"Yet I am always with you; you hold me by my right hand. You guide me with your counsel, and afterward you will take me into glory" Psalm 73:23-24 (NIV One Year Bible).

Chapter 34

October 22, 2014

So we didn't take into account movement sensor porch lights. We had cased the neighborhood when it was light out and had our homes picked out for "*Booing*," a new term for us because we never lived in a neighborhood before. We had been Boo'd by an unknown neighbor (basically a positive spin on ding-dong-ditch because you get a Halloween bucket of gifts).

House #1, porch light pops on, kids dart behind the only pine tree for two miles. I'm nearly wetting my pants laughing, standing in the pitch dark road until the old man appears from house #1's open garage and says, "I swear I heard the doorbell?!" Just then, three sets of headlights come veering around the corner, showing me in the road dressed in all black. The old dude eventually sees the Boo bucket, but Pete, still behind the pine, didn't think he did, so he puts on his tactical moves and re-rings the doorbell. Now I'm signaling with my flashlight for the kids to abort the mission all while cracking up the whole time. And this was just house #1...

October 23, 2014

Dad is really sick; his fever has his teeth chattering. I'm praying the fever will break and go away. His spirits are good, he keeps everyone laughing and putting everyone else first. He's always making us feel special. I asked if I should look to find other resources for the kids in the mornings, but he insists Mom can take over his tasks. I sit here and think of how, when the other day he texted me, I make him proud. Tears are streaming down my cheeks. I'm proud to be his daughter.

October 24, 2014
What a day today. *Oye.* It started at 5:10 am when my alarm went off and seemed to be go-go-go from then on.

These busy days keep me on my toes. I'm pooped. Although, if I helped one kid or old lady walking into school, it will make me smile. I'm where I'm supposed to be.

After school today I had to work a home football game. I worked the grassy knoll where the elementary-aged through high school get dropped off by mom and dad and left for hours, unattended. I shouldn't make it sound annoying, it was actually quite entertaining.

Kids become my fast friends. I had some little dude just come up and start talking to me. He became my "informant," and came to get me when there was trouble I needed to address. Then, I'd go walking towards the trouble and a huge group of like minded kids would clump up behind me. Honestly, it made me feel pretty cool. Besides sore feet and being a little chilly, it was a fun experience.

As the football game was dwindling down, I happened to spot a student who I knew had been suspended earlier today. I took a few steps away from where I was, radioed another security officer and asked to make sure he wasn't supposed to be there. Nope, he wasn't, it was in violation of his suspension. Well, this kid has major 'tude, so I wasn't about to go from "Cool Charly" with 5th graders, to getting blitzed. So I asked if there was another officer nearby to assist. I kept an eye on this kid the entire time as I was waiting for some backup. Next thing I know, my fellow officer is talking to him, the kid tosses his hands in the air and starts to walk away. Another security officer walks up and tells him to go the other way and we all three follow him out. Good times.

We were handed burnt wieners that were extras from concessions and the game was done; on home to take a hot bath (my Friday night "spa treatment" after working these games) and *ahhhh*, a quiet house. I hope and pray the kids are comfortable with their dad. He seemed alright when I dropped them off quickly before the game.

October 30, 2014

Seeking prayer for the days, weeks, and months ahead. I've been reaching out and asking, needing... prayer. That we'll look to the Lord and know He will carry us all through and guide us in these hard times. Dad is such a man of faith and the Lord is surely using him.

When people come to visit or even at the hospital, he shares. What a testimony.

We went to the high school's musical, and it was pretty cool. Although, the kids had mixed reviews. Anna was so thirsty, she asked when the "water break time was?" about ninety-seven times during Act One. DK had to pee, so he asked to go about thirty-two times, but we were mid-row in the balcony (where he'd only sit comfortably with my right arm tucked around his back because he didn't like the heights). Oh and Pete?

Bored-out-of-his-mind.

He looked like he'd rather be at the dentist than there, until the intermission when Anna got her drink, DK peed, and I explained all the work and that the kids were actually singing to Pete. Act Two was more successful, Pete was engaged until Anna and DK started to fall asleep.

We left early, but I still tried to give them some culture, all while supporting the kiddos at my "work."

October 31, 2014

I had to search the school for a kid for twenty minutes today, only to find him near his classroom returning to class. I ended up pulling him in the hallway for the attitude he gave his teacher...seems he can't poop in the restrooms that are close to that class, he has to go to some really far away one to concentrate. I had to hold my face back from cracking up. I wanted to say, what are you, five?

It's been decided that DK would rather we not talk all "wobbly" about Papa when all it causes is "wobbles" right now. This means Mom (me) gets choked up talking about things like "this will probably be Papa's last

Halloween" and "we hope Papa makes it until Christmas." I appreciate DK's honesty, and I feel it's important to be honest with them. As always, it's the best policy.

These are hard days, let me tell ya. Most of my thoughts are focused on Dad, if not how he's feeling, what I'm doing, and how bad I want to tell him all the details. I hurt for him, wishing he wasn't having all of this pain and suffering. Cancer plain *bites*.

Saturday (good Lord willing) I get to go shopping with some girl pals from church who I haven't seen in a long while, and I can't wait! Grace and Joe are watching the kids, and man, am I looking forward to a day away!

November 1, 2014
Mom and Dad came over to our house to help pass out candy for Halloween. Dad felt so puny and awful but had promised the kids and was not going to go back on that promise.

Dad even wore a funny hat over that he got while working a mission many moons ago and told the kids some stories. He then gifted the hat to us, and I proudly put it on the top shelf. We'll keep it here as a "Papa token," a conversation piece...

Dad knew, when I got on the floor with the kids, what we wanted. He said, "Liv, grab the camera." He started this tradition with me five years ago. He's always been the one to take the picture.

November 4, 2014
I'm struggling. Dad seems to be declining, rapidly. He's sleeping quite a bit and in so much pain. He has sharp shooting nerve pain. My heart wants to be so strong for him as he's been for us, but my heart is truly breaking. It hurts so deep inside. To see him suffer through all of this, but still manage a smile is beyond words. I want so bad to record him laughing, to capture his head tilting back in genuine laughter, to see his teeth flash, and his eyes squint in delight at a joke, even if only for a moment.

He keeps his faith strong, his will and testimony in place. He's said that if one person comes to Jesus through his journey, it's been a life well spent. He is so strong and convicted.

November 5, 2014

Yesterday, as I stood by the doors at school in the morning, one of nearly 2,000 students approached me, stopped in his tracks, pointed at me, flashed me a big smile, then proceeded to take his hat off. He then said, "seeing you every day reminds me..." and he kept on walking. I got the biggest grin on my face (that school rule, no hats - and I usually have to tell kids at least four times a day).

Then about five minutes later, a young gal who often yells, "CHARLOTTE!" when she sees me walks on by and greets me. She usually has something sweet or funny to say. Yesterday it was, "Your hair looks cute today!" I thanked her and stood there with a smile.

A boy with special needs walked on by and pretended, at first, that he didn't see me; it's like this game he likes to play. Then, at the last possible second, he looked back and waved sheepishly and said quietly, "Hi."

DK was too sick this morning to go to school again, and Grace has been gracious to take him these past two days. Since she was going to take Mom and Dad to Dad's CT scan, I decided it'd be best if I stayed home with him instead. I hemmed and hawed some before contacting my boss, but knew it was the right thing. Changing out of my work uniform and into "mom clothes" was a-ok, taking Pete and Anna to school was a-ok, and being home with DK today was more than a-ok. Took me back - to when, in all the years past, this was why I was here - what my purpose was. And it still is. I'm Mom, first and foremost, and it felt good.

Tonight at bedtime, Pete took off his shirt and was plopping into bed when he tripped and made a goofy gesture, making himself fall on his bed. I just stood there, watching this brick house of a kid, and found myself starting to laugh.

See, there are things. In all of this hurt I feel underneath, like right underneath the surface, that still makes me smile and even laugh. And I'm grateful for it. So when the tears start to come, I take deep breaths, and pray that I can keep it together, that Dad isn't gone yet, and I can do this. I pray that when he is gone, that I can do this.

I pray I can figure out where the kids can go in the mornings now, how we'll cope and manage all of it. I pray for each of my kids, too, as they will grieve and are already beginning to, that they know they can come to me and be open. This is all too much of big people stuff, and they have had a big serving of big people stuff already in their lives.

November 6, 2014

I had just turned the lights off and was dozing off, with Pete in the bed next to me (he said DK was snoring so loud, he couldn't sleep), when my phone rang. I saw it was Mom and got a little nervous. She just called to say hello, and I chatted with Dad, too. Looking at the clock, it's only 8:47pm, not midnight, so no logical reason to be alarmed. I'm just nervous.

Dad had quite a few hiccups with his last appointment. He keeps plugging along, though, grabbing shut-eye when needed. Prayers are pulling him through. So many people are praying for him. He got me laughing tonight on the phone, first when I was talking to Mom and he kept breaking into song in the background. Oh, how I wish I had a tape recorder. He breaks into song/hymns all the time.

My latest music download, Building 429 *Where I Belong*:

"Sometimes it feels like I'm watching from the outside,
Sometimes it feels like I'm breathing, but am I alive?
I will keep searching for answers that aren't here to find.

All I know is I'm not home yet, this is not where I belong.
Take this world and give me Jesus, this is not where I belong."

I listen and just raise my hands. This is all temporary. I need to keep my eyes fixed on Him.

November 7, 2014

I can't recall a time, in a long time, that my hands were shaking so badly.

I sat there, in the entrance to Danny's apartment complex, for the second time tonight; this time, waiting for "backup." I had seriously contemplated calling the police, even jotted down Danny's apartment address on a piece of paper, so it was in my hand, but called Grace and Joe instead. I figured if they were with me, Danny would be less likely to punch me or grab me by the throat. Something was very different tonight. I was honestly afraid - most wholeheartedly for my kids, who were still with him in that apartment...

As the weekends go, this is Danny's time with the kids. He's tried three times to get out of it. Not surprising, seeing as how he often skips or last minute cancels on his parenting time. He was hunting all week and to have to come home from that to "babysit," I mean, "watch his kids." So after finally being reassured that the drop off was his place, not his aunt's house, I swooped in and grabbed the kids from school and drove them down to his apartment before I needed to be back to work the varsity football game.

When we got there, Danny was distant, had the *large pupils*, but hey, he's often reserved when that happens. I had an inkling but didn't go with my gut. Of course what am I supposed to say, "Um, I know it's your weekend, and you haven't even spoken one word, but I sense you're in a mood, so how about the kids and I leave?" Maybe I should have... He asked a quick question to the kids about how Papa is doing, and I cracked a joke to one of the kids about the underwear they packed or something, and it seemed to bother him that we were laughing and hugging. Sensing something, as the kids walked away, I got Pete's attention and did the, "if you need me, you call me" signal. He nodded and walked on in. I pulled away, turned on down the busy traffic-filled street, and back towards the high school. Just as I pulled into a parking spot, I see a text, then two...from Danny.

"I'm really (cuss) off. My family, nor I, was given the opportunity to pay for the stuff Pete was selling for his upcoming class trip. Apparently, you and your folks paid, but my family and I weren't given the chance. What the (cuss words)! This is unacceptable. I would have driven up to town to get my family's money and give the money I had stored. Am I supposed to hold Peter accountable? Seriously, why don't you just take the kids and turn them away from me and my family."

Immediately my heart is with my kids. What is this? Are they scared? Why can't I be there to protect them? So I wrote back, "It said on the order form that payment was due at the time of placing the order. That wasn't kept from you, it was on the form."

He continues via text, irrational and seething. "That's (cussing). I'm glad you are so smart. Thanks for letting Pete down. I'm so (cuss) at you. You are supposed to help him."

I texted, "Why don't I come get the kids." But figured, enough of this texting business, I need to hear his voice; I need to hear the kids. So I call him. He goes *bonkers* on me. He's so incredibly irate with me about this money, with the order form. I spell out again, anyone else who ordered things paid at that time, it said it on the form. But he keeps on it. I tell him, do *not* hold Pete accountable for any of that, that was on you. He rants more about how it's my fault, that I'm a horrible person. So I tell him, go ahead and blame me, you've blamed me for fifteen years.

That was my mistake. I shouldn't have given him a nugget. "Why did you marry me? Huh? Why did you even marry me? When did it start, before we got married? (Cussing)!" he says to me. And that is when I put my van in drive, pulled out of the high school parking lot, and headed directly to his apartment. I said, "I'm going to come get the kids, you are swearing at me, and that is not cool. They don't need to be around that," to which he said, "oh YEAH? Well, I meant it."

After ranting at me some more, and me telling him I was on my way but needed to call my boss, him asking if I was as upset as he was, me telling him I wasn't actually mad at all, my only concern was how the kids were, he hung up on me.

I frantically called my boss, and it went to voicemail. I called my co-worker, and it went to voicemail. I contemplated the police, but instead, called Mom. She offered to come help but I knew Grace and Joe were that much closer. I needed help fast; I needed my kids sitting in their respective seats in the van right now, safe.

I pulled into the apartment entrance, a few minutes before Grace and Joe got there, and it felt like an eternity. I had all sorts of visions rushing through my head and praying, *"Lord God, please put a shield of protection over my kids..."*

Grace and Joe pulled in behind me, we parked, and Joe walked right up and buzzed the door. I called Danny, but he wouldn't answer. We got buzzed in (turned out it was DK who did), and all three of us headed in to find even which apartment was his. I had never been inside.

We find #3B, and I knock, standing there in my security uniform, Grace by my side, and Joe off to the side down the hallway. We can hear Danny talking guilt into the kids from behind the door. My eyes are fixated on Grace's while my body is pointed square at the door. Her eyes reflected my thoughts as she'd rolled them in response to what he'd just said to the kids. He said how he wished he had longer to spend with them, hoped they enjoyed the dinner he packed up since they didn't eat it, etc. Finally, the door opens and immediately I see DK had been crying. Pete was saying his goodbyes and trying to be Mr. Mediator and Anna was...well, Anna.

I didn't make eye contact, didn't say a word to Dan. I just greeted the kids and walked out. Grace grabbed DK in a tight hug to assure him. Pete and Anna started putting things in the van, and we parted ways. I called Mom to update her, then the kids and I had a really good talk about what happened and why I came back.

DK told me he thought about calling the police (insert deep breath).

Anna told me, "I lied to Daddy and told him I had to go to the bathroom, but just went in there (to hide away)."

Pete was saying how Daddy went off on him for not letting him pay for the order form. I mean, really?

I kept apologizing to them, for putting them in that situation. I used to be there to protect them, but I assured them that I will always be there; I will always swoop in. It wasn't appropriate, and they don't deserve to be treated like that. Anna chimes in and says, "well neither do you, Mom." I hemmed a second and responded, "well Anna-banana, that's why Mommy and Daddy aren't married anymore."

From there, Anna went to spend some time with Nan and Papa, and I took the boys to the football game. The boys stuck to me like glue, and I loved it. We didn't last the whole game, it was cold and the boys weren't dressed for it, plus today was just, well, kind of long, so we headed out. My boss made sure we felt safe and secure. He even let the boys sit on the sideline to watch the game. I appreciate him so much. All of the people I work with are so amazing.

I'm thankful to be home with my precious cargo. And oh, Danny is still texting me. I'm not going to respond. *Gracious Lord, please carry us. Please give me perspective and wisdom in this whole situation. Simply put, I praise Your Name for getting us out safe and sound.*

Chapter 35

November 10, 2014

Today was a much better day than expected. I should be thanking the Good Lord for that, for my plea this morning was, *"Help me, Lord."* I wasn't sure what else to pray. But as He does, He *did*.

I got choked up a few times today. I got some needed hugs and moved past the bumps.

I must admit, as much as I say the hurtful words of Danny don't hurt, eventually they do. I get emotional. Perhaps it's the adrenaline wearing off. It isn't so much the words (although he did call me "unclean" in the eyes of God), it's just this emotional warfare that he seems to enjoy placing on me.

I'm over the abuse. I've had enough. Let the kids and I live our lives and stop being manipulative and cold hearted. Is that too much to ask? The kids were scared to death Friday night, but it's somehow my fault according to Danny. Then the rants via text don't stop all weekend.

I got to spend tonight with Mom and Dad and loved it. I actually recorded part of our conversation because I wanna cling to Dad's voice, what we talk about and hearing his voice. I know I'll listen to all of these recordings over the next several years. I recorded him praying the first prayer when we ate dinner here at the new house. That's a keeper.

His voice... it's been my voice of reason and wisdom. He told me tonight he has a calm about him when it comes to the kids and my future. We're going to be alright... We are; we'll be alright. The sting of death is right there, looking at us, but there is a rested assurance in the Lord that we'll be alright financially, emotionally, and physically. We'll make it through this long season we've been in.

I'm so ready for winter to be done and it to be spring. I feel like I've been stuck in this freezing, cold winter for ten years.

November 12, 2014
I got to talk to Dad today on the phone. He said he needed some time to think, to get out. He wanted to test drive Mom's new car (she picked out a white one because it's his favorite color). He drove by houses he lived in as a kid and ended up at the cemetery. He told me (I'm swallowing a huge knot in my throat as I write this) that he went to the plot that he chose for him and Mom.

And stood there, taking in the view all around, looking at the ground, seeing the scenery from where he will lay, knowing that will be where he will be soon. It's so eerie in a way to think of him standing where he will be laid to rest.

I get instant chills to know someday when we visit his grave, we can picture him standing there. I have chills again.

November 13, 2014
Dad met with his oncologist today. His numbers continue to be low, his fatigue is increasing, and the bottom line is, the decision was made to not continue with any further chemo.

Any chemo would only do more harm than good, giving Dad discomfort he doesn't need. He's had enough of being poked and prodded, and it wears him out tremendously these days, going back and forth to appointments. Dad's cancer doctor thinks he has three to six months before hospice. Quality of life over quantity.

Dad is very much at peace with this decision. We are, too.

His oncologist initially went to shake Dad's hand and apologized for not being able to do anything further, but that hand shake turned into a very sincere, heartfelt hug.

November 14, 2014
Wow, just wow. What an outpouring of love and support from so many around us. This uplifting and constant prayer surrounding us is amazing. We are grateful for how God has brought everyone into our lives, be them family or friends. We cling to encouraging words, help, meals, and ways others comfort each of us.

Praise the Lord for Dad's continued peace. He's ready to "go home" and continues to be an amazing example of faith, wisdom, and love. We love him more than words could say. Although tears are constantly under the surface (I've told people not to ask me about Dad at work), there are also smiles in knowing the suffering is temporary and Heaven is forever. Last night Anna was having a hard time with things, and she and I were crying. Sitting on my bed, I said to her, "But think, when Papa goes to Heaven..." And her tears were interrupted by a huge smile.

She caught her composure and said, "Papa will get to be with Grandpa Will, and Dutch, and Grandma Gigi, and he'll get to meet Mary and Joseph!" I told Dad this today on the phone, and we both got choked up.

November 16, 2014
We had such a great day, having the ability to go see Dad and spend some time just visiting, on a Sunday afternoon, like always, was the best.

Dad was tired today - but didn't need to take a nap which is huge. We got choked up, laughed, watched football, and just enjoyed. He's the most amazing man I know. Someday when, and/or if I find another man who comes into my life, he will have *huge* shoes to fill to be anything like my dad. I pray someday I will, so that the kids and I can have a good man to help guide us on this journey. That would be pretty awesome. I need to pray more for this potential "dude."

I'm pretty tired from the weekend. The boys had a super fun sleepover on Friday night with two great boys, but I'm pooped. The boys are, too - it really showed today more in the attitude department. I'm hoping they will sleep good tonight!

November 17, 2014
It's been such a blessing to have so many people who are willing to help us in the wee-hours of the morning. This has been a gut bomb for me, wondering who to ask to help with the kids every morning before school. I'm not good at asking for help like this, but I have to.

People truly are gracious and willing to help. I need to work through my feelings and realize people *want* to do it. I have some amazing friends from church that have volunteered, our Pastor and his wife, and Mom and Dad's neighbors a few doors down who heard about our situation.

It's hard to get up and going. Everyone needs to be dressed and ready, even though their day starts almost two hours after mine. I drop them around 6:30 am and head to work. I still cry every single day. It's mixed emotions. I'm so grateful people are wrapping their arms around me and the kids to help, sad that it can't be Dad. I feel guilty that people are making sacrifices of their own time, and that the kids feel like they are lacking something consistent. I know it's less than ideal. Anna crying and telling me she misses me on the way nearly every morning breaks my heart. So does the boys asking if they can just go to Nan and Papa's, promising they won't bug Papa. I think my heart is on the outside of my body at this point.

Bottom line, with all the chaos and unknown, I'm just so thankful. Tears and all. The Lord isn't having me walk this journey alone. All of these folks love Him and He is using them in a mighty way. They are being the hands and feet of Jesus...

November 18, 2014
We hung out at Mom and Dad's today for a bit. We didn't want to tire Dad out too much. He put on a strong front, but I know he's exhausted. He's trying some medicine that's supposed to help with fatigue and pain,

so we'll see. The boys went out front and built a snowman with Dad's earmuffs and hat. They called it Papa.

Hospice is coming next week to talk with Mom and Dad. This is a big and hard step, but we all know it's time. *Lord, please provide peace that passes all understanding. For Dad, Mom and Grace as she continues to be right there with them to help. She's an incredibly selfless caretaker.*

November 28, 2014
I feel alone here. The washing machine is off-balance again, and I was telling Dad about it. But he got all wound up and told me I need to spend the money to replace it.

"The van breaks down. I know you want to store money away, but you have to get some things taken care of. You need a washing machine."

I know I need one. I'm just barely getting by and don't want to use up what little money I have on huge purchases like that. I get it. I know; I'm smart. I just don't like making big ticket decisions alone. I'm so scared.

I don't know when to date, when to put myself out there. Will any guy want to spend time with me? Dad is in the mindset where he just wants to fix everything. I think he's being ornery because he won't be able to fix it for me for much longer. I don't want our conversations to feel like this, though

Danny "gave" me Thanksgiving with the kids. I'm glad he did, but it's sad how quickly he's willing to just give away his time.

When Thanksgiving rolled around, Danny was texting me about how he gave it to me, and he was being really inappropriate. Dad says, "You need to learn to weed that out and look at the positive. The kids got to be with me (Dad) for Thanksgiving." I do, and I am so glad, so glad, and so were the kids.

But I still have to deal with Danny. He's a huge thorn in my side. I wish he'd move away, go away and leave us alone without the constant disappointment and harsh words. The kids still want to protect him, and I get it, that's their right, it's their dad. Of course I want them to have a relationship with him. But never has he been able to be counted on, ever. He's selfish and manipulative to where he has them feeling sorry for him. He's the adult. I pray I can get this court situation rolling for supervised visitation. Should I talk to the kids about it? They don't need more stress, and my brain feels like it doesn't either.

Lord God please help with all of this. You know it all. Help me sort through and get to the place I want to be.

Chapter 36

December 1, 2014

Dad made a greasy dinner with the kids again today. Such a gut bomb! But so worth it. This time I studied Dad closely (in case he needed to take a break, which he didn't) but also so I can carry on this tradition after he's gone. Soon, we'll make fudge at Mom and Dad's so Dad can have a taste. I hope he feels up for helping us.

"Now to Him who is able to do immeasurably more than all we ask or imagine, according to His power that is at work within us, to Him be glory in the church and in Christ Jesus throughout all generations, for ever and ever! Amen" Ephesians 3:20 (NIV One Year Bible).

December 2, 2014

I know many people have cool jobs, but one of the coolest things about mine from today was watching, on surveillance video, Dad dropping off all three kids to their school this morning. They know I watch the surveillance cameras now, so they wave!

December 3, 2014

Dad insisted on taking the kids to school today. When I took them over and dropped them off, I could see Dad standing in the kitchen window. What a sight. I, of course, pulled out in tears. We'll take the strong days, and cling to them, as long as they are here.

Right now I'm putting together my list for things to print to take downtown tomorrow. I'm going to go seek some free advice from the court system for getting Danny's changed to supervised visitation.

I'm wanting so badly for this situation to change. I want something positive to happen for my kids. I don't want them to get hurt or be emotionally damaged. I never want them to feel any of this is their fault... like he had convinced me of. I pray they learn and grow in compassion more than anything. They amaze me even now, just so young. These are lessons you never want your kids to learn, yet it will help build them into the humans God designed.

I pray that their eyes will be open to it, that they'll see and not fall prey.

I know it can be said, "Oh, but he's mentally ill..." Yes, I know. He's also manipulative, smart, and controlling. I wish him well, I really do. Why does he feel the need to continue hurting us? It's dark. So dark. DK, Pete, and Anna don't need darkness. They need light and newness, but it's heading in a different direction than that.

Dad has had a few really "strong" days, like Superman days, so for that, I smile. We stopped over tonight to see him, and he looked really good. I'm so glad. We walked in and he said, "Hey (funny name)!" to which I quickly matched with a, "Hey, (funny name)!" These days are even more numbered, we all know, so we'll take 'em.

I know I should keep these feelings quiet, just being honest with what's on my heart. I'm nervous about approaching this whole visitation thing. I've had a migraine for *days* with anticipation. Whatever I'm able to start rolling with the court system, he's gonna fight it. I want to be prepared and have my armor on. I pray I can stand and weather whatever comes. I feel like I already have had to wear a lot of armor, and I'm getting tired. I want to be able to stand and take it just long enough to save my kids from this, and then I can rest. Then, I can rest.

December 5, 2014
Today at work I nearly got jumped. Later, a student found me directing traffic in the parking lot to give me a piece of cake she made. Days like this is when I love my job.

December 7, 2014
We tried making fudge today but something was off. Dad kept blaming me for not using enough sugar, but I know I followed the recipe. The real blessing was that Dad was on his feet the entire time.

Although he's getting tired, and his body is weary, he continues to make us feel important, laugh, and provide wisdom and love like only he can. I look at him with such awe for all he has and is teaching my kids. While it hurts that he won't see them become teenagers or learn to drive or graduate from high school, he will be "right there" with us. He is such a big part of us, of helping mold me and my kids. Be it helping them order me a Christmas gift (they were all whispers and secrets, pointing and telling me to leave the room), simply leading by example, he's made such a tremendous impression on their lives.

December 14, 2014
It's been an emotional day to say the least. The kiddos and I picked Mom up for church this morning. It's been a long time since she's been to church because she's been taking such good care of Dad. He really encouraged and wanted her to go, so we did. We shared tears on the car ride there and seeing so many faces brought the need for extra Kleenex and hugs once we entered. After church, there were more hugs and words of encouragement. It was wonderful to be back. I'm so proud of Mom. That took courage, and she did it. God will keep carrying us through this time.

He's failing. His pain has increased, and he's been put on more pain medicine. *Oh Lord, please help manage his pain. We know he's on his way to You. I pray that these days and weeks leading up to it are comfortable for him.*

He shared a message he got today from an old friend:

"As I write this, I remember John Glenn's Mercury mission in 1962 or 63. Fellow astronaut Scott Carpenter manned the radio in the Command Post as Glenn lifted off from the launch pad heading for the darkness of space. If you remember, Carpenter stated to Glenn and the entire world - "God Bless John Glenn!" As you depart this world for Heaven, I want you to know that your family, fellow agents, friends, and anyone that he ever had the privilege to know you, will join me to say, "God Bless YOU!!!"

December 15, 2014
Wouldn't you know; I still have *no* idea if Danny got the paperwork from court. I'm full of anxiety, then giving it over to the Lord, then anxiety takes over again, and again while I'm trying to just hand it over to Him.

Danny sent a rather nice text today about Thursday night, spending it at his aunt's with the kids. I can take from that, he did get it and is now on-watch for his words. But I don't think he truly is.. Either way, I need to trust the Lord will carry me on this, even if I get to court (the day is right after Christmas) and lose. I'm praying I don't!

Anna just conked next to me. She's been having bad dreams about Papa these past few nights and didn't want to be alone. Last night, she dreamt he couldn't talk anymore. It broke my heart. I can't resist her saying that and asking to sleep with me (even though she snores like a 400-pound man and hogs the bed with her jiggly legs). But alas, she's only seven once.

Dad is going downhill. I catch myself fighting tears all the time. It can be a song, a saying, a truck that looks like his, or a flashback memory. I want to talk to him so badly, but he's resting a lot, and I don't want to wake him. So we'll just take the time we have left, whatever amount that is, and cling to it. I want to record him more, for he is such a HUGE part of our daily lives. And the pain of losing him is already so raw. Sometimes I can't fake it, the tears and ugly cry just come on out.

Now onto a new week at school, just this last one before Christmas break. I'm looking forward to that, for time with Dad, time with these precious, snoring kids (although by week two, I may pull my hair out). I just sit here, look at Anna, and snicker to myself; she's precious.

December 19, 2014
The kids and I got a chance to stop in and see Papa yesterday, and he said it was the highlight of his week.

The days are slipping, Christmas is next week, and I am feeling so many emotions. I don't want the time to go too fast. I don't want to share the kids with Danny, despite that being totally selfish of me. I want to be present in every moment, but then my mind goes to the court date on the 26th and what will come. How much longer will Dad be with us? This is his last Christmas. I NEED to treasure this time. I wish it would slow down.

December 20, 2014
Dad and I talked about Heaven again today, what a victorious place it will be. As much as Dad loves us, and is young, he is more than ready to meet Jesus. What a testimony. That conversation led me to ask Dad if he would do me a favor.

I asked if he would write each of my kids a letter before he goes. Sure we've gotten choked up and changed the topic before, but this? With this question, he broke down. He full on cried sitting in his recliner. I've only seen him cry one other time. He said between gasps, "ask me to do anything else, and I'll do it right now. I just can't...they mean too much to me...I just can't..." He could hardly get the words out. That reaction was enough.

December 21, 2014
I went to the neighborhood Christmas party last night. I hemmed and hawed so much about it but then ran to the store to pick up an ugly sweater to wear. I went from, "I should go" to "they won't notice if I don't." I am just me, everyone else in our neighborhood is married; I'm a third wheel.

I did eventually decide to go and had a decent time. I had all of these feelings, though. I don't know where I belong, I'm not married nor have a "date" to come along with me, someone to hang around so conversations aren't so awkward. I have no idea when I will even feel ready to date. That seems so far off. I'm just hanging out there, feeling super vulnerable. All

I end up talking about is how Dad is doing or the kids. That's about all I've got right now.

No one means to make me feel this way, they were super welcoming, it's just how I feel. Where do I fit? I'm the odd (wo)man out. *Lord, please give me some courage and confidence.* I feel so self-conscious in group settings like that, like I want to hide away. As I walked home in the dark afterwards, I had a moment of pride in myself. The first of many events I'll fly solo, but I did it. I went.

December 23, 2014
For days I've been waiting for Anna's last-minute gift, her purple tutu, to show up. Today, a package was delivered to my folks that I quickly put in my van and waited until now to open up and wrap. But in the FedEx box, wasn't a skirt. Puzzled, I pulled out gift after gift with labels for my kids from "Santa." And the most thoughtful, overwhelming card and letter were inside.

Whoever did this? They typed the letter and didn't sign their name so I wouldn't know... I've tried to figure out who, but then realized the lengths they went to remain anonymous.

Whoever it was? You made our Christmas incredibly extra special... I am humbled and overflowing with thankfulness.

December 24, 2014
The boys have been in cahoots with Papa over these past few weeks about my Christmas gift. They wanted to wrap it at home and give it to me tomorrow. Since this year is Danny's year with them for Christmas Day, we simply moved our traditions up by one day. Everything is the same except for the date on the calendar. One of the greatest traditions is reading '*Twas the Night Before Christmas*, which Dad read to us kids all growing up, every single Christmas Eve. The same exact book I now have.

December 25, 2014
Blessing of spending time together - lots of naps for Dad, but glad to be there. He is so ready to be with Jesus. I'm praying for peace in his heart

and mind over things he wishes he could do here on this earth, but can't. For the ability for all of us, who hold him so dear, to help ease his journey Home.

It was a hard day for me, as much as we tried to make yesterday *feel* like it was Christmas. It's hard to have to share the kids. It made my heart at ease to know that tonight when they got home, they equally missed me.

Another big piece has been taken away. Since Anna was the only one to receive gifts from Santa today, she believed it was because the boys weren't good enough all year. I couldn't bite my lip, I had to have an honest conversation with her. I knelt down next to her bed, hallway light shining into her dark bedroom. She now knows that Santa is not real.

The boys discovered this truth way back in the day when a basketball was hidden in a closet at our old house that was later gifted to DK from Santa. Of course, it was during the days of teaching about lying, so DK asked me, point blank, if I was lying about Santa, and I fessed up. Peter got pulled into the conversation because, if DK knew, Pete would too. And like anything else, I want them to hear the truth from me. The boys did a great job for years playing along for Anna. They have continued to get gifts from Santa. We don't get too carried away, for we know Jesus is the Reason for the Season, but there is a piece of innocence and fun in having Santa come.

They bit their tongues today and didn't respond when Anna was gloating to them that she did better all year and that's why she got gifts from Santa. Now all three of them know, but no matter what they will always have a few things under the tree from Santa. That's how my folks did it and I will, too.

I did get the best gift from the boys: A Green Bay Packers (Aaron Rodgers) jersey. I love it, despite them accidentally getting me a youth large and it fitting me like a freshly opened can of biscuits.

December 26, 2014

I found a note I wrote to myself in October 1996: "I want to be trustworthy, honest, good, pure, kind, gracious, modest, wise, courageous, and bold." At least I have the bold part down. Especially when I'm telling a story including my hand gestures and facial expressions!

December 30, 2014

Dad has always been on the same page as me - morally, family wise, our shared sense of humor and striving to leave others with a laugh rather sadness. But Dad hasn't been himself these past few months. He gets heated pretty easily, yet he has always had the patience of a saint. I want to get back to Dad's level of patience, myself, for my kids.

I can't model Dad because right now, he doesn't have patience for me. I hear him, I know it, but I just feel so hurt. He has never scolded me like this before. He scolded me about me taking Danny to court. He told me I'd lose. If I had asked him, he never would have filed the paperwork. It hurt when he called me an overprotective mom.

I was shocked to my core.

This is the same guy who protects us, non-stop in his sleep. I heard him out, tried processing it a bunch of different ways, but it hurt. Deep. Is he trying to protect me by pushing me away? I do believe he didn't want to hurt me about the court outcome as he prepared for me to lose. Ok, I get it, but I just need some support. Maybe it wasn't what he would have done, but I did it and was proud of myself, win or lose. I wished he could have been, too. This is a reminder to me that I'm my own person, and I can hold my head high. I believe in myself, and God has me in His hands. Call it overprotective, but he is, too. So that, I will take as a compliment.

Chapter 37

January 1, 2015

The kids and I were sure happy to ring in the new year with Mom, Dad, and extended family. It was a very relaxing night of games, food, and a John Candy movie, one of Dad's all-time favorites. Dad even managed to stay awake to see the ball drop. Though we know the time is fleeting, every moment is creating memories we'll look back on. Even photos snapped where we think we look bad or fat, we'll have them with Dad, and that won't matter.

But in these past weeks, his pain has increased to a "steady six" or greater in the night, and that is the last thing we want for him. No more pain, no more suffering, no more having to put on a good face for us. He's ready to go be with Jesus, and we want that for him, too. We can't keep him here; he's ready to go. With the pain, comes a tad ornerier than usual version of dad, which, as he says, doesn't sugar coat things.

I know that in his orneriness, the point he's making with me is to stop worrying. *Who cares?* Dan will be a bully, there will be many things out of my control, but "tying myself up like a pretzel won't change it." That's wisdom I need to cling to, even if it's hard to hear. I can't change anything; all I can do is continue to try to reach upward and try to make sure my kiddos have the best they can, given the situation.

Court has come and gone. Now we are waiting for an investigator to make the next call. The judge did chew on me a little, but he's objective and doing what he's there to do. He wondered why, just last March I would say the kids could be with their dad, as set by the guidelines, but now, nine months later, I want to change it.

I wish I could have said, *"Your Honor, you have no idea what it's like being married/then divorced to someone suffering from Bipolar Disorder and alcoholism."*

But I said what I needed to say, felt I put my best foot forward. Danny's attorney stood there and shook her head "no" at me while I talked. It reminded me of Danny when we'd go to church, during the sermons. I guess it was a funny turn of events that Pastor was one of the two people there to support me during court, and Grace, too. My biggest cheerleader, as always.

Danny's attorney said things that were hurtful and abysmal. I just stood there and listened as hives rose up my neck and onto my cheeks. The struggles from his point of view are much different than mine. Not surprising. What I was saying was not false, though. I had notes, pages of notes.

The judge ordered that the kids be interviewed by a court investigator. He heard my side, then Danny's, and said, "Well then, let's have the children interviewed, shoot, I'll even do it myself!"

Then the judge looked sternly at me and said, "They will be able to tell, within moments, if your kids have been coached."

He then turned to Danny and said, "And if they find out anything, things will change."

I'm happy with that.

Lord, thank You for holding me up, helping me to stand alone on my two feet, wobbly as they may have been. Thank You for putting that behind me.

January 2, 2015

I just dropped the kids off to their dad for the weekend. I have a migraine coming on. As I drove home, I talked to myself the entire time, cried, and realized why I have a migraine on its way:

1) I just dropped the kids off to their dad.
2) I'm nervous about heading back to work after two good weeks off. Silly, I know, but it seems like forever since I've been there.
3) My dad is dying, soon.

Those are certainly enough things to cause a headache.

The kids were ready to see him, with the exception of Anna-Banana. She's been in tears for about two hours not wanting to go. We took some selfies of me and her for her LeapPad that she can look at. She took her stuffed animal kitty cat and has Papa's t-shirt she sleeps with every night. I hope she's comforted by those things and can make the best of this situation. It breaks my heart to "have to" drop her off there when it's not at all anything she wants to do. She's nervous, she's afraid, she's got no one there (in her words). *I'm praying for her heart and protection over all three kids, Oh Lord.*

Danny has been telling the kids we have "many issues we need to work out" and "your mom never updates me on Papa, I don't understand." Well, my thoughts are that I don't owe you anything.

Dad is going down, I know. Yesterday he was completely out of sorts and today he can't even remember yesterday. He used his humor as he dozed on and off in his green recliner. UB, Aunt Gene, Mom, and I were talking and he dozed off, then before opening his eyes, lifted his left hand and waved.

Then said a few colorful words to make us laugh.

Typical Dad humor. To know now that he remembers nothing of it, not even the basketball game we were watching, makes me wonder if it's the medication he's taking now or his mind slipping. Either way, we'll love him through and are more than grateful he has no pain right now. I was talking with the kids about this earlier and about how he's "ready to go."

DK looked at me from the front passenger seat of the van and said, "We're ready to let him go, too, Mom." What a mature, wonderful eleven-year-old.

During my drive home just now, while in a tough crying match, I talked myself through the recent weeks with Dad. He's torn me a new one, told me he'll stay out of my business, and admitted he felt my filing the motion wasn't a good idea.

It hurt.

But, I know from where he's sitting, he wants to protect me. Just like I long to protect my kids.

He has always loved us kids with all he's got and makes every effort to spend time rather than money on me and my kids. That's what I long for with my crew, just the gift of time. Dad has shown me more in these eleven years since I've become a mom than anything else. He's taught me what to strive to be like as a protector, lover, and confidant for my kids. I could and can tell him absolutely *anything*.

It's my hope that this is the same type of relationship I'm building with my own kids. For the rest of my life here on this earth, I will do my best to live the way Dad would approve, the way God approves. I want to do my best, and although the kids and I will face struggles, temptations, trials, impatience, and hardships, we will make it through. We will. I need to keep reminding myself of that. The Lord has brought us this far and given us peace about our circumstances right now. I'd love to think the hardest of our times is behind us, but maybe not. I pray we can cling to and grow closer in our faith and relationships.

January 3, 2015

Danny cried in my driveway saying he spent money on alcohol that he could have used to feed the kids. I just...there is nothing to even say. I feel so hurt, yet thankful the kids will stay home if that's what's best right now. But wow, that statement hurt.

January 4, 2015
I was going to go home tonight but decided to stay at Mom and Dad's. Dad has been on and off confused and incredibly weak, so Mom called hospice and the on-call nurse stopped by. Everything checked out ok, so she left. His fever finally broke. With that, he had clarity and started asking questions about what happened earlier today.

"We also have joy with our troubles, because we know that these troubles produce patience. And patience produces character, and character produces hope. And this hope will never disappoint us, because God has poured out His love to fill our hearts" Romans 5:3-5 (NCV Mom's Bible, God's Wisdom for Mothers).

January 5, 2015
Define {Motherhood}: the act of having to go back outside in your pajamas and bare feet, only to find all doors of the minivan are frozen shut except the driver's door, to climb over armrests and booster seats to the way back of the van to retrieve the doll and Papa's shirt Anna can't sleep without.

January 6, 2015
Dad has had a few better days. He texted me tonight asking if we were alive over here. He's so funny. We were able to chat a while. I put him on speaker and Pete asked him

"If you were stranded on a desert island with just me, what would you do?"

Dad quickly answered, "I'd throw seashells at you."

Smiles and laughter all around, yep, that's Papa.

January 10, 2015
We went over to Mom and Dad's house this afternoon and ended up staying for supper. It was wonderful to visit with Mom's siblings. We shared laughs and good conversation. I can tell it is surely bringing up Mom's spirits, and Dad is enjoying the good cooking. Anna hasn't been feeling 100%, so we haven't been over to visit. It breaks my heart, but we need

to do what is best for Dad. In spite of his fatigue, he manages to make everyone around feel like they are the most important person in the room.

Danny cancelled his parenting time with no excuse; he just didn't want to. As much as this frustrates me, life is so precious, and I'll take all of the time I can get with the kids. We need to be close right now.

"You, Lord, give true peace to those who depend on You, because they trust in You" Isaiah 26:3 (NCV Mom's Bible, God's Wisdom for Mothers).

January 13, 2015
Just got all three kids signed up for baseball and soccer, so they are all pretty excited.

In years past, Dad has been a taxi driver, helping run the kids to and from practices and games. When his health started to waiver last spring, Dad would either show up in a wheelchair to watch or we'd be in constant contact via text, video or phone call so he knew play-by-play. Signing up this season is extremely bittersweet. I know I'll be on the lookout for him, his pronounced gate, carrying his red folding chair that he kept in his truck for baseball.

Selfishly, I also know how hard it is going to be to take three kids to different practices and overlapping game times. I will figure it out. It's all worth it, I saved up the money for months so they can do what they love. Watching them do what they love is worth all of the work and every penny spent.

January 16, 2015
I managed to start up the washing machine with my security uniform inside, not realizing I had left my cell phone in the pants pocket. I'm devastated. I quickly put it in rice and prayed it'd work. But alas, it was too far into the wash cycle before I realized it. Talk about wishing you could go back and do that over...

Dad is increasingly tired, he's struggling to want to sleep all the time, but his body is telling him he has to. As we've said many times, if this is how the Lord will call him home, through rest. I didn't ask tonight, but last I knew, he had no pain, so that's a blessing. We did get a chance to remake fudge with Dad a few nights ago. This batch turned out perfectly delicious. Dad was on his feet.

January 19, 2015
Talk about feeling ridiculously torn. The kids are sick, but do I stay home from work? I feel like I shouldn't. I'm hemming and hawing back and forth, but you know what? I'm going to stay home. What an inner conflict. I know I'm responsible to be at work every day, but what to do when this happens? I still feel so guilty, but I have to do what I have to do. Before I know it, these kids will all be grown up, and if I don't take the time now, I know I will regret it.

This balance of single momhood and working full time is tough.

Dad is in a lot of pain now. He's tired, and it's so hard to watch. Mom has been a trooper. I know it has made for sleepless, tear-filled nights for her.

January 20, 2015
Ok, Pete is gonna get it. I just found a fake snake under my pillow when I hopped into bed. I about croaked on the spot! Payback is in order for the little prankster! I wasn't actually that mad, I needed the hysterics to make sure my heart is still pumpin'.

With DK sick, we can't go over to visit. We just can't risk it for as much as we want to see him. Hospice has been there more and more.

He's so sick and tired of being sick and tired. Who can blame him?

Knowing he'll soon be in the Glory and rid of all sickness and pain is surely something to yearn for. I'm grateful to know where he's going and that he's ready. I'm praying he'll have calmness and peace of mind, as he's a bit ornery these days. I know Mom has so much on her plate. Having Grace there as the "nurse" 24-hours a day is an amazing gift. I know I couldn't do it like she does. She is so caring. I pray for her patience and peace, too.

January 22, 2015

Dad has had a change in mentality. He's very much ready to fully let go and pass. At this time, he just wants to rest and sleep peacefully, not prolong it anything further. Hospice knows and will work to make him more comfortable. The goal is to make his pain at a zero. I selfishly want all of this to go away, just *go away*, but we know it's not the Lord's will for Dad's life. Knowing he has peace, we do, too. I never ever would have thought it possible, but the Lord has brought us this peace. It's amazing, and my heart is so full.

It gives me some perspective. Despite Danny continuing to cancel his parenting time, we need to be together. I need to let go of my expectations. It's hard for me to do because every day with these kids is a gift - each day.

January 24, 2015

Pete was too sick for basketball practice, which Danny planned to take him to, but DK asked repeatedly, texted and calling to see if he could still have some time with him. After waiting and wondering, Danny finally returned the call saying he was too tired. I get it, I know he struggles, but his own son is begging for time with him...and he is too tired. What on earth does he think is going on in our world over here?

January 25, 2015

The kids and I were able to spend this afternoon and evening at Mom and Dad's. Dad didn't have a very good day. He's sleeping a lot and so disoriented. When he was talking, it didn't make much sense. Anna was so tender with Nan. She held her hand and they got giggling over a doll. It was so cute. It was hard, yet inspiring to watch my kids interact with Papa. They are amazing human beings.

January 27, 2015

The voicemail box on my phone said it was 90% full, so I started going through old ones and I have a bunch I want to save from Dad; they are treasures. I got welled up with tears as I listened to one from before he was diagnosed and he had just gone to get an oil change and wanted to see how

I was doing. Oh, how he'd love the ability now to do something as simple as wait at Barry's for an oil change.

January 28, 2015
Dad was asking about what he's been saying and doing lately because he doesn't remember. He said to take a video next time so he could see if for himself. I've been staying up on the couch now at Mom and Dad's so I can hear everything and react that much quicker should Dad or Mom need anything in the night.

It has been a good day for Dad; he's been coherent. He was even up in his recliner which is a welcomed sight. Things are slowing down; his body is weak. His face shows his pain, and it's so hard seeing his eyes. They tell of what's going on inside, despite the smile he still shows.

January 30, 2015
Anna just sat in my room and cried and laughed, her two front teeth still missing, about life at school as a first grader: how she tattles, and other kids tattle on her. She has such a heart, and these issues she has, they feel like a huge mountain to climb. She can't talk about her feelings in front of DK and Pete because they act like they are so tired of hearing about it. She knows she can talk to me, and I'll listen. Those precious little freckles and no teef...

I'm thankful that the Lord helped me set aside my exhaustion and, honestly, I'm not really in the mood to sort out drama, but I listened and encouraged. She has a smile and we worked it out, solved the world's problems the best we could for 9:26 pm on a Friday night. I pray I will find a good man to come alongside me, us, to help encourage and love us. However long it takes, we'll wait.

January 31, 2015
It's been a crazy week of running kids all over for practices. Dad has been having some restful sleep which is good. He's comfortable and pain is better managed. He's been coherent from what Mom has said. He got to laughing over us telling him his antics from last weekend. If hearts can smile, mine was a full, toothy grin. It was the best sight and sound. What

a gift, a sense of humor. I'm so thankful Dad has shown us what being able to laugh in all circumstances looks like.

Always leave them laughing...

Lord, we seek You and please bring comfort to all of us as we surround Dad. These times can get heavy and even confusing. Lord, please give us each the wisdom we need and peace we yearn for to get through this. How can we without You? Hold us up, please, if You will. Please.

February 2, 2015

The kids and I have spent the past few days at Mom and Dad's. With the pending snow, Mom asked if we just wanted to stay there following the Super Bowl. You would have thought it was Christmas for my kids. We had a snow day, too, as expected, so that was even more time to relax. The kids built a snow fort and visited with Papa when he was awake. I keep going back to last evening in my mind... There was a time when it was just him and I in the room (Dad is parked in his hospice bed in Mom and Dad's bedroom), and I just stood there and studied his face. His eyes were closed, he was conked, and I stood there, bedside, studying him.

Tears filled my eyes as I thought of how strong he has always been, of all he has done in his life for me and for my kids, and here he lay. DK stepped in, and we met eyes. He gave me the "it's ok, Mom," look and gave me a hug.

Dad was awake during part of the Super Bowl last night. Then today, was awake in the morning to visit. Pete and Anna entertained him with some yoga moves they saw in a magazine. Dad sat up in his bed, reading glasses on his nose, comparing the poses to that in the pictures. It was really cute. He then slept the afternoon away and woke up in the early evening. He's, honestly, really going downhill now. It won't be long.

When I leaned in to awkwardly hug him in his hospital bed (I mean, how is it not awkward when someone is laying down?), he said, "I love you, Charlotte." To which I whispered into his left ear, "Goodnight Dad, I love you." Eyes were met as I pulled away. Our eye contact said what our words never could. I think we both knew in that moment that these would be the last words we'd speak on this earth. He called me Charlotte; he said my name.

"Follow me one step at a time. That is all I require of you. In fact, that is the only way to move through this space/time world. You see huge mountains looming, and you start wondering how you're going to scale those heights. Meanwhile, because you're not looking where you're going, you stumble on the easy path where I am leading you now. As I help you get back on your feet, you tell Me how worried you are about the cliffs up ahead. But you don't know what will happen today, much less tomorrow. If I do lead you up the cliffs, I will equip you thoroughly for that strenuous climb" (Jesus Calling by Sarah Young).

February 3, 2015

With a very humble heart, and many tears shed, he's slipping quickly now. As prepared as we can be, this won't hurt any less. Mom and Grace had to call paramedics to help get Dad placed back in bed after trying to get up and to the "'head'" (as he calls it). He's having issues swallowing, and he's quite restless. At this point, the decline is eminent. It's the hardest thing in the whole world. I'm praying our hearts will be filled with celebration at his Homecoming.

In the van, Anna said, "It's like Papa is going to a new house." To which Pete quickly corrected her and said, It's not a new house. It's his *home.*"

February 4, 2015

We've been sitting and taking turns with Dad. He's at peace as he sleeps. He hasn't spoken or opened his eyes in two days. His breathing is labored, but we're so glad he's not in pain right now. I look at him and see the definition of selfless. How fortunate we are to know this love? He's lived this life so fully. He has always put others first and left everyone with a smile. I can hear him laughing.

While I got to sit with him today, I just sobbed and whispered that I didn't know quite how I would do all of this without him. He has always been my rock. He's helped me through it all, especially these hard moments as my marriage ended, I faced bankruptcy, losing our house, all of it. And now who do I have? Who can help me? I was reminded of Dad's and my conversation about a week ago that maybe the Lord is drawing me closer to Him through all of this, helping me rely on my Heavenly Father and not just my earthly one. It's so hard to swallow.

As I was sharing and reflecting with Dad laying there, unresponsive, Grace came in and asked that I not disturb him with my negative thoughts, things he can't help with anymore. I get where she was coming from, I know that hearing is the last thing to go, and he didn't need to be weighed down by my burdens. I just, selfishly, wanted to tell him what I was feeling, as I always had. I know he heard me. I collected myself and left the room. I sat in a wicker chair just outside the bedroom door that was closed while Grace helped the hospice nurse bathe him.

Chapter 38

February 4, 2015 (later)

Dad died today; he died. I just can't believe it's true. He's gone from this earth. Nothing but an empty shell was taken from Mom and Dad's bedroom today by two men in suits who never even met him.

I'm looking at the dark sky and full moon wondering what it's like for him now. Is he dancing? Is he resting finally? Is he singing as a bass with the angelic choir? Is he cracking jokes? Why did he have to go? When will I see him again? Do I have the strength to carry my kids through this? I have to. I have to trust God above to carry us.

Dad told me the day before yesterday how he planned to pay half of my rent every month. But things went downhill so quickly and he didn't get a chance to figure that all out. I shook my head "no" for him to be helping me after he's gone. He knew I'd never expect it. But he said, "that was just what I was going to do."

He wanted to help me; he wanted to protect me. I know he wants what's best for me, just like I feel for my kids.

Lord, grant me strength to be this single mom. Carry me; carry DK; carry Pete; carry Anna; carry Grace; carry Mom. In ways we can't express, carry us. Dad is gone from this earth. I smile, and then within seconds, cover my face with both hands and sob.

"Yet I am always with you; you hold me by my right hand. You guide me with your counsel, and afterward you will take me into glory" Psalm 73:23-24 (NIV One Year Bible).

February 6, 2015

I feel empty, like there's an organ missing, or half of my heart has literally been cut out of my chest. Earlier when I was folding laundry, I couldn't even pick up an article of clothing to fold it because I was hysterical.

I couldn't breathe.

All I wanted to do was talk to Dad. He's the one who would understand. He's my *why*. My fingers can hardly write this, my heart can hardly function. I got distracted watching tv earlier, a show Dad and I used to watch together. I'm sitting here in the pitch dark, the kids just left my bedside where we read devotions, and I can't even lay down to sleep. I need to because I have a huge headache coming. I can't do anything but just sit here in the dark.

February 7, 2015

Honestly all of this seems surreal. It just seems like it can't be true. Then waves of emotion come over me and it's like, *whammo*. It *is* true.

The kids and I went to Mom and Dad's. We'll be calling it that for a long time, kind of like changing a calendar year and it taking time to write the new year's number correctly on a check. I plopped down on the couch and looked over at Dad's green recliner, the big green one he's always teased about.

He'd say, "Guess what I'm doing? Sitting in this green chair I've got, have you seen it?" because that's where he was parked most all of the time.

He'd come walking out of the bedroom, or the bathroom doing his walk where he would act like he was trying to sneak up on you, even after you already saw him.

But he didn't.

I don't know how I will face visitation tomorrow. It will drain us all. I can't even fathom it. Just the thought of having to go makes me cry...

Then the funeral...oh, what a day that will be. Dad wants it all at our church in front of the stained glass windows; he planned it out. He used to say that he didn't want it at a funeral home because those are for *dead people*. He wanted it at our church home, where babies are baptized and life's joys are celebrated. Oh, and we had to have potato salad, because who doesn't have potato salad at a funeral luncheon?

February 8, 2015
Right as the visitation was getting started, Danny came up to me and said, "Your relationship with your dad is what caused our divorce." I swallowed deep and tried to let it roll off.

How could he say something like that to me right now? I can't spend my exhausted energy that I have left on this. I literally have a sore throat and feel like I have a fever. I think it's just all of this, the weight of it all hitting without me even realizing it.

I'm really struggling with a migraine and pray I'll get through it ok. Everyone surrounding our family has been such a tremendous gift. Dad was *one in a million*, so that's the song I put on his photo montage.

February 26, 2015
I just heard that all of the furniture, that Danny insisted on taking from our farmhouse right after I filed for divorce, went to auction and was all sold off. Our sofas, tables, chairs, dressers, bed, etc. I guess he had put it all in a storage unit that he couldn't make payments on. It was all just material stuff, and it's not like I figured I'd see it again or get it back. But was it worth it to make us go without a place to sit until I could scrounge a few dollars together at garage sales or hand me downs? I just shake my head.

March 15, 2015
I knew it had been a while since I'd written, I haven't written since Dad died. Wow, I'm finally ok with saying those three words. *My dad died.*

Since he died, I believe I've experienced about every emotion known to man. At first I just couldn't believe it was true. I mean, my dad has always been my rock, he couldn't possibly be gone, laying in that casket. I kept waiting for him to open his eyes and say, "fooled you!" in a *Spaceballs'* voice.

Then came the mix of hysterics, brought on by folding laundry, listening to music, or a bad day at work followed by having to make eighteen phone calls to deal with my Medicaid dropping me for no reason... Then some anger came. Never in my life have I been truly angry with God. But I did fall on my knees and just ask those questions. *WHY Lord, WHY? Why him? Why now? Why this?* Sometimes I cry out, asking on my drive to work in the wee hours of the morning, *"WHY, Lord?"*

I wanted to ask Dad about my taxes. I have wanted to call him pulling out of my work parking lot to tell him about my day, like I always used to. Buying baseball gear for the kids and starting practices was hard. Trying to do it all on my own, without him is harder.

The day I got hit the hardest with all of the above was March 4, the one-month anniversary of him going to Heaven. On that hysterical day, I was, honestly, inconsolable, and I was embarrassed the kids had to see it.

I now feel more peace in my heart and mind, and for that, I'm grateful. He would want it this way.

Fast forward to today, sitting in church in a pew we often sat with Mom and Dad over the years. The registration pads had just been handed out, and we were listening to the morning announcements. Ever since I can remember, Dad had written "Fred Schwartz" down as a visitor. Some Sundays the registration pad would pass him by, or Mom would grab it to make sure he didn't do it. She'd give a wrinkled eyebrow and cross it off. Dad would act like he had no idea where it came from, then look over at us kids or his grandkids with a guilty smile.

But then came the time when Papa couldn't make it to church anymore. He was too sick, so he'd stay home and catch church on his laptop. Pete decided to keep the tradition of Fred nearly every Sunday since Papa couldn't. Well today, something miraculous happened. I wrote in our names, passed it to Pete sitting next to me, where he, of course, crossed off our names and wrote in visitor Fred. The pad gets passed to Mom and I look from the corner of my eye to see her put a line through it in pen... but not today. Mom wrote her name, then on the line underneath, wrote "Fred Schwartz Jr." My full, toothy grin I'm sure would have matched Dad's if he were there.

March 17, 2015

Our meeting with the court investigator went better than I expected. It ended up feeling like the investigator and I teaming up to build Danny up so that he knows he's important to these kids. They love their dad, they always have. They genuinely want time with him. It felt less like an attack, and more like a healthy conversation with a lot to take away. The kids want time with Dan I want to help build that, however long it takes, as long as he's honest about how he feels. We both left encouraged and even rode the elevator down together. I pray he will have a clear heart and make his time with the kids a priority. That's honestly all I've ever wanted, for him to be a dad.

March 24, 2015
I'm exhausted.

I wish I could say it's a Tuesday thing, or a Monday thing, but it's an every-day-during-the-week thing. Going from working an eight-hour day to picking the kids up from school and working my second, and more important, full time job: being MOM.

Fortunately, I can get through some days without the tears, but with others it can be the teeniest reminder. I'll be perfectly fine one moment and the next with crocodile tears on the tips of my fingers as I wipe them away. It comes on a lot while I'm driving. It's probably because that's when I can listen to the radio and hear songs Dad used to listen to. He loved all sorts of different music. We joked about my "country western" music, but over time, I got him to like a few songs, especially "Whiskey Lullaby" by Alison

Krauss and Brad Paisley. Even just a phrase of a song he probably never heard will pop out, and next thing I know, I'm sobbing.

I miss you Dad.

"God, I don't know what I would do without your promise to uphold me in every way" (Turn Your Eyes Upon Jesus devotional).

Chapter 39

October 26, 2018

This feels like a life-defining moment. I'm leaning over the steering wheel with the glow of the dashboard reflecting off my face. Both feet are bare and pushing down the brake pedal as I sit in reverse, completely stationary. The backup camera is lit with Peter working diligently to hook up the camping trailer. It's only been one season and already we are preparing to sell our dream trailer. It really was. But I know in my heart that I bit off more than I could chew. It wasn't just for camping; it was my way to prove to myself that I could do it on my own: pull my own trailer, back it up, do everything on my own. I was even able to get my own loan through the bank; I didn't need a co-signer. *I did it*. I can take pride in that. *I did it*. But now, I've got to be reasonable and honest with myself... it's more stress than its worth.

After many cold moments of all four windows down so I could hear Pete's call, "back up a tiny bit, Mom," I couldn't help but reminisce about this point in my life. There are so many life definers for me. Why did this seem like such a big one? It might seem super silly, but as I sit here, hunched over the steering wheel watching all three kids in the rearview mirror, a smile flashes on my face. I'm overcome with feeling like...I've arrived.

I've learned so much about myself in these past few years. I am capable. I will make mistakes and have made plenty, but by the grace of God, I am His. God works through our human weakness. I know He has a plan for my life and telling my story feels like part of it. I've been at tremendous peace since deciding, *now* is the time to write my book, my memoir. Now is the time for healing, for growth.

We have *NEVER* gone without food, shelter, warmth, a working vehicle or love. To everyone who has stuffed cash or gift cards in my purse, taped random gift cards to our front door, "boo'd" us with amazing things on our front porch. For all who have helped me pay for my kids to play sports and their equipment. For surprise cleaning my entire house. For purchasing my kids Christmas gifts. Helping me get food assistance worked out, even contacted a State Representative on my behalf. The free turkeys at Thanksgiving, overpaying me for making Christmas ornaments and earrings to help make ends meet. For Starbucks gift cards, hot meals delivered out of the blue. During my recovery from brain surgery a year ago, holding us up in prayer and constant help. For the rides for my kids, hugs, words of encouragement, freezer meals to keep so we had food all week. For those times I've gotten less than $10 to my name and still had three days before a paycheck and the Lord provided with gift cards, cash, a flow of eggs and milk (delivered to our front porch). For letting me ugly cry in front of you.

You know who you are. *I am eternally grateful.* This journey I've been on, my kids, too. Without all of you in our lives during this time, we wouldn't be where we are now. You have truly been the hands and feet of God.

We have been humbled, grateful, and blessed. Beyond any words, I thank you.